DILEMMAS OF
BLACK POLITICS

DILEMMAS OF BLACK POLITICS:

Issues of Leadership and Strategy

Edited by

Georgia A. Persons
Georgia Institute of Technology

■ HarperCollins*CollegePublishers*

This book is dedicated in loving memories of Lucious, Bettie Jean, and Agie Lee Shakespeare Persons.

Executive Editor: Lauren Silverman
Project Editor: Melonie Parnes
Cover Design: Kay Petronio
Production Manager/Assistant: Willie Lane/Sunaina Sehwani
Compositor: ComCom Division of Haddon Craftsmen, Inc.
Printer and Binder: R. R. Donnelley & Sons Company
Cover Printer: The Lehigh Press, Inc.

Dilemmas of Black Politics: Issues of Leadership and Strategy

Library of Congress Cataloging-in-Publication Data

Dilemmas of black politics: issues of leadership and strategy /
   edited by Georgia A. Persons.
      p. cm.
   ISBN 0-06-500509-0
   1. Afro-Americans—Politics and government. 2. Afro-American leadership. 3. United States—Politics and government—1989–
I. Persons, Georgia Anne.
   E185.615.D55 1993
323.1′196073—dc20   92-19599
                                                              CIP

93 94 95 9 8 7 6 5 4 3 2

Contents

Preface

*T*his book had its genesis in a series of informal discussions in Memphis, Tennessee, at the October 1989 annual meeting of the Southern Political Science Association. As small groups of us—some previously strangers, some old acquaintances—sat around over meals and other refreshments, the conversations inevitably turned to the state of political affairs in our respective venues. Some of us were from places like Virginia and Georgia where state and local political races and governing regimes were in the national news. Black candidates were seeking top posts in campaigns in the Virginia and Georgia gubernatorial races and the mayoralties of New York City, New Haven, Connecticut, and Seattle, Washington, among others. All of us were inquisitive about the emerging thematic thrust of these then ongoing campaigns and how they tended to pivot around the issue of race in new and interesting ways. We were in general agreement that something different was emerging, and one member of the group applied the appellation of deracialization. Thus we were able to depart from Memphis with a tentative analytical framework for understanding an apparent emergent dimension of black politics. Some new collegial relationships were forged out of these discussions.

The second stage of preparation for this book was set when the original Memphis group was extensively expanded when we next met in Atlanta at the March 1990 annual meeting of the National Conference of Black Political Scientists (NCOBPS). There is a saying among black political scientists that while we may specialize in areas such as comparative politics, international security affairs, public policy, scopes and methods, and so on, we all study black politics. That commonality of interest was evident at the Atlanta meeting as the formal panels on mayoral elections and other panels devoted to the changing state of black politics frequently had standing-room-only crowds and were characterized by much heated debate. While there was diversity of opinion and much questioning of presenters and other discussants, there was no even split in the debate. The more popular position was that the emergent trend of deracialization presented an interesting, but indeed troubling dilemma for black politics—its study and practice—in that it appeared to separate in new ways political strategy from political and policy agendas. The rather clear consensus on a new dilemma in black politics as expressed at the NCOBPS meeting gave decisive impetus to this volume.

Two members of the Memphis group, Charles Jones and Michael L. Clemons of Old Dominion University, are contributors to this volume. Several individuals from the NCOBPS meeting—Joseph McCormick, Saundra Ardrey, Robert Smith, and Alex Willingham—have contributed chapters as well. Many others, too numerous to name, contributed by way of their participation in numerous discussions, formal and informal, by telephone, mail communications, and published interviews with various journalists and reporters. Some contributors to this volume were not participants in either the Memphis or Atlanta sessions, or in the subsequent media-sponsored public debate, but were involved in research which seemed most appropriate for this effort. To all of the individuals referred to above, I am extremely grateful. I must also thank the reviewers of the manuscript: Russell L. Adams, Howard University; William Boone, Clark/Atlanta University; Sharon Watson Fluker, Vanderbilt University; and Jerry G. Watts, Trinity College (Hartford). All of the contributors are appreciative of the help given by Lauren Silverman, Executive Editor, and Melonie Parnes, Project Editor, of HarperCollins, without whose expertise this book would not have been published.

I must offer special thanks to two new colleagues whose words of compliments, encouragement, and support have been particularly touching as I pursued this project: Gayle Tate of Indiana University, Bloomington, and David Covin of California State University at Sacramento. I will never forget either of them.

Georgia A. Persons

About the Contributors

Georgia A. Persons is associate professor of political science at Georgia Institute of Technology. Her areas of research include African-American politics, public policy, and urban political development.

Saundra Ardrey is associate professor of political science at Western Kentucky University. Her areas of research include urban politics and African-American politics.

Michael L. Clemons is assistant professor of political science and director of University Planning and Institutional Research at Old Dominion University.

David Covin is professor of political science and director of the Ethnic Studies Program at Sacramento State University. His areas of research interest include African-American politics and Latin-American political movements.

Marilyn Davis is associate professor of political science at Spelman College. Her areas of research include African-American politics and women's studies.

W. Avon Drake is associate professor of political science and director of African-American Studies at Virginia Commonwealth University.

Charles E. Jones is associate professor of political science and director of the Institute for Minority Issues at Old Dominion University. His major areas of research are African-American electoral politics and politics in the new south.

Robert Holsworth is professor and chairman of political science at Virginia Commonwealth University. His areas of research include African-American politics and state and local government issues.

Joseph P. McCormick II is associate professor of political science and director of Masters in the public affairs program at Howard University. His major areas of research are black electoral politics, black mass opinion, and public policy.

Robert C. Smith is professor of political science at San Francisco State University. He has published extensively in the areas of black political thought, black electoral politics, and black mass opinion.

Alex Willingham is associate professor of political science at Williams College. His areas of research include political theory and ideology, African-American politics, and electoral systems.

Zaphon Wilson is assistant professor of political science at Appalachian State University in Boone, North Carolina. His major research interests are African-American politics and southern political development.

Chapter
1

Introduction

Georgia A. Persons

Certainly for the past two decades or more, the presence of blacks in electoral politics has been associated with system challenge and social reform efforts. Electoral politics became the arena for institutionalizing protest, or so it was assumed. While black electoral politics emerged out of the civil rights movement and other protest activities, it also both drove and was buoyed by national-level political developments, which generally created both a political climate and tangible supports for the pursuit of political, economic, and social justice for black Americans.* These national-level supports included, among others, the Civil Rights Acts of 1964 and 1968, the Voting Rights Act of 1965, and the Great Society program of the Lyndon Johnson years. The decade of the 1960s in particular, with some carryover to the early 1970s, was a period of creedal passion in which the general tempo of politics nationally was characterized by a sense of urgency in bridging the gap between the American creed of equality and justice and, in part, the starkly contrasting conditions and status of black Americans.

However, the social movements of the 1960s and early 1970s waned as the period of creedal passion that had helped sustain them inevitably passed (Huntington 1981). This development, coupled with the social and political backlash of the late 1970s drained the black political struggle of much of its vital energies. A second major setback came with the declining political fortunes of the national Democratic party in its loss of the presi-

---

*Throughout this text we have chosen to use the terms "black," "African-American," and "people of African descent" interchangeably.

dency in 1972, and most critically, in 1980. The intervening years of the Carter presidency constituted a brief period of hope, as blacks had been undeniably pivotal to the Carter victory in 1976. However, Carter had notions of cutting federal spending for social programs and increasing defense spending, and generally never championed the black agenda with the fervor expected of him by blacks, or at a level requisite for forging a national commitment to this agenda. Carter's defeat in 1980 gave rise to explicit questioning of the perceived burdensome tie between the fortunes of the Democratic party and its embracing of racial policies (Weisberg 1986; Carmines and Stimson 1988).

The Reagan years were a period of undeniable losses for black Americans. On every policy front—housing, income support, education, employment, affirmative action, and so on—the Reagan regime pursued actions which significantly reduced or vitiated levels of support vital to the well-being of low-income blacks specifically, and all blacks generally. The Reagan regime explicitly pursued two courses of action that were enormously damaging to the interests of black Americans. One was the trivialization and sometimes mocking of issues of race, and the concomitant destruction of significant public sentiment regarding the propriety and need for concern about matters of racism in American society and its consequences for the status and life chances of black Americans. The second major point of attack was clearly quite deliberate in its intention. The Reaganites in and outside of government set about to disparage the tradition of liberalism in national Democratic party politics to the point of creating shame and disdain for this political sentiment among many of its previous adherents. If matters of race were trivial and even farcical, and if liberalism as a political philosophy was bankrupt and illegitimate, upon what moral and philosophical foundation could blacks hinge their hopes and policy demands?

Recognizing the devastating impact of the Reagan first term on the black agenda, and perceiving that the national Democratic leadership was attempting to fashion a conservative course to counter the new Republican stridency, Jesse Jackson, in 1984, audaciously ran for the Democratic nomination for president in an apparent hope of correcting the course being set by the Democrats as they presumably headed back to the White House. Jackson's candidacy did not so much succeed in "framing the issues of the black agenda" as had been hoped for, as it created a new dilemma for the Democratic party. Jackson's candidacy moved to the national levels of the Democratic party an insurgent-style black politics that had heretofore been restricted to big-city black mayoralties. Indeed, at this level, insurgent-style black politics had actually been beneficial to the national Democratic party, both in relation to the posturing of the party vis-à-vis the Republican party, and in terms of providing a philosophical stimulant and constituent support for a generalized urban policy agenda which had beneficiaries well beyond big cities and the black community.

However, by moving insurgent-style black politics to the national level, Jackson created an untenable strategic dilemma for the Democrats. Jackson's candidacy, in effect, joined the issue of race and the subordinate status of blacks within society at large and within the Democratic party specifically, and attempted to force philosophical and policy resolutions of these issues. Although the party had paid rhetorical and policy homage to this issue over the past several decades, the essentially vested interests inherent in the party's total philosophical tenets and its practical politics as well, ultimately mitigate against any such resolution. One impact of Jackson's candidacy was that many Democratic operatives became convinced that by being wed to a large black constituency with a noisome leader at its helm, the party would continue to lose white voters to the Republicans, especially in the South. Jackson lost his bid for the Democratic nomination, did not clearly succeed in enhancing the policy position of blacks within the party, and the Democrats lost the presidency. Jackson ran and lost again in 1988, but reshaped his campaign into one with a more centrist and racial crossover appeal; though he continued to vacillate between waging a mainstream candidacy and leading a protest action (Reed 1986; Walters 1988; Barker and Walters 1989; Morris 1990).

Jackson's efforts had a paradoxical effect. On the one hand, Jackson's two presidential campaigns succeeded in subtly influencing many, even his detractors, in that he effectively got the nation ready for the idea and acceptance of blacks pursuing high political office. On the other hand, Jackson presented a political strategy and model which showed great potential, but which was to be explicitly rejected by the national Democratic leadership and by ambitious black politicians. Jackson's candidacies and the relative successes of each one effectively gave impetus to alternative models of black politics, ones in which candidates pursue a politics of racial reconcillation, presenting the non-negligible currency of race in a newly minted coin. Thus new opportunities for national political prominence and presumably national leadership have been seized by the victories of L. Douglas Wilder as governor of Virginia, David Dinkins as mayor of New York City, and others.

While the emergence of a new cadre of black elected officials is welcomed by some as the way out of the dilemma of blacks in the Democratic party, this new politics of racial reconciliation is, at the same time, troubling. It is troubling because it creates a dilemma within the black community. This new politics of racial reconciliation plays on black pride and thus has a strong emotional and symbolic appeal. It also plays on the desire of many whites to be able to demonstrate their commitment to racial equality, at least at the level of participatory politics. However, its major deficit is frequently its apparent lack of adherence to even a generalized form of the black agenda, and its embrace of a generally conservative agenda. The central concerns and thrust of a black agenda pivots around the plight of the black underclass, whose plight generally is neither recognized nor addressed by the new black politics of racial reconciliation. While the dimunition of explicit racial appeals by black candidates is not necessarily a strategy to be disparaged, the absence of an alternative populist or other reformist agenda does provoke concern in many quarters.

What we saw with the elections of November 1989, in which blacks captured top political executive positions in Virginia and several major cities, was the apparent emergence of a new variant of black politics; a politics of deracialization. These elections were viewed with a great deal of concern and ambivalence by some segments of the black community. These elections constitute a dilemma in that they suggest that blacks must make a major trade-off between achieving more and higher political offices, and pursuing a politics with a marriage between strategy and a reformist agenda.

A series of elections in 1990 helped to give even broader appeal to the use of deracialized strategies in black electoral politics, and suggested that a new era in black politics might have indeed emerged. The effort by Andrew Young to capture the governorship of Georgia was closely watched as an expected repeat of the Wilder victory in Virginia. While Young patterned much of his strategy on the Wilder campaign—downplaying his own racial identity, embracing mainstream issues, courting the support of even the most unlikely rural white voters, taking an affirmative stance on the abortion issue—Young managed to make it into the Democratic runoff, but lost to the 16-year incumbent Democratic lieutenant governor. Young's loss was due to a range of factors, including the fact that despite his stellar credentials he was an outsider to state-level politics. However, the opinion polls consistently reflected an electorate divided along racial lines. The state most completely identified with the "New South" was not prepared to elect a black governor.

Undoubtedly, the campaign that most dramatically illuminated the possibilities and limitations of the new black crossover politics was the 1990 North Carolina Senate race in which Harvey Gantt challenged long-time incumbent and arch conservative, Jesse Helms. This race gripped the attention of the nation. Gantt waged a gallant and strong challenge to Helms and the racist-tinged traditional southern-style politics that had characterized much of the state's politics. Gantt was aided by the thaw in the Cold War which substantially vitiated Helms' traditional anticommunist rhetoric as well as an apparent deeply rooted readiness for change on the part of a considerable segment of progressive whites and most blacks in the North Carolina electorate. Although Gantt lost, it was clear that much change was underway, not only in North Carolina, but in the nation as a whole.

The Gantt race was particularly important in that it began to alter some of the prior resistance of blacks nationally to some aspects of the new black crossover strategy. First of all, Gantt appeared to be much more progressive in his issue stances than either Wilder or Young. Secondly, the very prospect of a black candidate unseating Jesse Helms was so inviting as to offset most other concerns about the status of the black agenda. Unseating Jesse Helms became a galvanizing effort which joined many white and black observers nationwide. In the end, however, as one black political scientist lamented, "Helms' victory served to restore our faith in racism."

Clearly much of politics is about opportunity and winning for white and black politicians. The campaign of Gary Franks from Connecticut for election to the U.S. House of Representatives demonstrated the opportunities created by the black crossover phenomenon. He won the election to represent a district in which only a mere four percent of the voters are black. Franks ran as a conservative Republican, reflecting the continued emergence of conservative black politicians who were most recently given the spotlight during the Reagan years. Franks' election thus adds a new dimension to the growing cacophony of black ideological voices, and at the same time, contributes to a dilemma for black politics. This dilemma is provoked by sentiments of racial pride on the part of many blacks in regard to the election of a black to high office, in the face of substantive politics which are significantly detrimental to black interests as traditionally conceived.

These contests and elections based on deracialized black politics clearly signal some major changes in black electoral politics, perhaps even a new era in black politics. They give cause for an assessment of the significance and meaning of these developments. That kind of assessment is the major objective of this book. However, more than anything else, this book is intended to provoke critical thinking about, and reflection upon, black politics in the present era and its institutionalization to date. Like all books, this one is limited both in what it attempts and what it achieves. However, the effort has been a joyful one. The hope of all of the contributors is that we have made some contribution to the continuing quest for understanding the plight of African-Americans and that we have advanced the contributions of scholarly efforts in enhancing such understanding.

The first three chapters, constituting Part One of this volume, are devoted to questions of leadership and strategy. Chapter 2, by David Covin, is meant to serve as a lens through which to view the entire volume. Covin takes as his fundamental point of departure Du Bois' consideration of the question of leadership in the first decade of the twentieth century. With this chapter we are reminded of the historical centrality of leadership, and questions of the directions of that leadership to the quest by African-Americans for freedom and equality. We are also reminded of how the concept of leadership has been defined and redefined over time. While we see in this chapter the consistency of the desire for and theme of racial uplift in conceptions of black political leadership, we also see how conceptions of black leadership essentially are ideal constructs which rarely fit perfectly with the extremely complex and rapidly changing reality of black life in the United States.

In Chapter 3, the collective experiences of black mayors is shown to reflect clearly the extreme difficulty of setting and pursuing a consistent notion of leadership and political goals, given the exigencies of electoral politics (and personal ambitions) in a changing urban America. In this chapter, "Black Mayoralties and the New Black Politics: From Insurgency to Racial Reconciliation," the author shows how the present dilemma surrounding black crossover politics was sown in the constraints and limitations of insurgent-style black political leadership. Thus what we saw as the emergence of deracialization in the elections of 1989, and its apparent triumph in the elections of 1990, had actually been an emergent strategy in black mayoral politics for some time.

In Chapter 4, Joseph McCormick and Charles Jones present a discussion directed towards "Thinking Through the Dilemma of Deracialization" as an electoral strategy and as a philosophical grounding for framing a political issue agenda. In this chapter we are informed of the (early) distinction between deracialization as an agenda setting strategy and deracialization as an electoral strategy. While the distinction is admittedly somewhat a matter of emphasis, the early use of the term "deracialization" was within the context of framing issues which were central to the black agenda in ways that provoked empathy and support from other major groups. What the reader will readily discern from several chapters in this volume is how an electoral variant of deracialization has triumphed in which candidates deny or diminish the significance of their racial identity, and adopt a repertoire of issue positions which are tangential, nongermane, or opposed to the black agenda. It is this latter context of deracialization as an electoral strategy which is primarily addressed in this volume.

In Part Two of the volume, we turn to a focus on the practice of racial reconciliation and deracialization within the strategic calculus of black politics. In Chapter 5, Drake and Holsworth assess varied attempts at calculated cooperation initiated by black politicians in Richmond, Virginia, since the mobilization of the black community in the early 1970s. The Richmond case is particularly interesting as it gave rise to the *Richmond* v. *Croson* decision in which the Reagan Supreme Court struck down minority set-aside policies that had come to be a hallmark of achievement of the new black politics at the municipal level. The authors analyze the ways in which political accommodation was variously pursued by black officials in Richmond and how various affirmative action policies ultimately served as instruments of elite racial reconciliation. While minority set-aside programs were a product of black insurgency politics, in a significant sense acceptance of this policy represented an effort at racial reconciliation on the part of white business interests. One might also view acceptance of minority set-asides as acquiescence in a rather limited form of social reform, as a substitute for a more profound level of social reform. From the Richmond case we gain insights into combined aspects of black leadership in action, in pursuit of realization of an agenda for reform, within the context of "calculated cooperation," which might well be the future of black-white political relations.

In Chapter 6, Saundra Ardrey assesses the resurgence of black mayoral leadership in Cleveland against its historical dimension as the locus of one of the earliest achievements of the new black politics. Cleveland was one of the two cities (the other was Gary) which gave birth to insurgency as a style at the very early stages of the new black politics. Its first black mayoralty was a rather short-lived one, 1967–1971. Subsequently, insurgency in Cleveland politics was kept alive by the political leadership of one George Forbes, who served many years as president of the Cleveland city council. Forbes thus spent much of his political capital, however, and was unable to achieve victory in the mayoral race. Given the historical context of Ardrey's analysis, we gather significant insight into: (1) the fragility of black political mobilization when it is organized largely as an individualized following, as was the case of the early Stokes mayoralty; (2) the limitations of insurgency as a political style, and ironically, the corrosive effects of this style even within the context of black voter support; (3) the almost magnetic appeal of a deracialized black candidacy in a context long accustomed to racially divisive politics.

In Chapter 7, Charles Jones and Michael L. Clemons illuminate the deracialized political strategy which contributed to the Wilder gubernatorial victory. The authors also present a theoretical model to explain the success of black candidates in majority white settings. We see from their analysis that a successful deracialized strategy is dependent upon many factors, chief among them: (1) a successful political apprenticeship in which the candidate has held other elective offices; (2) genuine party support which ensures key political endorsements; (3) the assumption by the media of a role as ombudsman in mediating the political debate, and discouraging the projection of issues in racially divisive ways; (4) a deracialized issue agenda on the part of the black candidate; and (5) a "wild card" factor, or some unpredictable factor which emerges during the campaign and causes a major turn in the fortunes of the black candidate. The Jones and Clemons analysis also shows that despite the generalized euphoria provoked by the Wilder election, in the end, a black candidate can be successful in a majority white setting, if all things break just right. Even then, victory may well be rather tenuous, as was represented by the "razor thin" margin of the Wilder victory.

The effort by Andrew Young to capture the governorship of Georgia in a deracialized campaign set in the midst of several racially driven challenges to statewide electoral processes is the focus of Chapter 8 by Willingham and Davis. The gubernatorial contest of Andrew Young in Georgia offers an interesting contrast to the Wilder case. Young, too, brought an impressive set of credentials to his gubernatorial race: extensive name recognition, powerful connections, editorial support of the state's leading newspaper, previous electoral success, adequate financial support, and a wholly deracialized issue agenda. These factors were not, however, sufficient for success. In contrasting the Wilder and Young cases, we see the significance of an uneven level of political development between the two states, the disadvantages for Young of not having previously held a statewide office, and the offsetting effects of several racially charged electoral issues prevalent in state politics during the course of the gubernatorial contest. More importantly, we see that deracialization in statewide political contests is not a strategy that guarantees that the limitations of race can be overcome.

In Chapter 9, Zaphon Wilson provides critical insights into the Gantt-Helms race in North Carolina, focusing on the overlapping factors of social change and racial fears which combined to structure the dynamics and the outcome of that U.S. Senate campaign. The North Carolina senate race provides another contrast to the Wilder case and an interesting complement to the Andrew Young case in Georgia. Both North Carolina and Georgia are more "deep south" states in their cultures and political orientations than is Virginia. Whereas Virginia has a major northern tier that provides a northeastern cosmopolitanism to its politics, Georgia and North Carolina both have political cultures driven by dynamics more internal to the states and disproportionately fueled by their respective, though common, historical pasts. We see in both the North Carolina and Georgia cases a tortuous passing of traditional society, a tradition long shaped by a strict segregation of the races, among other factors. While the civil rights movement significantly influenced the traditionally conservative political dynamics in Georgia politics—with a greater mediating impact in Atlanta than elsewhere in the state—the conservative political dynamics of North Carolina have been continually reinforced by a stoking of anticommunist sentiments which overlapped with and embraced an antithesis toward any social reform efforts which challenged traditional conservative mores.

Thus, Wilson frames the contest between Harvey Gantt and Jesse Helms as a contest between a traditionalist and modernizer ideology with regard to the role of government in addressing problems of the economy and socio-economic redistribution. Although racial fears were at the heart of the Gantt-Helms contest, such fears were also a kind of proxy for fears regarding a broader set of concerns—including jobs and employment, implications of educational reform, the future composition of the economic base within the state, the distribution of wealth and power—stimulated by an apparent process of inelectable change underway within the state. We see from the analysis that a deracialized political strategy provided a tantalizing prospect for ushering in a new political order. We also see, simultaneously, the limitations of such a strategy in overcoming resistance based on fears beyond the issue of race, as well as the ease with which racial issues can be deployed against a black candidate in a context in which race has traditionally been a major factor in defining politics.

In the analysis of the Gary Franks election, the focus of Chapter 10, we see a second variant of the deracialization strategy. The first variant is defined by a shift in tactics among liberal black Democrats from a traditional and expected insurgent-style politics, which pivoted around a social reform agenda, to race-neutral and mainstream issues, with retention of an otherwise liberal Democratic philosophy. The second variant, exemplified by the Franks candidacy, involved campaigns in which black candidates ran as conservative Republicans of the Reagan-Bush genre and advanced issue positions which have frequently been used as thinly veiled, antiblack voting cues. While the first variant of deracialization might be seen as a gesture of racial reconciliation directed towards building a common ground between black and white voters, the second variant embraced issue positions which have traditionally formed the basis for divergent interest identification between blacks and whites. Thus the Franks election raises profound questions of just what is black politics.

Persons argues in Chapter 10 that the Franks election must be understood in a broader context than the politics of deracialization and questions of what constitutes black politics. The author argues that the Franks election was part of a broader movement engendered by the Republican party to establish a conservative black leadership cadre to serve as an alternative to, and ultimate replacement for, the traditional civil rights leadership. Within the pragmatism of partisan voter support, the Republican strategy seeks to siphon off 20 to 25 percent of the black vote in order to ensure Republican victory in congressional campaigns, in addition to their controlling the presidency. However, the broader objectives include: altering perceptions of the nature and causes of the black predicament; delegitimating one set of demands made on the political system by African-Americans and legitimating an alternative set of demands; and ultimately legitimating a different set of policy responses to a broad range of domestic policy issues.

Part Three carries in its title the implicit conundrum of black politics in the present era: enduring dilemmas or inevitable transitions? This section brings the volume full circle with two concluding essays. The first, by Robert Smith, focuses on ideology as both the foundation of black politics and as its enduring dilemma. This essay serves as something of a lens for looking backwards over the previous chapters. In the analyses and discussions of the preceding chapters, we have, in effect, seen the outcome of various leadership foci and strategic efforts stemming from at least two major ideological perspectives. The Smith essay defines and clarifies the role of ideology as a foundation of political activity. We are also reminded that diversity in ideology and the rich variety of politics engendered by this diversity within the black community constitutes a major dilemma in the efforts of African-American leadership to develop and sustain movements of racial solidarity to deal with the subordinate status of the group. Thus Smith analyzes, historically and conceptually, the dilemma of ideology in black politics and seeks to explain its significance and implications for politics in the black community.

In a synthesis of the major points in the analyses of the component chapters, the editor, in Chapter 12, argues that deracialization represents yet another manifestation of an historically changing relationship between black political leaders and the mass-level black population. The editor also takes a look forward at the prospects for, and implications of, a reconstituted black politics as we approach the turn of the century. The major thrusts of change within contemporary black politics, of which deracialization is a main manifestation, are placed within the broader context of change in American politics generally. This essay also examines ways in which the two Jackson candidacies restructured black politics by rendering obsolete a traditional dependent leveraging strategy developed out of a leadership group consensus, and supplanting it with an independent, solo political broker model, ripe for exploitation by adherents of a mainstream deracialized black politics. While the chapters of this volume have focused primarily on black electoral politics, in the concluding chapter, the author turns to the articulations of the leaders of two mainline civil rights organizations for signs of the likely future foci of at least one level of black political efforts. In at least one case, we discern a rather telling concern about the need to reaffirm the significance and transcendence of blackness as an identity and cultural phenomenon.

While a total transformation of black politics is not foreseen, the author concludes that there is ample evidence to suggest a greater crystallization of black politics along two major tracks: electoral politics, and what we might call black advocacy politics. Deracialization will likely become the preponderant pattern of black electoral politics, leading increasingly to a politics of symbolism, which provides a necessary gratification for African-Americans, and which offers, as well, affirmation of the principles and myths of the egalitarian nature of American politics. Black advocacy politics will become the primary domain of the traditional civil rights organizations and other black activists. While both concluding essays of Chapters 11 and 12 reflect, by implication, on the question of what can be done to resolve the present dilemmas of black politics, they more directly address the question of what might we expect in the near future. We fully understand that the latter question is a far easier one to contemplate.

REFERENCES

Barker, Lucius and Ronald Walters. 1989. (eds.) *Jesse Jackson's 1984 Presidential Campaign: Challenge and Change in American Politics.* Urbana, IL: University of Illinois Press.

Carmines, Edward G. and James Stimson. 1988. *Issue Evolution: The Racial Transformation of American Politics.* Princeton, NJ: Princeton University Press.

Huntington, Samuel P. 1981. *American Politics: The Politics of Disharmony.* Cambridge, MA: Harvard University Press.

Morris, Lorenzo. 1990. (ed.) *The Social and Political Implications of the 1984 Jesse Jackson Campaign.* New York: Praeger.

Reed, Adolph, Jr. 1986. *The Jesse Jackson Phenomenon: The Crisis of Purpose in Afro-American Politics.* New Haven, CT: Yale University Press.

Walters, Ronald W. 1988. *Black Presidential Politics in America: A Strategic Approach.* New York: State University of New York Press.

Weisberg, Robert. 1986. "The Democratic Party and the Conflict Over Racial Policy" in *Do Elections Matter?* Benjamin Ginsberg and Alan Stone (eds.). Armonk, NY: M.E. Sharpe.

Part
One

ISSUES OF LEADERSHIP AND STRATEGY

Chapter
2

Reflections on the Dilemmas of African-American Leadership

David Covin

INTRODUCTION

This essay is a discourse on African-American leadership in the twentieth century. It takes two sources as its points of departure: (1) W.E.B. Du Bois' formulation of the Talented Tenth in the first decade of the twentieth century, and (2) conversations during the spring of 1989 with members of the California Legislative Black Caucus.

The conversations were based on 28 questions taken from 6 of Du Bois' positions in his conception of the Talented Tenth. Originally scheduled as half-hour interviews, the sessions with the legislators flowered into something richer. The appointments stretched out, ranging from 45 minutes to more than 2 hours. In my notes I found a lode of ore important enough to be given a unique treatment. The notes revealed California legislators at the height of their legislative powers, reflecting on the character of African-American leadership, informed by the probing vision of W.E.B. Du Bois. It was an essayist's dream, and in the tradition of that art of "trying," or "essaying," I have attempted to mine the depths of a many-faceted subject.

In choosing this approach I have necessarily opted not to conduct a "scientific" study. Instead, I have rested my observations on the art of government as seen through the eyes of the leader.

It is a possibility that the dilemmas faced by black leadership in the United States are, and have been, deeper and more salient than those faced by most leadership elements on the planet, now or ever. This is without minimizing the severity of the questions faced by any leadership group.

Societies set the conditions under which leadership may emerge—values and beliefs, procedures and structures, the social settings themselves. An unusual agglomeration of such conditions has been set before African-American leaders. Forbidden access to official or legitimate leadership for most of the period marked by European settlement by the dominant beliefs, values, procedures, and structures of society, African-American leadership has emerged in singular circumstances.

"Leaders" such as Denmark Vesey and Nat Turner, Harriet Tubman and Sojourner Truth, were anathema to the whole social system. They led, and black people followed them, but their leadership was resisted by the dominant forces of the social order. It was not official leadership. It was not legitimate to the dominant social order. It was counter-leadership.

Indeed, "legitimate" African-American leadership—leadership sanctioned by the governing power—only emerged when the prevailing social order was successfully challenged by the Civil War, and the civil rights movement. The success of such challenges identified "officially" the absence of legitimate black leadership and the subsequent "official" need for it. Means were developed to place black people in office, to make their leadership "official," sanctioned by the society. Yet even *legitimate* African-American leadership must operate in a context controlled by others, a context, more importantly, where the perceived interests of African-Americans are greatly at odds with the perceived interests of much of the remaining population.

What notions of leadership develop under such convoluted strictures? How, given these twisted limitations, is leadership to emerge and be chosen?

The most noted examination of these questions was made by W.E.B. Du Bois at the turn of the century. His formulation of the Talented Tenth has been supported, derided, analyzed, and castigated. Yet, while his conceptions were neither fully articulated nor systematic, in the almost 90 years which have passed since his initial explorations of the questions, no treatment has been offered which shares an equal prominence.

I have set out in this essay to see how Du Bois' leadership prescription jibes with those of contemporary black California legislators. The legislators are not representative of black leaders or politicians at large, but they form an important group and I have tried to probe in some depth how they perceive what they do. I have tried to sift out whether any theory of leadership—even inchoate—has emerged from their practice of office; a theory which might challenge, sustain, or supplement that of Du Bois.

The legislators I talked with all came from districts with majority black populations and electorates. Their views are of particular significance with regard to the question of the deracialization of politics considered in this volume. Do their constituencies want their politics deracialized? Do these political leaders—who specifically represent African-Americans—have a deracialized perspective on politics? These are central questions upon which their views can shed valuable light.

The first part of this essay places Du Bois' formulation of the Talented Tenth in its time and place. It also lays out the central features of that conceptualization as I have treated it.

The second part is a short consideration of important differences between the circumstances of African-Americans as viewed by Du Bois in 1903, and as viewed by the legislators in 1989.

The third section identifies six positions derived from Du Bois' conception of the Talented Tenth and compares them with the legislators' views on the same points.

The fourth section concludes the essay with some reflections on contemporary African-American leadership.

THE TALENTED TENTH AND THE WORLD OF ITS ORIGIN

It is important to put the early thought of W.E.B. Du Bois, whence the concept of the Talented Tenth originated, into its context. We have, in this latter day, a tendency to look at Du Bois, Washington, and others as if they wrote from and for our time. This temptation is all the greater with regard to Du Bois because he lived into our time, was—as it were—one of us. But his early writings did not spring from our circumstances—and part of the measure of our accomplishment as a people—even though it is minimized, derided, and despaired over—is that we came so far within his lifetime. By examining the context within which he wrote we can recognize what a great distance that is.

Du Bois' own work is a brutal reminder of the times when he came to Atlanta to work, to try to realize his dream of uplift for his people.

Considering the conditions of black people in the South as a whole, Du Bois writes of "black serfs."[1]

He speaks of black colleges by saying,

". . . they had scattered haphazard throughout the South some dozen poorly equipped High Schools and miscalled them universities."

Black people are ". . . backward and ungraceful. . . ."

Their minds are ". . . wildly weak and untrained. . . ."[2]

Du Bois says progress is often ". . . a surging forward of the exceptional man, and the lifting of his duller brethren slowly and painfully to his vantage-ground."[3]

It is clear from his narrative that he witnessed most black people as these, "duller brethren."

Looking . . . at the county black population . . . it is fair to characterize it as poor and ignorant.

. . . at least nine percent are thoroughly lewd and vicious. . . . over eighty percent are poor and ignorant, fairly honest and well meaning, plodding, and to a degree shiftless. . . .[4]

Du Bois was paradoxical because he was a product of his times, the last third of the nineteenth century, and a maker of his times, the first two-thirds of the twentieth century. We tend to see him through the world he very prodigiously helped to shape, rather than through the one which shaped him. But in examining his ideas, particularly his early ideas, we must examine the soil in which they were planted.

Using today's vocabulary, the late nineteenth century was highly racist, classist, and sexist. It was assumed that there was a natural hierarchy, that on the very top of it were Anglo-Saxon males, that even among Anglo-Saxon males there were some who were head and shoulders above the rest, destined to lead, the fairest artifact produced by the hand of God. The variegated working class and women were conceived of as below the lordly scions of Western European heritage. Constituting the floor, far beneath everyone else, to whose level no one else could ever fall, were the sons and daughters of Africa.[5]

Great as his mind and soul were, Du Bois could not help being influenced by all of these ideas.[6] He was, after all, eminently schooled into the rarest heights of that tradition: undergraduate degree from Harvard; graduate study in Berlin; Ph.D. from Harvard. At a time when a majority of white males in this country were largely unschooled, Du Bois walked away from Harvard with a Ph.D.

Du Bois' first priority was to serve his people, the African race.[7] It was towards that end that he directed his transcendent talent, his stupendous energies, and his long life.

He set out to get others to accept not only what he knew about himself, but also to help other young, black men who had the capacity to achieve. What distinguished him from most other prominent thinkers of the time was that he believed there was a significant body of black men who had the requisite capacity: the Talented Tenth.

Keep in mind that the contemporary science was dominated by thought which relegated black mental capacities to perpetual inferiority, a body of thought popularly reinforced by the postulates of Social Darwinism.[8] For Du Bois to assert that one-tenth of the black population (or at the very least one-tenth of the black *male* population) had the capacity to distinguish itself intellectually placed him in the heretical position of saying that the white and black populations showed the same intellectual profile.[9]

This may not seem an extraordinary stance to us today, though, quite frankly, in the popular mind it is. Despite much noise to the contrary, Jesse Jackson's major disqualification for the U.S. presidency has had nothing to do with his never having been elected to public office. Keep in mind the "Bradley effect" of current polls involving one white candidate and one black candidate. Indeed, in a 1973 study, the leading (and most educated) officers in the Sacramento City Police Department responded to a questionnaire almost universally by saying that black people were mentally and morally inferior to whites.[10] But however unextraordinary Du Bois' position may seem to some today, it was outrageous at the turn of the century. It was contradictory to all the evidence—the established, confirmed, scientific record. That record established incontrovertibly that black people were inherently inferior. Also, it violated the tenets of common sense, because as anyone and everyone could and did observe, black people were demonstrably inferior. That recognition was reinforced in the daily lives of anyone who contacted black people or heard about them. Du Bois is candid about these observations.

Characterizing black awareness, Du Bois says of his fellows, that they ". . . dimly perceive. . . ."[11]

Categorizing the black residents of one county, he says, "Careless ignorance and laziness here, fierce hate and vindictiveness there; these are the extremes of the Negro problem. . . ."[12]

Such a state of affairs should not be surprising. When Booker T. Washington gave his Atlanta Exposition speech, slavery had ended only 30 years before. But the legal conditions that had accompanied slavery had been brought to a close only 28 years earlier. They had been continued for two years after the end of the Civil War by the restorationists and the Black Codes. And more than that, for 18 of the 28 years following the end of de jure slave conditions, circumstances had been worsening for black people. By 1895, in many places throughout the South, conditions for black people, with the exception of chattel slavery, were not far removed from what they had been before 1865—in law and in fact.

In addition, these conditions, both legal and factual, were accompanied by unprecedented violence and social terror to teach the post-slavery generation of black people what their true place was, and to keep them there.[13] They had to be taught through terror, violence, and bloodshed, the lesson their forebears had learned in slavery. Moreover, a majority of black people then alive had either been born in slavery or were the children of people who had been born in slavery. That they constituted a rural peasantry of the most oppressed, exploited, subjugated, and debased kind there can be no doubt.

How Du Bois could see in one of ten from this population the makings of college graduates was beyond the ken of most of his contemporaries. We must not forget that. Sweet Auburn, a street that at one time served as the center for black uplift and ambition in Atlanta, had not blossomed. Fisk, Howard, Lincoln, Wilberforce, Prairie View, Southern, Xavier, Tougaloo, Spelman, Morehouse, Tuskeegee, Hampton, Clark, Atlanta, Morris Brown, and all the rest of the historically black colleges and universities, did not have close to a century of tradition behind them. Neither the NAACP nor the Urban League existed. Marcus Garvey had not come forward. There had been no Harlem Renaissance. Black physicists and

mathematicians and Pulitzer and Nobel Prize winners were literally in-
conceivable. What the "New Negro" meant then was simply a black person who had not been born under slavery and therefore was dangerous to
the white population and had to be intimidated, controlled, or killed.[14]

Yet one out of ten of such a beknighted population, said Du Bois, could
master higher mathematics, the highest forms of European culture, could
compose symphonies and write learned monographs, could become leaders and molders of men and women. His conceptual accomplishment was
mind-shattering. But we must not see it for what it was not.

In 1903 W.E.B. Du Bois was not egalitarian. He did not expect that
many people—in any group—had considerable intellectual capacity. He
did not say that people who were intellectually capable were in any way
superior to those who were manually or in some other way capable, but
he left no doubt as to which of these sets of people should lead, and guide,
and mold.

> . . . true training meant neither that all should be college men nor all artisans,
> but that the one should be made a missionary of culture to an untaught people,
> and the other a free workman among serfs.[15]

> Patience, Humility, Manners, and Taste, common schools and kindergartens,
> industrial and technical schools, literature and tolerance—all these spring
> from knowledge and culture, the children of the university.[16]

In Du Bois' eyes, who, then, constituted the Talented Tenth, and what
is their role?

Who are they? They are ". . . men taught to think. . . ."[17]

And what is their role? ". . . to maintain the standards of the lower
training by giving teachers and leaders the best practicable training; and
above all to furnish the black world with adequate standards of human
culture and lofty ideals of life."[18]

It was, he said,

> . . . not enough that the teachers of teachers should be trained in technical
> normal methods; they must also, so far as possible, be broad-minded, cultured
> men and women, to scatter civilization among a people whose ignorance was
> not simply of letters, but of life itself.[19]

Interestingly enough, in this latter quote, Du Bois refers to "cultured
men *and women,*" (emphasis added) which is inevitable, as Harold Cruse
reminds us, once one looks at the record.[20]

Du Bois' emphasis on the Talented Tenth was to develop a vanguard,
an advanced cadre of the race's most capable people who would then
educate and lead the rest.

The first point he had to establish was that there were such people,
that black people existed who could learn, express, teach, and implement
the highest forms of culture and learning. That position was a direct
contradiction of the popular wisdom. A second point was that these people
existed in such numbers as to be a leadership element for the black population—10 percent.

The next point was one of Du Bois' major bones of contention with Washington. Du Bois believed that this education of the Talented Tenth should receive the highest priority because it was they who must educate and lead all other black people. How can black people go to trade schools if they have not been taught to read and write and cipher? Answer: they cannot. Who is going to teach them to read and write and cipher? Answer: graduates of the colleges and universities. Who is going to found and staff the trade schools? Answer: graduates of the colleges and universities.

Moreover, Du Bois always persisted in the idea that education did not consist exclusively of learning skills, but that it necessarily also included a view of the world, of culture, and ideals. Who were to impart such an enrichment of life if not the graduates of colleges and universities?

The education of the Talented Tenth, for Du Bois, was a prerequisite, a necessary precondition for the uplift of the race. Somebody had to initiate and lead the process. Those people should be capable, the race's "exceptional men," as Du Bois put it.[21] And they should receive the best and most complete kind of education. They then would be in a position to serve the rest of the race, to pull it up after them.[22]

Du Bois believed that the first priority should be given to the development of colleges and universities, and the training of black people through them, because from that set of conditions all other developments would follow. Moreover, he believed that the race *could not* be developed without the leadership of its best men.[23]

Du Bois saw the Talented Tenth as college-educated. He saw them as professional people who used their professions to serve African-Americans. He saw them, and this is clear, as teachers of teachers, and to what extent also teachers of, ". . . common schools and kindergartens, industrial and technical schools," is not as clear. But there is no doubt that teaching, especially teaching teachers, was one of the foremost obligations of the Talented Tenth in Du Bois' mind.

The most concise statement of the role/responsibility of the Talented Tenth as conceived by Du Bois was the development of the race, or in Du Bois' formulation, the uplifting of the race.

One may look at Du Bois' own life at the time to see what he saw as the leader's role. Du Bois was not reticent about recognizing himself as a leader. Du Bois' profession at the time he wrote *The Souls of Black Folk* was college professor, a teacher of teachers.

It is also true that the opportunities for other kinds of leadership, elected or appointed officialdom, for example, were decidedly limited. Even Booker T. Washington, the preeminent African-American leader of the time—and who, to some extent, held leadership philosophies antithetical to Du Bois'—was a teacher and an educator, himself embodying Du Bois' perception of the leader's role.

Du Bois looked at the particular circumstances of his people in his place and time and formulated a conception of leadership addressed specifically to them.

THE SETTING OF CONTEMPORARY VISIONS OF LEADERSHIP

Just as it is important to set the context of Du Bois' thought, it is important to contrast the most salient differences between that context and the environment of the black leaders considered in this essay.

Probably the most important factor is the fundamental change in the condition of the African-American population. It is a population that has grown in absolute numbers, quintupling its size, and it is a population which has moved physically. It is no longer as it was in 1903, an almost entirely rural, southern population. Instead, a directly contrary situation prevails in one respect: it is almost entirely an urban population. Moreover, a significant component of that population lives in the North. When Du Bois wrote of the Talented Tenth going as missionaries to an "untaught people," he meant, literally, that, *going* into the back country of the rural South, as he had during his summers at Fisk, to find and teach the rural folk who lived there, remote, out of the flow of the modern world. Indeed, when he returned to such scenes and others, prior to writing *The Souls of Black Folk,* he found conditions as bad as, and worse than, they had been when he had taught in the South fifteen years earlier.

Today, a missionary going to such sites would find few African-Americans. Such a missionary would be directed to Harlem, Auburn Avenue, the Southside, Watts, Hough, Liberty City, and so on. There she or he would find a dense African-American population, very much a significant component of contemporary life.

The change of the black population has also been marked by a tremendous diversification. Du Bois could say of his contemporaries, ". . . over eighty percent are poor and ignorant. . . ." One can no longer put 80 percent of the African-American population, nationally, or in any significant region of the country, into one such category. African-Americans live in large numbers in the north and the south, east and west, cities and suburbs. Present in all the professions and trades, blacks have great and little wealth, and all the differences between those extremes. African-Americans are scholars, and illiterate; politicians and apolitical; governors and junkies; generals and privates; communists and conservative Republicans; Jews, Buddhists, Christians, Muslims, atheists, Bahai. As a population group, African-Americans are larger than the populations of most countries of the world and every bit as varied.

The leadership opportunities available to today's African-Americans far exceed anything found by Du Bois in 1903. Black people occupy seats of government, and act as spokespersons for national points of view. Such is the world inhabited by contemporary African-American leaders, and their perceptions are shaped by it.

Placing these views in their respective contexts, Du Bois' in 1903, and those of African-American members of California's legislature in 1989, may help us explain and understand some of the major differences and continuities between them.

SIX IDEAS ON LEADERSHIP

I have compared the contemporary leaders' views with Du Bois' on six positions taken from Du Bois' articulation of the Talented Tenth and its role. They are: (1) leadership is solely the responsibility of the college-educated; (2) teachers, or at the very least, teachers of teachers, are, *ipso facto,* part of the black leadership structure; (3) college or classroom teaching is primarily a leadership function; (4) leaders are particularly prepared to guide and direct the African-American masses; (5) African-American leaders must think in terms of racial uplift; and (6) African-American leadership—as distinct from other American leadership—has a specific role in dealing with the particular problems faced by African-American people. It is worth noting that the last two positions have no place in a politics of deracialization.

My comparisons show that on the first of the positions, leadership is solely the responsibility of the college-educated, the legislators are unanimously and explicitly in complete disagreement with Du Bois. On the second and third positions concerning the roles of teachers, or teachers of teachers, while the legislators do not speak directly to them, by implication they disagree with Du Bois. On the fourth position, that leaders are particularly prepared to guide and direct the African masses, the legislators' comments indicated three positions: (a) not responsive to the question, (b) disagreement, and (c) agreement. On the sixth position, that African-American leadership—as distinct from other American leadership—has a specific role in dealing with the particular problems faced by African-Americans, two-thirds agreed and one-third disagreed, though the explanations of disagreement tended to minimize the degree of disagreement. *Deracialization, it seems, is problematic at best for these leaders.* On the fifth position, that African-American leaders must think in terms of racial uplift, the legislators were unanimously in accord with Du Bois. *And this position has no place in a deracialized politics.*

The comparisons show that there are more points of disagreement than agreement on the six positions among Du Bois and the legislative leaders. The major points of disagreement are on the role of the educated and of teachers of teachers, or teachers as principal elements of black leadership. There are minor points of disagreement on the unique role of black leaders *qua* leaders, and the specific responsibilities of black leaders.

The points of agreement, however, are the most critical. They are: the role of leaders in racial uplift, the specific role of black leaders in dealing with the particular problems of black people, and some agreement with the unique role of black leaders *qua* leaders.

All three of the major points of disagreement can be directly related to changes in the conditions of the African-American population between the two periods.

The legislators do not—as Du Bois does—associate leadership exclusively with college training. Uniformly, they disagree that black leadership should be restricted to college-educated people.

Diane Watson says, "Some of the most profound leaders, for example, Fannie Lou Hamer, had or have little education."

Elihu Harris (now Mayor of Oakland) says, "There are so many different levels of experience. Some people get experience in the military. Others learn skills that have utility. Leadership should be based on the capacity to serve—on skills—whether acquired from college or not."

Black people are no longer almost entirely an illiterate, backwater, abased peasantry. They are almost entirely urban, literate, and sophisticated in the ways of the world.

To a significant degree, the cadres whose creation Du Bois championed in 1903 now exist. Eighty-five years later African-Americans have thousands of Ph.D.s, and make up millions of college graduates. Annually, black people assemble in hundreds of professional conferences all over the country—and the world. African-Americans write books, plays, films, music; publish their own newspapers and magazines, and produce films, plays, and television programs. African-Americans pontificate on national television and write syndicated news columns. Among today's black leaders are a governor, scores of mayors, members of Congress, and dozens of state legislators. Blacks have mastered every facet of Western civilization, many of Eastern civilization, reclaimed African civilization, and created some new ones.

The times have changed. There is no need "to create" a Talented Tenth—they exist.

As a result, African-Americans do not place the same priority of emphasis on college education. The *a priori* condition required by Du Bois—the creation of the Talented Tenth—has been met. African-Americans are free to focus on later, developmentally subsequent, concerns.

Perhaps equally importantly, however, African-Americans no longer play—or expect to play—the same role in their own education that they played then. Du Bois wrote of a single generation that put 30,000 black teachers in the South. Now, black teachers no longer teach a majority of black people, indeed, not even a significant percentage of them. And the numbers of black teachers are diminishing. That African-American education would be left almost entirely in the hands of whites was a possibility Du Bois did not envision.

> Southern whites would not teach them; Northern whites in sufficient numbers could not be had. If the Negro was to learn, he must teach himself. . . .[24]

That has not been African-Americans' fate. Blacks have not taught themselves, and as Carter G. Woodson said long ago, blacks have been woefully miseducated.[25]

The legislators speak to the black reality. African-Americans do not educate themselves as they do not have the numbers of teachers needed to educate themselves. They speak to other roles for black leaders.

Senator Watson says,

> The primary role of black leadership is to provide guidance and direction, to represent variations and problems, to speak out for their concerns, to be instruments of change. We should take as our motto, 'Lift as you climb,' from W.E.B. Du Bois.

Bill Greene says, "The primary role of black leadership is to lead. In all respects. Not just in a given area."

Assemblyman Harris puts it this way. "The primary role of black leadership is to set the agenda, to determine direction, to articulate the needs of the black community."

There is another way to look at this anomaly from our vantage point in the twentieth century: teachers are not leaders.

In Du Bois' formative years, by the sake of their educations alone, black teachers were identified, *ipso facto,* as leaders. There were so few of them that—by definition—they were part of the Talented Tenth.

Today this is no longer the case. While black teachers certainly are viewed more favorably and have higher status within the black community than their counterparts have in the white population, they are no longer assumed to be leaders, no longer expected to lead, and aspiring leaders neither emulate them nor pursue teaching as a career.

Du Bois imagined teachers as the molders of future generations. And to a significant degree they still are, or can be. As such molders, he invested them with heavy responsibilities, leadership responsibilities.

> [I]t is the problem of developing the Best of this race that they may guide the Mass away from the contamination and death of the Worst. . . .[26]

Du Bois believed that the Talented Tenth must first be educated that they might uplift their brethren. And how were they to do that? He is not altogether clear, though he gives some indications, but he does indicate that education is to constitute a significant portion of this uplift.

> The Talented Tenth of the Negro race must be made leaders of thought and missionaries of culture among their people.[27]

They do other things as well.

> In the professions, college men are slowly but surely leavening the Negro church, are healing and preventing the devastations of disease, and beginning to furnish legal protection for the liberty and property of the toiling masses. All this is needful work. Who would do it if Negroes did not?[28]

On these points we are clear: Du Bois saw the Talented Tenth as college-educated. Teaching other black people was a central part of their responsibility. They were to use their educations to help uplift the race.

The legislators see leadership not as a function of formal education, but—as much as anything—as a function of political consciousness. They do not identify teaching as a major leadership responsibility.

Senator Watson informs us that,

Black leadership is spawned from conditions—issues. Some of the most effective leaders came out of the movement, at the grass roots. Leaders should be people who can conceptualize, strategize, develop a plan of action.

Senator Greene comments,

Leadership should be chosen by its ability to produce. It should prove itself. They should make an effort to get freedom, work to acquire leadership. Leadership which has been given is dangerous. It can't be trusted.

And, interestingly, he goes on to speak as if he were a spokesman for Du Bois himself.

Leadership should be developed from the kind of education one gets at a Black institution—from the associations there, learning history, knowledge of how to analyse the composite experience, including experience from the community. Black institutions are fundamental elements of leadership development.

Harris tells us,

Leaders should be chosen based on merit and demonstrated capacity to lead. Those who demonstrate the capacity should be given increased responsibility.

In all this the legislators do not once mention the teachers of teachers, or teachers. Greene speaks to the role of black educational institutions in *forming* leaders, but he does not identify—even by implication—the faculty of such places as leaders themselves. Senator Watson has a Ph.D. and teaching was her first career. Yet she does not identify teachers as leaders.

Indeed, these leaders are exercising one important kind of leadership in which they believe: elected political office. This was a kind of leadership virtually unavailable for Du Bois, Washington, and other African-American leaders of the time.

The case is convincing that, on the matter of the legislators' unanimous opposition to Du Bois' positions on the role of the college-educated and teaching as central components of African-American leadership, the difference can be attributed overwhelmingly to the differences in the overall circumstances of the African-American people. The analysis is different because the circumstances are different.

On only one point are the legislators in unanimous agreement with Du Bois: black leadership must think in terms of racial uplift.

This response speaks to a continuing race consciousness in African-American leadership; despite *Brown* v. *The Board of Education,* the civil rights movement, the march on Washington, and the Civil Rights Acts of 1964, 1965, and 1968. Despite their very own presences in the California

State Senate and the California State Assembly, these legislators believe that African-American leaders have a specific responsibility to the race as a whole, and that they must think in terms of lifting up the race collectively. "Lift as you climb," said Senator Watson. The analysis is the same because collectively—in comparison to other significant groups—the circumstances are the same.

Internally, the composition of the black population has changed significantly. Externally, in comparison with other major groups, the aggregate position of the black population has not changed significantly.

The two positions on which the legislators show some significant differences *with each other* point to the perceptual subtleties which arise from the complexity of the contemporary racial question.

One of those positions looks at the responsibilities of African-American leaders—as distinct from other American leaders—with regard to the specific problems which confront African-Americans as a group. Du Bois was unequivocal. African-American leaders have a specific responsibility with regard to such problems. "Who would do it if Negroes did not?"

Senator Watson sees other possibilities, possibilities not envisaged in Du Bois' day. She says,

> White leadership can be as good for Black people as Black leadership. People with similar life experiences, right alternatives, sensitive, committed. Such people can be leaders of all people.

Yet as she continues her discourse, her position seems qualified. Looking at a specific set of conditions, she says,

> With regard to gangs and drugs in Black neighborhoods. Black leadership must be responsive and responsible. It must address conditions and issues. It must set about making an impact. *This is absolutely obligatory.* (Emphasis mine)

But she also explains in more detail her initial response to the question.

> Networks and coalitions are necessary. Leadership must provide resources and expertise. That requires joining hands across racial lines.

Still, it is black leadership which has a special charge. She says,

> Black leaders ought to take hold of the problem and do something about it. The primary role of Black leadership is different from the primary role of white leadership. Black leadership requires more sensitivity. Because it is part of an oppressed group.

Dr. Watson has assumed and maintained her leadership role in a very complex society, one that has undergone unprecedented change, including relations between the races. She has known good and bad white leaders, good and bad black leaders. Indeed, she has known white leaders who have served black constituencies well, and black leaders who have served them badly. She is also familiar with the demographics; that there are not enough black teachers to teach all African-Americans; that blacks live in such varied settings that the elected and appointed leadership which serves the black population will not always be black. She wrestles with the question that given this intricate set of circumstances, how are we to manage?

Despite these worrisome problems, Senator Greene sees the issue differently. He sides with Du Bois' position.

He tells us,

> White leadership is not just as good for black people as black leadership. White leaders can't sense the core of things. It's such a challenge to know our situation that it's unlikely a white politician will believe or go through what's necessary to obtain our goals. The white American experience goes back into European history. We are African-Americans. It is important to go through the means to know who and what we are. We're descendants of Africans. That's how we understand our role. What it means to be leaders.

Yet, later, the Senator seems to echo Dr. Watson's point. He says, speaking about drugs and gangs,

> Black and white leaders should be at the forefront of developing a response. People against whom the problem is perpetuated should be at the forefront, but it is a social problem of the whole society. . . . There is no difference in the responsibility for putting it down. . . . There is no difference between the primary role of black and white leaders.

Then he makes a telling point. "The task is tougher for us and we have fewer resources." He makes another observation of equal importance. "Black leaders don't have a fully developed constituency."

He is making the case on very specific grounds, that this is a fight black leadership cannot win alone. That point, however, does not obviate African-American leadership from a special responsibility to its constituency in these matters. Senator Greene speaks to this special obligation by saying, "People where it's happening should be at the forefront. We are its victims."

Clearly, both of these senators perceive a dilemma. They see a welter of horrid circumstances from which—for a number of reasons, including wealth and social power—black people cannot possibly extricate themselves alone. They see some white leaders of goodwill. Nevertheless, they believe that leaders chosen by and for black people must take the lead in forging solutions to the specific problems which confront black people. They share this cluster of orientations. Yet what these orientations mean to each of them is different. Watson says white leadership can be just as good for black people as black leadership. She then qualifies her statement in such a way as to render it an assertion, which seems to rest more on inner conviction than on her own considered evaluation.

Greene, on the other hand, says white leadership cannot be just as good for black people as black leadership. He goes on to say, however, that the specific problems faced by black people are social problems, and as such, all leaders have equal responsibilities to address them. There is no difference in responsibility between black and white leaders, he says, with one caveat—which completely obliterates his point about equal responsibility. That caveat is that because African-Americans are most directly affected by specific "social problems," we have the greatest responsibility for them. This whole matter of the differential responsibility of leaders by race seems to be a matter on which Senator Greene has reached no final conclusion. The way he wrestles with it illuminates its complexity. It is a question highlighted by other selections in this volume. If there are responsibilities based on race, what does it mean for black people to have politics deracialized?

Senator Greene agrees with Senator Watson that African-American leaders alone do not control enough resources to combat the problems effectively. He also points out another dimension of the question, which delves into the relationship between black leaders and their constituents. African-American leaders, he says, do not have a fully developed constituency. It is not as highly mobilized as the constituencies of the other legislators. It does not consistently apply the kinds of pressure to which this country's official leadership responds. This situation has frightful implications for a deracialized politics. If black politicians self-consciously deny identification with the specific interests of African-Americans, who can be impelled to address those interests?

The underdeveloped African-American constituency has at least two major leadership implications. One is that it leaves African-American leadership relatively free to develop and pursue its own agendas, irrespective of the priorities of its electorate. The other is that it leaves non-African-American leadership *absolutely* free of concerted pressure from the African-American constituency, and therefore at liberty to deal with African-American leadership in any way it deems fit. It also frees black leaders to pursue policies of deracialization when they feel that such policies will further their own political objectives or careers. It is an option which they can pursue, because their constituencies do not hold them accountable. This reality places black leaders clearly on the horns of a dilemma. On the one hand, their underdeveloped constituencies give them great personal latitude. On the other hand, the very same attribute leaves them virtually powerless in the arena where they must contend with their white colleagues for public policy priorities, particularly in so far as those priorities reflect the specific needs and concerns of the black population. To the extent, however, that their policy priorities are non-racial, they can seek and obtain a significant array of white support for those priorities.

Elihu Harris' consideration of the respective merits of black and white leadership leads him to say,

White leadership is not just as good for Black people as Black leadership because nobody can be as good to you as you are to yourself. The responsibility of Black leadership with regard to gangs and drugs is to get directly involved. To play a positive role—to lead by example. Leaders must return physically to the community.

His position is much less tortured than either Greene's or Watson's. Yet he, too, feels a need to comment on the particular quality of black leadership. He observes,

> The primary role of Black leadership is different from white. Black leadership is often informal. It lacks institutional power. Much of it is social in nature (religious leadership).

Harris stands foursquare with Du Bois on the specific responsibility of African-American leadership, but he alludes to some of the same constraints which trouble Watson and Greene: black leadership lacks institutional power.

Du Bois' position on the relationship between leaders and followers partakes of his unmistakable elitist posture. Du Bois believed that leaders ought to lead, and that they ought to know where they want to go. This view, by the way, is very much akin to Harold Cruse's.[29] Such a model conflicts with the normative one popular in the United States which posits that elected leaders should represent the views of their constituents. That the popular U.S. normative model is naive in the extreme contributes in no small measure to the ludicrous and often pathetic character of public life in this country. This popular model does not address such perfectly obvious questions as: Whose views of a leader's many and diverse constituents (even within the same political party), is the leader to represent? What happens to the people whose views are not represented? Does the leader represent the constituents' views or their interests? Who determines, and by what methods, the interests of constituents? What does the leader do when the interests (and/or) views of the leader's constituents conflict with each other? All these questions also bear specifically on the politics of deracialization as such politics affect the *presence* of African-American interests and perspectives in the political arena.

These matters did not arise to trouble the early Du Bois because the position he articulated, with respect to the Talented Tenth, was that leaders lead and followers follow.

Du Bois felt that the Talented Tenth should use their superior educations to inform and uplift the masses, to pull them in the right direction, which they knew but the masses did not.

One of the characteristics of black leadership, however, and one which Du Bois himself exemplified throughout his life, has been its diversity. To the extent that it has pulled its sisters and brothers, it has pulled them in different directions.[30]

Du Bois' model of leadership in 1903 was, for black people, elitist. The role he ascribed to the Talented Tenth is an elitist one. It is altruistic, service-oriented, and non-materialistic, but elitist nonetheless.

Du Bois' visualization of the Talented Tenth assumed a unified black leadership. That seems a curious assumption for Du Bois to have made, as insistent as he was—even during this period—in recognizing the virtues of black leadership diversity.[31]

Senator Greene and Assemblyman Harris were in direct disagreement with each other on this point. Senator Greene rejected Du Bois' leadership model. He comments.

> Black leadership should get political direction *primarily* from their interpretation of the wishes of their constituents. Leaders have to understand the need, the want, the station, the right of the people they represent. The constituency is necessary for everything the leader produces. Political thinking is collective. It is not individual.

Keep in mind that Senator Greene has already told us that the African-American constituency is underdeveloped. This condition places heavy emphasis on the leader's *interpretation* of the wishes of constituents, because they will not tell the leader their wishes with the same consistency, frequency, and intensity of more fully developed constituencies. Nor do such constituents examine the leader's actions with the same consistency, frequency, and intensity. This condition can enable the leader to minimize the actual differences within the constituency because of the importance of the leader's *interpretation* of constituent wants. In other words, because of the peculiar characteristics of the African-American constituency, an emphasis on responsiveness to it, or representation of it, may be less than it appears, since this representative function relies so heavily on the leader's interpretation or sensitivity to the constituency.

Senator Greene's assessment of the character of political thinking—that it is collective—is a deep and powerful observation. It approaches what Hannah Arendt refers to as the *public* dimension of political life—its collective nature—which makes it specifically political. This central perception, however, does not deny the premise that collective thinking can go on within the leadership. Indeed, Senator Greene goes on to make this very point. He says, "Even a veto can be overridden." He's asserting that individual actions in political life are not complete. The kind of collective thinking that results in the legislature overriding the individual executive is a direct expression of collective political thinking or acting that goes on entirely within the governmental or leadership apparatus. It is collective thinking, but not necessarily tied to the larger body politic, to the constituencies.

Unlike Senator Greene, Assemblyman Harris embraces Du Bois' view. He argues that,

> Black leadership should get political direction *primarily* from their own understanding of political, social, and economic conditions. Black leadership has the responsibility to develop a vision for the future of the race and lead on the basis of that vision—and their constituents should sometimes act as a corrective.

Harris says,

> The intensity, the scope of leadership (in preparing themselves) is different. Leadership generally requires one step beyond. Otherwise, what distinguishes leaders from followers?

On these two positions we can see the legislators grappling with the question of what it means to be an African-American leader in a society much more complex, and with an African-American population infinitely more varied, than the one Du Bois described in 1903. In one sense, African-Americans are much more folded into the society at large than they were in 1903. Yet it is also unmistakable that they have retained a distinct identity, and collectively, a distinct social place. How to handle that specific identity, with its concomitant conditions, in the midst of a heterogeneous society is a central problem for African-American leaders. It is one on which these leaders have come to quite different conclusions, to the degree that they have come to any conclusions at all.

Nevertheless, one of the most surprising elements of these conversations was that while the legislators disagreed with Du Bois directly on three of the six positions, agreed with him on one, and were split on the other two, they disagreed with each other on only two positions.

Even the positions on which they disagreed, especially on the role of black leaders on specific problems, did not place them at loggerheads. There was a considerable degree of overlap in their thinking, particularly between California's two black senators.

LEADERSHIP FOR OUR TIME

What accounts for these contemporary black legislators' agreement two-thirds of the time on central questions regarding black leadership? There are a number of possible contributing explanations, many of them worthy of comment. I will start with one often identified by political scientists.

Leaders, political leaders, undergo a process of socialization and political socialization which leads them to share certain values and perceptions.[32] On such matters they have much more in common with each other than with members of the population at large. Indeed, in their conversations, Senators Watson and Greene both spoke frequently of "the rules of the game," how things were accomplished in the legislature, and the necessity of mastering the process and the techniques required to get things accomplished. They also commented avidly on how they and their African-American colleagues in the legislature had mastered such matters. Senator Watson specifically cited Willie Brown, Speaker of the California State Assembly. She said that though one might not always agree with him, one could not help respecting his mastery of the legislative process. Most elected political leaders go through a long apprenticeship as political workers, activists, party supporters, aides, and candidates, during which they are inculcated in the specific mores of the U.S. political establishment. Elihu Harris spoke to this point when he mentioned rewarding competent people with increasing responsibility. He mentioned, specifically, appointed and elective office. Hence, one source of such agreement between the leaders may well be their common acculturation into political leadership, and, specifically, to the activist ranks of the Democratic party and to the California state legislature.

Another important factor to consider might best be called a modal interpretation of African-American life in the United States. Despite the great variety of our population, there is much evidence that, particularly in the political arena, a modal view among African-Americans exists. To cite just a bit of it—continued support of the Democratic party by more than 80 percent of the African-American electorate; within the Democratic party, the greater than 70 percent support of the African-American electorate for Jesse Jackson in the presidential primaries of 1984 and 1988. Diane Pinderhughes has done some important work that shows the African-American electorate's attitudes clustering on the left end of the political spectrum while the white electorate's attitudes cluster at the center.[33]

More anecdotal evidence can be found in the work of African-American scholars and thinkers. Bill Strickland, in a 1980 address concerning the conditions of African-Americans, said that while he was preparing his remarks he reviewed the Black Agenda for the Black Political Assembly in Gary during 1972. He found no need to update it because it said everything he wanted to say, and said it better than he could. *The essential conditions had not changed.*[34] During the same conference, Harold Cruse said that everyone in attendance could summarize the essential conditions of the black population, that we could identify the problems, that we would all be fairly much in agreement—and that we would all be right![35]

Simply put, there is a widespread, perhaps modal, agreement among African-Americans about the essential conditions of our existence. It may well be that agreement, which in part, the three legislators share, and which contributes to the accordance of their responses. The agreement concerns the comparative position in U.S. society that black people share, which has remained consistent since Du Bois wrote *The Souls of Black Folk.*

This interpretation lends credence to the way Cruse followed up his 1980 remarks about our almost universal agreement on the particulars of our condition. We all know what the problems are, he said. The question is, what are we going to do about them?

That is where we disagree. That disagreement may well be reflected in the legislators' differing responses. They agree about what we face. Their disagreement is over what to do about it.

What leadership style should African-Americans adopt?

Cruse says—his 1968 interpretation would still stand today; witness his *Plural But Equal,* written in 1988—we suffer the crisis of the Negro intellectual, which is essentially a leadership crisis (observe the parallel between his ideas of leadership and Du Bois'). If leaders fail to lead, or lead in the wrong directions, we can expect our central problems to remain, and to remain in their essence much the same. They may improve slightly, or they may even become exacerbated, but in their essence they will remain much the same. Hence, the diagnoses which were made in 1968, and 1972, and 1980, still stand today.

Du Bois spoke not only to the composition of the Talented Tenth, but also to its mission. While these contemporary African-American leaders are not in accord with Du Bois on the necessary composition of African-American leadership, they do share his concern for racial uplift. The principal reason for that shared concern is that no leadership cadre has emerged which has eliminated the need for it. The external situation which black people faced at the turn of the century is one that, in the aggregate, they still face today.

The stumbling block before these leaders is not where potential leaders should come from. They agree that such leaders should come from all sectors of the society and that political consciousness should propel them into the quest for leadership. Nor is there a point of contention in what these leaders' ultimate objective should be. That objective is *racial* uplift. These legislators, coming from the constituencies they represent, do not have a deracialized perspective on politics. Where their consensus fractures—or at least is dimly perceived—is on the question of means. How are leaders to bring about racial uplift? Not through teaching; they were agreed on that. But how?

Through making laws? Since these people are all legislators, that is a reasonable assumption. But none of them said that. They have all been legislators long enough to know that making laws—*at least the kinds of laws they are able to get passed*—is not doing the job. What then? The only specific alternative offered was Harris's admonition to move back physically into the community and lead by example—but example of doing what?

These leaders no longer incorporate many of Du Bois' leadership conceptions into their philosophies because they face, in part, a different reality. They agree on many leadership questions. Even when they disagree they often cite similar concerns. Nevertheless, the crisis Harold Cruse alerted us to in 1968 and lamented again in 1988 persists.

What Cruse labels a crisis of leadership is, to a degree, a crisis of conceptualizing the role of leaders. Now, that is a very narrow edge to sustain a crisis, but it is a critical one. In the Madisonian model, one role of leaders is to fight each other and to combine against those who would wrest away their social position. Unfortunately, in lieu of alternatives, too many contemporary black leaders have seized upon it. They may be people of goodwill, but they have no leadership theory specific to their condition that directs them. Or they have so completely adopted the U.S. model that their leadership theory or orientation minimizes the role of any special racial component in politics.

For the legislators in these conversations, no systematic conceptualization of how to address the collective position of the black population has turned up. That leaves them at loose ends about what should be done to obtain solutions for problems upon which they are agreed. Within the context of the United States perhaps the most difficult problem for black leaders is conceptualizing a way in which they can be effective. If they serve society at large they don't necessarily serve black people; (the predominant failing of deracialization), and if they serve black people, the society at large will expend stupendous energies to limit their effectiveness. This is a leadership conundrum. The best efforts must be applied to resolving it, and such efforts must be applied continually because the particular circumstances which sustain it continuously change.

Du Bois argued for *teaching people to be leaders.* In that teaching, he argued, specific attributes ought to be stressed. Absent some theory of identifying or preparing potential leaders—*because we do not condition or control the social and political mechanisms through which the society at large shapes leaders*—we must accept as leaders whomever we get, with whatever predispositions they have been encouraged to develop, with no grounds for challenging their credentials to lead except *ex post facto* ones.

This would not be much of a problem if black interests and the interests of the society at large were congruent, but we have several hundred years and a very long record of the contemporary period that establish incontrovertibly that this is not the case.

What are we to do?

Du Bois developed a theoretical perspective about black leadership from the specific circumstances of his time. There is no corresponding effort arising from and addressing the decidedly different conditions of the contemporary era which has a collective appeal to African-American leadership. Hence the consensus that African-American leaders share about our condition, as exemplified by these legislators, bears no fruit because there is no plan—even one they can disagree about—for leading us out of this morass.

This recognition may help—though little more than that—to explain some of the quagmire in which we are mired. Our leaders, for the most part, are extremely capable people. But even the most powerful engines on a ship without a rudder will keep turning it in circles.

NOTES

The interviews with the legislators were conducted in their offices at the California State Capitol during March and April of 1989.

1. W. E. B. Du Bois, "On the Wings of Atlanta," *The Souls of Black Folk* (New York: The New American Library, 1969), 112.

2. *Ibid.*, 116, 119, W. E. B. Du Bois "Of the Training of Black Men," *The Souls of Black Folk* (New York: The New American Library, 1969), 123.

3. *Ibid.*, 127.

4. W. E. B. Du Bois, "Of the Quest of the Golden Fleece," *The Souls of Black Folk* (New York: The New American Library, 1969), 169.

5. Du Bois himself writes of these conceptualizations. See "Of the Dawn of Freedom," and "Of the Training of Black Men," *The Souls of Black Folk* (New York: The New American Library, 1969). See also Thomas F. Gossett, *Race: The History of an Idea in America* (New York: Schocken Books, 1965).

6. In Du Bois, "On the Wings of Atlanta," 116, for example, Du Bois writes of "the rule of inequality," and he also writes, showing his true feelings, that it is *almost* but not quite as silly to try to make a blacksmith out of a scholar as to try to make a scholar out of a blacksmith. His early correspondence, especially from Germany, reveals such sentiments. See Herbert Aptheker (ed.), *The Correspondence of W. E. B. Du Bois: Vol. I Selections, 1877–1934* (Springfield: University of Massachusetts Press, 1973).

7. *Ibid.*, 24, for example, "I am very anxious therefore on my own account but especially for the sake of my race, to try to obtain this degree."

8. Thomas F. Gosset, *Race: The History of an Idea in America* (New York: Schocken Books, 1965), 144–175.

9. Virginia Hamilton (ed.), *The Writings of W. E. B. Du Bois* (New York: Thomas Y. Crowell, 1975), 50.

10. *Citizens' Advisory Committee on Police Practices Report,* Sacramento, California, August 1973.

11. Du Bois, "Of the Training of Black Men," 138.

12. W. E. B. Du Bois, "Of the Black Belt," *The Souls of Black Folk* (New York: The New American Library, 1969), 157.

13. This is Leon Litwak's interpretation. See his lecture, "Race Relations from Reconstruction to the Civil Rights Movement," 1988.

14. Joel Williamson, *The Crucible of Race* (New York, Oxford: Oxford University Press, 1984), 111.

15. Du Bois, "Of the Wings of Atlanta," 117.

16. *Ibid.*, 118.

17. *Ibid.*

18. Du Bois, "On the Training of Black Men," 129.

19. *Ibid.*

20. Harold Cruse, *Plural But Equal* (New York: Morrow, 1987), 181, "In . . . 79 Black colleges surveyed for 1926–27 by the United States Bureau of Education, 5,944 of the 12,090 students were women."

21. Hamilton, *Writings of W. E. B. Du Bois,* 50, "The Negro race, like all races, is going to be saved by its exceptional men."

22. *Ibid.*, 53.

23. *Ibid.*

24. *Ibid.*, 128.

25. Carter G. Woodson, *Miseducation of the Negro* (Philadelphia: Hakim's Publications 1933).

26. Hamilton, *Writings of W. E. B. Du Bois,* 50.

27. *Ibid.*, 55.

28. Du Bois, "Of the Training of Black Men," 134.

29. While Cruse is most insistent on this point in *The Crisis of the Negro Intellec-*

tual (New York: William Morrow and Co., Inc., 1967), it is also a consistent theme of *Plural But Equal.*

30. This is a constant theme in Cruse's works, articulated forcefully in *The Crisis of the Negro Intellectual* and maintained in *Plural But Equal.*

31. See especially, W. E. B. Du Bois, "Of Mr. Booker T. Washington and Others," *The Souls of Black Folk* (New York: The New American Library, 1969).

32. See, for example, Peter Bachrach, *The Theory of Democratic Elitism* (Boston and Toronto: Little, Brown, and Co., 1967), especially "Elite Consensus," 47–68.

33. Dianne M. Pinderhughes, "Realignment, Dealignment and Black Politics," paper presented at the National conference of Black Political Scientists, April 2–5, 1986, Chicago, Illinois.

34. The Working Conference on the Black Political Party, October 15–18, 1980, Sacramento, CA.

35. *Ibid.*

Chapter
3

Black Mayoralties and the New Black Politics:
From Insurgency to Racial Reconciliation

Georgia A. Persons

INTRODUCTION

The November 1989 elections appeared to have marked the beginning of a new era in black electoral politics. Several African-Americans were elected as mayors of major American cities—New York, New Haven, Seattle, Cleveland, and Durham, North Carolina—and in a most historic development, L. Douglas Wilder was elected as the nation's first black governor in the state of Virginia. The fact that in each case these men won in majority white jurisdictions made these developments only somewhat unique as blacks (Congressmen Dellums of California, and Wheat of Missouri, for example) had previously been elected in majority white election districts. However, what gave the 1989 elections such prominence were their manifestations as a clustering of events which collectively posed a challenge to dominant theories of American electoral politics generally and black politics specifically. Prior to these elections, the predominant pattern and constraint in the election of black candidates had been their emergence from concentrated, predominantly black (population) locales, with the corollary of a strong and persistent reluctance of white voters to support black candidates.

Coupled with this seemingly anomalous development, the factor which sparked concern and debate, first among analysts of black politics and later incorporating journalist/observers and laypersons alike,[1] was the apparent deliberate absence of familiar appeals to black voters, as well as the absence or diminution by the winning candidates of campaign issues which could be interpreted as addressing "the black agenda." Thus, in effect, the 1989 elections conveyed a new set of signals, a new political message. Interpretations of the strategic contents and significance of the 1989 elections as manifestations of an emergent political strategy of deracialization is the specific focus of Chapter 4 in this volume. For the purposes of this chapter, the 1989 elections serve as a reflective backdrop for attempting to understand the evolution of the new black politics. The analysis and discussion presented in this chapter assume that the 1989 elections constituted a significant political development with implications for the future practice of black politics, and constituted as well a new and important reference point for the analysis and understanding of politics in America.

From the vantage point of early 1990, the 1989 elections appeared to portend, or at least to crystallize in our understanding of things past, the end of an era in black political struggle. The possible end of an era and the implications inherent in such a magnitude of change provoke concern and the quest for explanatory factors, because profound questions of the status of blacks in America remain unanswered. Yet, one also senses other profound changes under way which promise to affect, in non-negligible ways, the future status of blacks in America. Some of these changes are occurring external to the black community, such as the growing number of newly immigrant groups and their increasing influence socially and politically. The social and political emergence of newly immigrant groups is not only altering the ethnic mosaic of major urban areas, but in many instances strains the social order and threatens to redistribute political power, just as blacks had achieved some limited successes in exacting rewards from the political system. Moreover, the socio-political dynamics of a culturally significant and politically distinct, multiethnic society are likely to be far different than those attendant to a society which, in relationship to the quest for black political empowerment, was in the main, culturally and politically defined by a bifurcation along racial lines of black and white.

Other dynamics, which are indeed ominous, are present within the black community. There is a widening gap between the black underclass and the rest of black America (Wilson 1978; 1987). This widening gap seems impervious to the social and political thrusts around which the black community has been mobilized and directed for the past several decades. In short, the successes of black political empowerment seem unable to deliver on the expectations and promises so fervently anticipated a few decades ago. Yet, what we have conceptualized as the new black politics simultaneously appears to be facing imminent transition and possible eclipse, leaving significantly unaltered the status of large segments of the black community.

The *primary* objective of this chapter is to illuminate a single question: in examining the evolution of black mayoralties, what developments, or patterns of developments, signalled the nature of strategic changes embodied in the 1989 elections? The focus is on black mayoralties as the embodiment of the major achievements and constraints of the new black politics. The focus on black mayoralties particularly affords illumination of the evolution of the new black politics from its early manifestation as an insurgent movement to its seeming "maturation" as a variant of "politics as usual," in which the significance of traditional racial appeals and social reform efforts apparently have been diminished.

In examining the collective evolution of big-city black mayoralties, three simultaneous and overlapping developmental paths are apparent:

1. *A pattern of insurgency* characterized by challenges to the prevailing political order, embrace of a social reform agenda, and utilization of a pattern of racial appeals to mobilize a primary support group of black voters;

2. *A pattern of racial reconciliation* in which, in some cases, black candidates woo white voters by simply diminishing, avoiding, or perverting racial appeals, while in other situations black candidates exploit the images of insurgent-style candidates to enhance by contrast their own appeal as racial moderates; in both instances black candidates expect to reap the benefits of racial symbolism and concomitant black voter support in a white-on-black contest;

3. *A pattern of institutionalization* which underlies all black mayoral successes in that the number of black mayoral successes has increased over time, and their longevity and succession in office have increased, reflecting their grounding, though in varied manifestations, in the systemic fabric of American politics.

The argument is advanced here that, within the context of the institutionalization of black mayoralties, and simultaneously the parent phenomenon of the new black politics, the apparently anomalous nature of the 1989 elections, in fact, reflects an ongoing evolution from a pattern of spirited insurgency to a pattern of attempts at racial reconciliation evident in black mayoral politics specifically, and black politics generally. Data for this chapter were drawn from extant studies of black mayoralties and the author's own research on black mayoralties in Atlanta, Washington, D.C., Gary, Newark, and other cities.

THE RISE OF THE NEW BLACK POLITICS

If we seek to understand change of significant magnitude, we need to understand the past as the standard against which to assess and interpret the new. What analysts and laypersons alike have, for more than two decades, characterized as the new black politics—its promises and expectations—has defined for many a *preferred conception* of black politics; though as the point will be made later, this conception has not in reality embraced all of what has in effect passed—to use a racially laden pun—as black politics. In its conceptions and early manifestation the new black politics represented a major strategic shift in tactics used by blacks. Analysts generally identify three shifts in black strategic activities which have occurred in the recent past: the first of which occurred between 1955 and 1957 in the movement for civil rights; the second in 1966–1967 with the black liberation movement, and the third in the period 1970–1972 with the movement to black electoral politics (Walters 1980). The latter and current period has been characterized as the era of "the new black politics" (Preston et al. 1982). The new black politics sought to shift black strategic efforts away from various modes of protest and civil disobedience to electoral politics as the means of achieving black political and social empowerment. Varying forms of representation are presumed to bestow varying benefits upon the group seeking representation (Pitkin 1967). It was assumed that with the achievement of descriptive *and* substantive representation, that is, the election to office of individuals who mirrored the racial background *and* political philosophies of blacks, that significant social and political benefits would accrue to the black community.

The new black politics represented primarily a strategic concensus, the pursuit of electoral politics, that has proven to be a consensus open to rather broad interpretations in terms of specific strategies. However, in its initial conception, the new black politics was a strategy presumed to be anchored in a consensus on objectives as well; indeed assumed to be so strongly shared within the black leadership corps that it constituted a cause of the intensity of the civil rights movement. The early promises and expectations of the new black politics were eloquently captured in an ambitious definition proffered by William Nelson:

> At bottom the new black politics is a politics of social and economic transformation based on the mobilization of community power. . . .

> The new black politics represents an effort by black political leaders to capitalize on the increasing size of the black electorate; the strategic position of black voters in many cities, counties, and congressional districts, and the growing political consciousness of the black community. It constitutes an immensely serious effort to build bases of electoral strength in the black community *and organize black political interests around the power of the vote* (emphasis added) (Nelson 1982).

Perhaps the singular achievement of the new black politics has been the election of black mayors in many of the major cities in America as well as in hundreds of small towns, totalling some 293 black mayors in early 1990. Prior to the election of Douglas Wilder as governor of Virginia, big-city black mayors were the most visible black elected officials; their responsibilities to the citizenry are much greater and more comprehensive than that of most other local officials, and their influence less subject to dilution than representatives in Congress. Thus the election of a black mayor, particularly a big-city black mayor, constitutes a major socio-political achievement, a highly symbolic achievement, as well as highly visible evidence of black strategic efforts. Yet prior to the 1989 elections, questions were being raised about the efficacy of black mayors (Preston 1990), reflecting recognition that the expectations and promises of their regimes were not being realized.

THE INSTITUTIONALIZATION OF BLACK MAYORALTIES AND A CHANGING POLITICAL ORDER

Institutionalization as a Political and Social Process

Social scientists use the concept of institutionalization to capture a dynamic in the processes of socio-political development when political leadership, governmental bodies, the rules and procedures of governance, and general methods of politics become accepted and widely supported by the polity (Polsby 1968). Institutionalization is assumed to have occurred when methods of politics, political leadership, governmental institutions, rules and procedures of governance reach a significant level of stability, as characterized by orderly, predictable, and infrequent changes, and in some cases, obtain a presumed permanent status. Institutionalization is characterized by predictability in patterns of recruitment of political leadership, professionalization of personnel and standards within governmental bureaucracies, infrequent and orderly change, and adaptability of political processes and institutions to change. The key factors to successful institutionalization are broad-based public support and acceptance, stability of functions, procedures, and political leadership resulting in a stable leadership corps.

The concept of institutionalization has been used explicitly as an analytical framework for studies of the U.S. Congress, which is said to have institutionalized over time as turnover in its membership has declined, as members have served longer terms, and as representation has become more stable (Polsby 1968). The concept has also been used extensively in the study of developing societies, particularly in reference to the processes of political development in post-colonial regimes, as the procedures and institutions of representative democracy have taken hold (Nordlinger 1971). It is therefore a useful concept for understanding the interplay of social and political dynamics pertinent to the realization of politically defined objectives.

The concept of institutionalization is particularly useful in observing and understanding the process of representation of diverse interests. It is useful as well in understanding changes in institutional arrangements in response to broad-based social change. Institutionalization thus implies a developmental process incorporating changes and adjustments in the dynamics and structures of political processes over time, bolstered by the critical element of broad-based, mass-level acceptance and support. As such, it is something of a "settling in" process for a new political order, a

movement towards stability and permanency, and not an immediate oc-
currence. Thus, in regard to black mayoralties, the mere election of a large
number of black mayors is not automatically tantamount to institutionalization, although such electoral successes may well be manifestations of
broad-based public acceptance and thus reflect some of the preconditions
of institutionalization.

Today, when one speaks of the election of a black mayor, reference
is not necessarily made to the comparatively simple development of 1967
when the nation's first black mayors were elected. In the late 1960s and
early 1970s, the election of a black mayor was generally the outcome of
a black candidate challenging the "white power structure" in a bruising,
racially charged contest. Twenty years later, the election of a black mayor
may occur as the result of a number of different political configurations:
(1) the election of a first black mayor for a given locale based on the
mobilization of a majority or critical near-majority black population (the
dominant pattern of the early cases); (2) the election of a first black mayor
in a predominantly white setting (this variant emerged early in Los Angeles in 1973 and has now been repeated in several locales); (3) the election of a black successor to an incumbent black mayor whose statutory
term in office has ended; or (4) the election of a black successor in the
unseating of an incumbent black mayor. Thus, there is now considerable
diversity in the circumstances surrounding the election of black mayors,
yet all reflecting the results of a pursuit of electoral politics.

In regard to big-city (population 150,000 and above) black mayors,
there have been roughly five electoral waves. The first wave occurred
with the election of black mayors in Cleveland and Gary in 1967, and
Newark in 1970. Cleveland lost its first black mayoralty in an unsuccessful
effort to elect a second black mayor in 1972. The second wave occurred
with the election of black mayors in Detroit, Atlanta, and Los Angeles in
1973, and the District of Columbia in 1974.[2] The third wave brought black
mayors to New Orleans and Oakland in 1977, and Birmingham in 1979.
The fourth wave occurred in 1983 with the election of Harold Washington
in Chicago, Wilson Goode in Philadelphia, and Harvey Gantt in Charlotte,
North Carolina. The black mayoralty in Chicago was lost in 1989, subsequent to the death of Harold Washington during his second term in office.
In Charlotte, Harvey Gantt was defeated for reelection by a white female
Republican. Baltimore was added in 1987, initially by default with the
election of then Mayor Shaeffer to the state governorship, and the automatic ascendancy of the black deputy mayor to the position of mayor.
Harvard-trained attorney and Rhodes scholar, Kurt Schmoke became the
first elected black mayor of Baltimore in 1987. The fifth and most recent
wave occurred in November 1989 with the election of black mayors in
New York City, New Haven, Seattle, Durham, North Carolina, and again
in Cleveland, Ohio (see Table 3.1).

During the 20 years or so since the election of the first black mayor
in a major city, several electoral junctures have been reached, including:

Table 3.1   BLACK MAYORS OF CITIES WITH POPULATIONS OVER 50,000,
(1990)

Name	City	Population	% Black
David Dinkins	New York City	7,071,000	25.0
Thomas Bradley	Los Angeles, CA	3,259,000	17.0
W. Wilson Goode	Philadelphia, PA	1,642,000	40.2
Coleman Young	Detroit, MI	1,086,000	63.1
Kurt Schmoke	Baltimore, MD	763,000	54.8
Marion Barry	Washington, D.C.	626,000	70.0
Michael White	Cleveland, OH	573,800	45.0
Sidney Barthelemy	New Orleans, LA	554,000	55.3
Norman Rice	Seattle, WA	493,800	9.5
Maynard Jackson	Atlanta, GA	421,000	66.6
Lionel Wilson	Oakland, CA	356,000	46.9
Sharpe James	Newark, NJ	316,000	46.9
Richard Arrington	Birmingham, AL	277,000	55.6
Richard Dixon	Dayton, OH	181,000	37.0
Jessie Ratley	Newport News, VA	154,000	31.5
Carrie Perry	Hartford, CT	137,000	33.9
Thomas Barnes	Gary, IN	136,000	70.8
John Daniels	New Haven, CT	129,000	31.0
Chester Jenkins	Durham, NC	110,000	47.0
Edward Vincent	Inglewood, CA	102,000	57.3
Noel Taylor	Roanoke, VA	100,000	22.0
Walter Tucker	Compton, CA	93,000	74.8
Melvin Primas	Camden, NJ	82,000	53.0
John Hatcher, Jr.	East Orange, NJ	77,000	83.6
George Livingston	Richmond, CA	77,000	47.9
Edna W. Summers	Evanston Township	72,000	21.4
Walter L. Moore	Pontiac, MI	70,000	34.2
Ronald Blackwood	Mt. Vernon, NY	68,000	48.7
E. Pat Larkins	Pompano Beach, FL	66,000	17.2
Carl E. Officer	East St. Louis, IL	51,000	95.6

Source: Joint Center for Political Studies, Washington, D.C., U.S. Bureau of the Census, 1986
population estimates.

successful reelections in many cities; long-term incumbencies of first black
mayors in Detroit, Los Angeles, (Gary and Newark); voluntary succession
in Atlanta; and involuntary succession in Gary, Newark, and New Orleans.[3] These electoral waves and junctures embody the developmental
paths of insurgency, racial reconciliation, and institutionalization.

Insurgency as Strategy and Style

Among black mayoral aspirants, particularly in the early stages of the new
black politics strategy, insurgency served as the predominant campaign

strategy; and later insurgency served as a style of leadership for many elected mayors. Generally, insurgency as strategy has been associated with the initial election of a black mayor in a given locale, and as a leadership style, has been adopted and retained by first black mayors throughout their tenure in office. (The retention of insurgency as a leadership style in long-term black mayoral incumbencies is discussed below.) Insurgency was characterized by direct challenges to the prevailing political order, encompassing explicit criticisms and attacks on elected officials, institutional processes, civic leadership structures, and the resulting mobilization of interests and bias in local political contexts.

As a tactical strategy, insurgency was driven by imperatives of time and place, and the prevailing demographics. The nature of the times was such that blacks were not only systematically excluded from elected positions and other posts within local political establishments, but their exclusion was also supported by a prevailing ethos which rendered their desires and efforts to obtain access to the political process to be illegitimate demands on the local political order. Prevailing patterns of voting behavior were such that a black candidate could not expect to receive more than a very small percentage of white votes, dictating an almost exclusive reliance on black voters, many of whom were not registered or generally unaccustomed to participating in politics, especially politics that deliberately threatened the prevailing political order. Given this convergence of conditions and circumstances, even in the absence of specifically social reform issues, insurgent black candidates were perceived as social reformers, a residual benefit which continues to accrue to most black aspirants for political office.

The early pattern of insurgency pitted a black candidate against a white candidate in a racially heated contest (Nelson and Meranto 1977). The basic pattern has been one of mobilization based on racial appeals with the successful black candidate garnering a solid black bloc vote supplemented with the crossover of a small percentage (rarely exceeding 20 percent) of white voters (Bullock 1984). Thus, the overwhelming majority of early black mayors were elected in cities with a majority of near-majority black population. In most cases of the initial election of a black mayor, either substantive issues were subordinated to overt racial appeals (frequently by both black and white candidates), or positions espoused by black candidates were of a social reform nature, racially exhortatory, and clearly directed towards black voters. White candidates in these races resorted to "save our city" racial appeals or adopted a newly "race-neutral" position of desiring to "represent all of the people" (Hahn et al. 1976; Pettigrew 1976).

As a strategy *insurgency promoted black political mobilization and provoked white resistance.* The result in most locales was that, subsequent to the election of a black mayor, the initial period of transition and displacement was characterized by severe racial polarization (Levine 1974; Eisinger 1980). Racial polarization subsided over time, but in many locales remained sufficiently ingrained to make for a tendency among whites and blacks to define most issues within a racial context (Persons 1985). However, severe racial conflict has not been a constant attendant to the election of first black mayors, although reasons for this significant deviation are not clear. The case of Atlanta, which became severely racially polarized, disputes the theory of the mediating effects of a previously prevailing biracial coalition (Persons 1985). The racially polarized 1983 election in Chicago, almost 20 years after the nation's first election of a big-city black mayor, disputes the temporal factor as an explanation, as does the contrast of the Philadelphia election of 1983 in which racial polarization did not occur. A highly plausible explanation may rest on whether the black mayoral contender espoused an explicitly social reform agenda or otherwise made strong and explicit appeals to the black community, thereby clearly challenging the prevailing political order.

In the case of Chicago, much more was at stake than a comparatively simple racial and political displacement. Harold Washington ran against the white ethnic-dominated political machine, which had variously dominated Chicago politics for almost half a century, and the prospect of his election carried a particularly severe threat (Akalimat and Gills 1984). Moreover, Chicago has long been held by many observers to harbor a most invidious form of racial tensions, in no small part attributable to the organizing tactics of the old line political machine that was founded and sustained by drawing on heightened ethnic appeals, making exclusion and oppression of blacks both politically expedient and socially acceptable. Thus the socio-political dynamics in Chicago in 1983 were very similar in nature and effect to those which prevailed in many cities two decades or more earlier.

The early black mayoral elections signalled a potentially significant level of social reform. These elections meant major change in the most important and visible local leadership corps. They also meant the representation and entry of new claimants to local political arenas. Most early black mayors explicitly articulated a social reform agenda in their campaigns, emphasizing issues of police brutality, the hiring of blacks in municipal jobs, increased contracting to minority vendors, improved low-income housing choices, improved and equitable delivery of public services, and a more open government relative to groups formerly shut out of the local governing process. While strong social reform agendas clearly caused concern among white voters, such an explicitly articulated agenda was not always necessary for mobilizing the black vote. In most initial black mayoral elections, for most black voters, the symbolic significance of the potential to elect a black mayor tended to override concerns for the specifics of issue positions. Moreover, in most black versus white mayoral contests, most black voters have understandably automatically associated descriptive representation (electing a representative who mirrored their racial and general social characteristics) with substantive representation (the support for and advocacy of issues and interests of greatest concern to them). Well beyond the early stage of insurgency politics, some black mayoral candidates and candidates for other offices as well have factored the significance of this symbolism into their strategies and, discounting the importance of explicitly stated substantive issues for black voters, have directed issue-specific appeals almost exclusively to white voters (Ransom 1987; Keiser 1990).

After the initial election, the crucial next step in the process of institutionalization is reelection. This is a particularly critical step for insurgent black mayors if social reform efforts are to be established. Some new dynamics emerge at this electoral juncture, presenting something of a strategic dilemma for the incumbent. However, perhaps the most interesting development is that at the stage of reelection we begin to see the many faces of the coin of race and its varied uses in black politics. Reelection efforts of insurgents have been characterized by the continued resistance of a significant number of white voters to black mayoral rule, manifested in efforts to develop more effective strategies against a second black electoral victory (Watson 1984). This occurred in Atlanta in 1978, and Chicago in 1987. In both instances, overtly racist campaigns were launched by white challengers to "save our city" from continued black governance. Moreover, there is the added problem of maintaining the monolithic clout of a well-mobilized black community in the face of major white and black challengers. First black mayors know well the dynamics of a black versus white contest, having experienced this in their initial elections, and having benefitted from having a "white ogre" as an opponent. One might thus conclude that the dynamics of a reelection contest involving a strong black challenger might require an adjustment in strategy; this is not necessarily the case.

The pairing of two black contenders in a multicandidate race suggests a need to create a distinction between the two while preserving the monolithic black vote in support of a single black candidate. This leads to a highly tenuous situation for both black candidates, as a split in the black vote may result in a loss of the mayoralty to a white candidate. The black challenger may, of course, seek to build a pivotal base of support among white voters with a smaller supplement of black votes. Such a strategy by a black challenger would simply reverse the conventional first black mayor strategy.

Coleman Young of Detroit faced this situation in his first reelection bid in 1977. Young's black opponent sought to make Coleman Young the issue: his frequently abrasive political style, his lifestyle, and his frequent use of rough language were labeled as inappropriate for the leadership of Detroit. Young's strategy was to label his black opponent as a "black, white hope." Young's black challenger had received only five percent of the black vote in the primary, but had forced Young into a runoff on the strength of his white support (Rich 1989). The appellation of "black, white hope" embodied the message which many incumbent black mayors, at one time or another, have sought to convey: competition is a threat to the tenuous political hold of black mayoralties and may result in a major setback for the black community—the loss of the newly won mayoralty to a white contender. The strategy of Young's challenger also has become a familiar one as the appeal of the mayoralty has become a means of fulfilling the personal and political ambitions of many black aspirants. In the Detroit case of 1977, racial appeals of essentially the same type as were used in the initial election continued to serve the incumbent despite the change to a black versus black contest. For strategic purposes the black challenger was depicted as the surrogate "white ogre," an interesting turn of the coin of race, and an interesting means of sustaining insurgency.

Also interesting is the fact that in some locales, structural factors, that is, the absence of statutory limits on the number of consecutive terms a mayor may serve, have played a major role in institutionalizing insurgency through facilitating long-term incumbencies of first black mayors. The result has been that some first black mayors have succeeded in "institutionalizing" their individual presences in office. This has been the case in Detroit and Los Angeles where incumbent black mayors have been re-elected for five consecutive four-year terms. (Los Angeles is not here characterized as an insurgency mayoralty.) Similar situations prevailed in Gary and Newark until both incumbents were defeated in 1986 and 1987, respectively. (The latter two cases are discussed later in regard to the dynamics of black mayoral succession.)

We might assume that long-term black mayoral incumbency might provide insights into the experiences of black mayoralties beyond the immediacy of the racially charged, initial transition and displacement to a period of normalcy, when the routine issues of governance come to dominate the local political agenda in a less racial context. Based on a study of the Young mayoralty in Detroit (Rich 1989), one can identify two major, somewhat distinct dynamics of long-term incumbency. First, there is the continuation of racial appeals in mobilizing the black community with the use of a kind of racial ostracism in efforts to differentiate the incumbent from his black challengers. Concomitantly, there is the continuation of clear, racial divisions in voting patterns regardless of the race of the challenger. In other words, the insurgent incurs the wrath of many white voters and that condition prevails indefinitely. Second, there is a distinct change over time in the type of issues that dominate the local political agenda, with a shift away from general social reform issues to basic issues concerning the overall economy of the city and its fiscal stability. However, despite successful mayoral efforts in garnering the active support of white economic elites in responding to these issues, and despite the fact that the white business community belatedly provided very strong support for the Young mayoralty, the majority of the mass-level white electorate remained generally unsupportive. For example, a crucial vote on a tax increase to save the city of Detroit from insolvency in 1981 was supported by white business elites, but won exclusively in the black wards of the city.

For the primary support group of black voters who sustain long-term insurgencies, the full range of advantages are not clear. Long-term insurgencies may assist the larger process of institutionalization by transcending the difficult period of initial transition and displacement to firmly establish a new, more inclusive political order. On the other hand, long-term incumbencies may well discourage or otherwise eliminate viable black successors. The long-term dominance of a single black mayor may serve to stymie the development of a black leadership corps independent of the incumbent, resulting in a decline in the number and efficacy of black activists who seek to monitor local government, and help keep it accountable and inclusive. Thus, by adversely impacting the local black leadership structure, the longevity of a single black mayor may serve to obstruct democratization and accountability, and may thereby hinder the move towards institutionalization of substantive black interests and participation.

There are also indications that the "institutionalization" of a single black mayor may otherwise have transforming effects on the local political arena. The District of Columbia is a case in point. Both scholarly and lay observers point to the existence of a machine-style politics attendant to the three-term mayoralty of Marion Barry, crediting Barry with influencing political and electoral processes across the board, including city council and school board elections. The Barry machine repeatedly undermined viable black mayoral successors by arousing mass-level black concerns about the danger of creating prime conditions for a "white takeover." Barry successfully used insurgency to build and sustain a political machine that was held together in the traditional mode of political machines: by patronage in the dispensation of city jobs and contracts, and firm control of the political mobilization, recruitment, and candidate slating processes. The retention of insurgency as a leadership style for long-term incumbents is no doubt attributable to the reluctance of a political leader to risk an obvious change in tactics and style, or perhaps a perceived inability to relinquish this posture, given the political exigencies prevalent in a particular political context. For whatever strategic or other considerations, insurgency is a continuing use of the coin of race even when population dynamics and other factors do not afford the likelihood of a white takeover (Persons and Henderson 1990).

We see that insurgency has served as a useful strategic resource in the mobilization of the black population requisite to the election of most first black mayors. In a game of low-resource electoral politics, insurgency tactics are a powerful means of creating vitally needed political resources. Having adopted the political style of an insurgent, many black mayors, in tending to their maintenance needs, use the spirit of insurgency as necessary, as long as it is a winning currency. We also see that as a matter of style and image, insurgency can be utilized as a way of undermining and delegitimizing all challengers, black and white, to an incumbent first black mayor. However, as a strategic political tempo and leadership style, insurgency can be difficult to maintain over time. It can effectively give way, in some cases, to the exigencies of governance, lose its social reform content, and subsequently serve as a rhetorical tactic for rallying necessary black electoral support. In some cases its demise is facilitated by the dynamics of black mayoral succession.

Black Mayoral Succession and the Passing of the Old Order

Black mayoral succession is of great significance in the process of institutionalization as it suggests the move towards permanency in securing the black political presence in American urban politics. One of the more interesting aspects of black mayoral succession is that this sequence has to date been a limited one. Perhaps indicative of a still nascent institutional process is the fact that the still dominant pattern in the election of black mayors remains the first-time election of black mayors in an increasing number of cities. However, the succession stage has not been stymied due so much to a large loss of black mayoralties as it has been equally stymied by long-term incumbencies of several first black mayoralties.

It appears that the black mayoral succession stage constitutes the defining stage of the new black politics. At this stage we see a fully charged political dynamic in which the new black politics as a sociopolitical phenomenon has been launched and is effectively "on its own." Thus, we see the emergence of critical contradictions internal to the black community that constrain the fostering of serious system challenging action. We also see critical decisions being made by key players in the political game, which in effect set the tone and thrust for the future practice of black politics. Specifically, assessment of the succession stage yields added insights into the following:

1. The pairing of two blacks in the absence of a "white ogre" or a surrogate "white ogre"
2. The move towards racial reconciliation as a strategic means of differentiating politically between black competitors
3. Situations in which white voters hold the decisive swing vote even with black population majorities
4. The emergence of nascent, class-based cleavages within the black community, resulting in the subordination of political thrusts by low-income blacks to the imperative of black solidarity as manifested in black bloc voting
5. Yet another face of the coin of race with the use of race as its stereotypical stigma by black candidates seeking racial reconciliation as a strategic move

There are two variants of black mayoral succession, both of which have occurred to date. Voluntary succession occurs when an incumbent leaves office at the end of a term as set by statute, or otherwise declines to seek reelection and is succeeded by a black. Involuntary succession occurs when an incumbent is defeated or otherwise removed from office and is succeeded by a black. Although the succession sequence has been a limited one to date, the city of Atlanta has experienced its second succession election. The discussion below focuses first on the dynamics of voluntary succession in Atlanta and New Orleans, and second on involuntary succession in Gary and Newark.

Voluntary Succession: Atlanta and New Orleans

In Atlanta, the October, 1981, election to succeed first black mayor Maynard Jackson was at once a serious test of the black community's ability to hold on to the mayoralty and a bitter reminder to whites of their displaced political status. For many whites the election became a "last ditch" effort to recapture city hall. The reported sentiment of many white elites was that the Jackson succession election was the last hope of electing a white mayor of Atlanta in the then foreseeable future. Nonetheless, in a style peculiar to Atlanta's historical political culture, the succession campaign was expected to be carried out in a manner devoid of any racial overtones. As one observer put it, "everything was racial, but nothing was racist!"

There were three major challengers in the Atlanta succession race: former Congressman Andrew Young and former Public Safety Commissioner A. Reginald Eaves, both black; and one white candidate, popular state legislator Sidney Marcus. Despite the fact that the black population had reached the level of 56.6 percent, making a black victory a theoretical certainty, this situation did not preclude a white victory in the event of a severely split black vote. This possibility was enhanced by the fact that Young and Eaves appealed to different segments of the black electorate; Young to solidly middle- and upper-middle-class blacks, and Eaves to low-income and marginal middle-class blacks. This nascent class cleavage has long been intermittently evident in Atlanta's politics as many low-income blacks, excluded from the historically discriminating black social and economic elite circles, at times have sought to displace those blacks who were, relatively speaking, "to the manor born."

Eaves was clearly identified with the insurgent regime of Maynard Jackson's first mayoralty, and had been the lightning rod of white ire and much discomfort among the old-line black leadership. Eaves had been appointed the "superchief" by Jackson, with authority over the police, fire, and emergency management departments. This move led to prolonged racial polarization, a legal challenge to the constitutionality of the city charter, and Eaves' eventual resignation under a cloud of scandal surrounding promotional examinations for police officers. Thus an Eaves candidacy continued the thrust and political tempo of insurgency.

Interestingly, *The Atlanta Constitution* ran a major news analysis series on poverty in Atlanta during the campaign, in conjunction with an assessment of the changes that had occurred during the previous eight years of black mayoral rule. It is not clear what the motivations were for the series, but it could have served to further incite a counter-mobilization among low-income blacks, thereby enhancing the possibility of electing a white candidate. The legal requirement that a mayoral winner receive a real majority (as opposed to a plurality) of the total vote all but dictated that one of the black candidates would face the white challenger in a runoff, given the racial demographics of the city and the generally racial voting patterns that had characterized the city's politics in the past. Eaves would have been, by far, the easier black candidate to defeat in a runoff with a white challenger, as many middle-class blacks would likely have supported the moderate white candidate out of a sense of "voting responsibly without regard to race." However, Young was the leader in the general election[4] with 41 percent of the vote. Marcus and Eaves received 39 and 20 percent, respectively.

In the succession runoff race, Atlanta was back to mayoral "politics as usual" with a black versus white contest in which the stakes were starkly clear. Most observers agreed that there were no major issue differences between Young and Marcus, and not surprisingly, substantive issues gave way to explicitly racial overtures. In the end, Andrew Young was endorsed by the *Atlanta Constitution* and won with 55.1 percent of the vote. There was roughly a 10–15 percent crossover vote for both Young and Marcus. Otherwise, voting occurred along racial lines, giving Young a decisive advantage because of the black population majority in the city (*Atlanta Constitution* 10/29/81). The business community had supported the white candidate, displaying a continued resistance to black control of city hall, which historically was controlled by the white business community via politically moderate white mayors. In that regard, the dynamics of the succession election demonstrated that the transition and adjustment to black mayoral governance in Atlanta had not been complete.

However, despite the refusal of the white business community to support Andrew Young's bid for mayor, in a grand gesture of racial reconciliation in the early days of his mayoralty, Young informed the white business community that he could not govern without their support (Stone 1989, 110). Insurgency was dead.

In contrast to the heated succession race, Andrew Young's reelection race in 1985 was a political nonevent. All three challengers to Young were political neophytes and virtually unknown. There was no "great white hope" candidate, nor was there a serious black challenger. Young easily won with 83 percent of the total vote in a race with a very low turnout of 32.3 percent compared to a 64.0 percent turnout in the 1981 runoff election (*Atlanta Constitution* 10/28/85).

In the New Orleans succession election of 1986, there were also three major challengers: two blacks, State Senator William Jefferson, and Sidney Barthelemy, a former city councilman and former state senator; and white candidate Sam LeBlanc, a senior-level local government employee. Despite a black population of 51 percent, a split in the black vote in New

Orleans could have easily resulted in a white victory. As in the Atlanta case, nascent class-based cleavages were evident in the New Orleans succession race. New Orleans has the distinction of having three socially and politically significant "racial groups": whites, blacks, and Creoles, who are very fair-skinned blacks (Schexnider 1982). Jefferson appealed mainly to low-income and dark-skinned blacks, while Barthelemy appealed to the largely middle-class Creole group. Barthelemy also assiduously courted the white vote.

As had happened in the Atlanta succession race, the specter of the New Orleans succession race as the last opportunity to elect a white mayor appeared strongly to influence the dynamics of the campaign. While whites could not independently elect a white mayor, they could nevertheless determine which black candidate would win the mayoralty. Thus Barthelemy assiduously courted the white vote and won the primary with 41 percent of the white vote, despite the presence of a white candidate, and faced Jefferson in the runoff. This black versus black contest had thus become a significantly class-based contest between low-income blacks and middle-class blacks (who are disproportionately Creole). Substantive issues in the runoff contest were upstaged by issues of personality, and the racial factor, around which the outcome of the election pivoted.

Initially, New Orleans' first black mayor, Morial, had unsuccessfully sought to get the voters to change the city charter to allow him to seek a third term in office. This effort and Morial's generally combative style had generated significant antagonism among whites. Thus, when Morial endorsed Jefferson, Jefferson was viewed by many whites as the black candidate to defeat. Barthelemy won the runoff with 58 percent of the total vote, 85 percent of the white vote, and 25 percent of the black vote. Analysts and observers suggest that with the near certainty of another black mayor, New Orleans white voters aligned themselves with the black candidate who was not "cut from the same political cloth" as the city's first black mayor (Watson 1984). The heavy white crossover vote was not only pivotal, but decisive.

In both the Atlanta and New Orleans succession races, the nascent black class cleavages were fleeting, and dissipated with the transformation of the election contest into the traditional black versus white contest. This does not, however, suggest the insignificance of this cleavage. Rather, the nascent and apparent fleeting nature of black class cleavage likely reflects the cross-cutting conflicts created by the perceived, overpowering significance of black racial solidarity and bloc voting. This exemplifies how the need for black racial solidarity, as a precondition for repeating even symbolic black political gains, tends to submerge the diversity of interests within the black community.

As has been noted earlier, the coin of race has many faces. While black mayoral candidates will use racial appeals to mobilize the black community to the point of labelling a black challenger a surrogate "white ogre," some black candidates will also use race as a specter of fear in mobilizing white voters against a black candidate with a "radicalized" or insurgent image. One variation of this occurred in the New Orleans succession election, another variation occurred in the second succession election in Atlanta.

The second succession election in Atlanta occurred in October, 1989, and pitted first black mayor Maynard Jackson against Fulton County Commission Chairman Michael Lomax, also black. Lomax had originally come to Atlanta as a special assistant to Jackson during Jackson's first term as mayor. Using his experience in city hall under Jackson, Lomax remained in the city to plow his own political fortunes. While Lomax had done well on the county commission, and was generally well received in both the black and white communities in the county, he had always been plagued with the image of an ultra-elitist who was basically uncomfortable being around most blacks of all socio-economic statuses. Lomax's image problem was, in turn, reflected in his standing in the polls taken during the mayoral campaign.

The earliest polls taken during the campaign showed Lomax trailing Jackson by 22 percentage points. Five months prior to the October election, Jackson had increased his lead by 34 percentage points, with a 58 to 24 percent lead over Lomax (*Atlanta Constitution* 5/7/89). Lomax had been able to increase his standing among whites, but was unable to claim support from a majority of any racial or income group. Lomax's standing among whites was not insignificant: he led Jackson among white voters 44 to 32 percent. Jackson led among black voters, 69 to 16 percent. Blacks comprised 61 percent of Atlanta's registered voters, while whites comprised 39 percent, a demographic mix which actually permitted blacks to vote in bloc and independently elect the city's mayor. There were no white challengers in this second succession race.

Former Mayor Jackson was by far the more popular of the two candidates although both Jackson and Lomax were seen as being well qualified to be mayor. Jackson enjoyed broad support among all demographic groups. Interestingly, Jackson also enjoyed solid support from the white business community. In his first term, Jackson had clashed with this group and reconciliation had not occurred prior to his leaving office. However, Jackson had moved early in his new campaign to cement good relations with this group, and he had succeeded. The white business community had responded positively with political support, and substantial financial support as well. During his years in private law practice Jackson had moved to the prestigious and overwhelmingly white, north side of Atlanta. Place of residency and race are by design such important co-factors in political and social sensibilities among Atlantans that this was not an insignificant move on Jackson's part (Bayor 1989). To his benefit, Jackson projected an air of consummate confidence, maturity, and leadership ability, all enhanced by an imposing physical presence. Lomax appeared too young in comparison. The challenge for Lomax was to create a major chink in Jackson's political armor and he chose a most interesting tactic.

Lomax chose to exploit the social and political tensions, which were also largely racial in nature, that had attended Jackson's term as the city's first black mayor, a tactic that simultaneously permitted Lomax to enhance his own strength among white voters.

Lomax chose to exploit the crime issue and to attack Jackson on the high crime rate which had prevailed during part of his first mayoralty. Like most big cities, the high crime rate during Jackson's first term was nothing new, but rather reflected a pattern of highs and lows over the years. In fact, the city was experiencing a crime wave which placed it first in the nation, even during the second succession campaign. The issue of crime during Jackson's first term was also connected to his firing of a white police chief and the appointment of the city's first black police chief. This action singularly led to severe and prolonged racial conflict in the city (Persons 1985; Eisinger 1980). Thus, to raise the issue of crime during Jackson's first mayoralty was to reopen old political and social wounds.

More importantly, Lomax chose a television advertisement campaign to exploit the issue. One ad featured a white woman declaring her fears about the safety of the streets of Atlanta under a new Jackson mayoralty. Another ad featured former State Governor Carl Sanders recalling the death of his secretary, who was murdered on the city's streets one evening after working late. Another ad featured prominent black Atlanta business-man Jesse Hill declaring his concern for the safety of Atlanta's streets during a new Jackson mayoralty. Lomax, in effect, sought to consolidate white voter support by manipulating the racially charged issue of crime in a predominantly black city. The net result was that in a contest between two black challengers, absent a "white ogre" or surrogate, there was still a return to racial and racist appeals. Jackson won with little difficulty, after Lomax withdrew just prior to the date on which he would have had to declare officially his candidacy for mayor and simultaneously relinquish his county council chairmanship.

In the first Atlanta succession race we see the demise of insurgency as it becomes clearly identified with the specific plight of low-income blacks in the Eaves candidacy, and we witness its subordination to the overriding consideration of racial solidarity and the subsequent triumph of the representational interests of the black middle class. We also witness the death of insurgency by abdication in the Andrew Young victory. In the second Atlanta succession race, we see yet another face of the coin of race with race used as a stigma by the weaker of two black contestants and as a grand gesture of empathy with the stereotypical fears of many white voters. We also see a former black insurgent win with both the overwhelming support of blacks and the overwhelming financial support and political endorsements of the white business community. The common thread in each of these variations is the move towards racial reconciliation, first as a means of political differentiation, and later as a more distinctly philosophical perspective not born of any clear "strategic necessity." In the New Orleans succession race, black class cleavages emerged as well in an association with insurgent politics. However, black middle-class representational interests triumphed due to political differentiation tactics by a black contestant, and a corresponding vote by whites against black insurgency politics. The era of black insurgent politics had passed, just two decades since its emergence.

Involuntary Succession: Newark and Gary

Within the span of a twelve-month period, two of the country's longest-serving first black mayors were defeated in reelection bids; Gibson in Newark in May, 1986, and Hatcher in Gary in May, 1987. Both incumbents faced strong black challengers in the absence of a white challenger, and thereby were faced with a relatively new and different set of dynamics in their reelection bids. In Newark, which is roughly 47 percent black, all three challengers to Gibson were black in a non-partisan, mayoral contest. In Gary, Hatcher's challengers for the Democratic nomination in a heavily Democratic, 78 percent black city were also all black. In both Newark and Gary, the most important factor in these succession contests seems to have been the absence of a "white ogre." In both cases, this missing element appears to have catalyzed a different dynamic, which significantly contributed to defeat and involuntary succession.

Gibson was initially elected mayor of Newark in 1970, winning with 60 percent of the vote in the heady and hopeful period (three years) following the Newark riots. He was reelected in 1974 with 55 percent of the vote in a bitter, racially charged contest against Anthony Imperiale, whom Gibson had defeated in his initial win. Gibson won again in 1978 with 68 percent of the vote. Gibson faced a black challenger in his fourth race in 1982, winning with 52 percent of the vote despite the fact that he and his major challenger were under federal indictments on charges of corruption. In 1986, the deficiencies in Gibson's record became a liability. Unfortunately, the generally continuing decline of the Newark economy was paralleled by Gibson's tenure in office.

Gibson's 16 years in office provided a convenient time frame for asessing the economic well-being of the city. Between 1970 and 1985, the city had a population loss of 68,050 residents, a decline of 17.8 percent. The steel fabrication plants, breweries, and other factories, which once boosted the local economy, had closed or declined. Unemployment in Newark in 1986 was 11.2 percent overall, and triple that for some segments of the black community. During the period 1970–1986, the number of movie theaters in Newark had declined from 14 to 6; hotels from 32 to 6; bowling alleys from 15 to 0; restaurants from 937 to 246; and food stores from 377 to 184 (*The New York Times* 5/24/87). Interestingly, *The New York Times* asserted that Newark's economy had begun to rebound with a burgeoning downtown and plans for major corporate relocations from Manhattan to Newark. However, many of Newark's neighborhoods remained blighted and the office real estate boom was not expected to aid the poor.

Gibson had made clear his political ambitions over the years. He had twice, but unsuccessfully, sought the Democratic nomination for governor, in 1981 and 1985. He had achieved the stature of a nationally prominent politician in Democratic party circles, which had been both necessary and beneficial to the city during Democratic administrations. Those ties had facilitated the rewarding of the low-income black voter base so crucial in the calculus of national Democratic party politics. However, under the Reagan regime, the city of Newark, like most major cities, had lost substantial federal funds previously provided under the Community Development Block Grant program and the Comprehensive Employment and Training Act program among others. Thus Gibson was rendered vulnerable against a strong black challenger and defeated by Sharpe James, who emphasized economic revitalization, improving the image of the city, increasing the housing stock, and more effectively combatting crime. Ironically, in many respects, the issues resonated Gibson's campaign in 1970. In another interesting irony, Gibson was endorsed by his old white opponent, Anthony Imperiale. Sharpe James carried all five of the city's wards, garnering 55 percent of the total vote to Gibson's 40 percent (*The New York Times* 5/15/86).

In 1986 there was no racist "ogre" to assure automatic black support for Gibson based on an obscuring of issues by the shield of racial solidarity. There are no indications that Gibson's opponent made special efforts to woo the support of the white community, despite the fact that the black population comprised slightly less than 50 percent of the total population. The combined black and Hispanic population totaled 70 percent of the electorate. The white vote was not pivotal to victory in this election. The mayoral contest thus pivoted around substantive issues regarding the future of the city, as espoused by two black contestants, with the record of the long-term black incumbent used pejoratively as a central theme. Interestingly, the black challenger's theme did not reflect a politically conservative turn, for the black incumbent was no longer perceived as radical. The challenger's theme was explicitly directed toward issues deemed critical to the needs of the black community in particular, and towards improving the image and economic vitality of the city in general, much as Gibson had promised over the years. The critical exception in 1986 was that the record of the long-term black incumbent was the standard against which blame was assessed, and the challenger was welcomed as a "refreshing breath" of new leadership.

In relationship to the Newark succession election of 1986, the outcome of the Gary succession election in 1987 was very much one of *déjà vu*. Richard Hatcher, initially elected in 1967, was the longest serving black mayor in America. Like Gibson, Hatcher had the misfortune of presiding over a city that declined along with the steel industry, upon which its economy depended. Gary had also lost substantial population, 60,000 or 29 percent, since 1967, as well as its taxi service, movie houses, many restaurants, and many other businesses (*Indiana Crusader* 3/14/87).

Hatcher, too, was indisputably a black politician of national prominence and stature, and was widely respected beyond Gary for his efforts on behalf of the national struggle for black political empowerment. Many national-level black politicians campaigned on his behalf, but to no avail. Hatcher lost to a black challenger who promised to improve the functioning of the city government and the general welfare of its citizenry.

In part, Hatcher's embattled position significantly reflected the consequences of the long-standing refusal of major components of the white elite structure to accept the transition to black mayoral governance. Hatcher had never won the support of the white business community or the white ethnic-dominated Democratic party. In the case of the business community, their split with city hall had actually preceeded Hatcher in that they had earlier objected to mayoral efforts in support of striking steel workers (Lane 1979). They were, of course, not satisfied with Hatcher's initial election and when Hatcher faced reelection in 1971, in a last-ditch effort to forestall their political displacement, the white business community and the party machine endorsed a black moderate candidate in opposition to Hatcher. Apparently in response to the prospects of an extended period of insurgent black mayoral leadership in Gary, the business community moved to abandon the city by building a mall in the adjacent suburb of Merrillville. Within fewer than 10 years after Hatcher's initial election, all 4 department stores, more than 100 smaller businesses and 2 major banks had closed operation in Gary and moved to the suburban mall (Lane 1979).

Moreover, Gary was a classic example of a company town, originally established as the locus for a major U.S. Steel operation and company housing areas for its employees. U.S. Steel and ancillary industries dominated the economy of Gary and the Lake County region. Subsequently, the fortunes of the Gary economy waxed and waned with the fortunes of U.S. Steel. Unfortunately, the waning of the local steel-based economy in Gary paralleled many of Hatcher's later years in office. For example, during the period of 1979–1982, employment at U.S. Steel in Gary dropped from 25,000 to 8000, and by 1987 had declined still further to 6000 (*Post Tribune* 1/17/86). Although Hatcher had not inherited a hollow prize, as some analysts predicted that black mayors would (Feemstra 1969), in the end, he was left to preside over one.

While black political rule had not come exclusively at the price of a loss of economic vitality (as there was no causal relationship between black political dominance and the decline of the steel industry), ironically, blacks in Gary were forced to entertain the option of trading political dominance for the prospect of improving the economic lot of the city. Thus, when the state legislature proposed a consolidation of the many separate governments in Lake County into the single political entity of Metrolake, which would have subordinated Gary residents politically and racially, many blacks in Gary speculated that such consolidation was perhaps what the city needed for economic revitalization. Metrolake would have consolidated some 70 governmental entities into a single metropolitan government of 405,000 in population, with 60 percent white and 40 percent black, excluding Merrillville. Although the consolidation effort failed, Mayor Hatcher was able to garner only minimal support at public rallies in opposition to the consolidation (*Post Tribune* 10/28/86, 11/3/86).

In the end there were many ironies in Hatcher's defeat. First, according to some observers, conditions in the city were in objective ways considerably better than four years earlier when, in 1983, Hatcher had narrowly won reelection. Crime was down, there was a generally better economic climate, large layoffs of city patronage workers had stopped, and some new jobs had been created in the local economy (Isadore 5/31/88). While many in the black community considered Hatcher their personal savior, many black elected officials and other local black leaders asserted that they had been "iced" by Hatcher over the years as he had moved to consolidate his power base. Thomas Barnes, Hatcher's successor, had been a member of Hatcher's initial team of key campaign workers in 1967, had been elected to three terms as the town tax assessor, but had broken with Hatcher in 1983 to support Thomas Crump, who lost by 2,700 votes. Hatcher had run an entire slate of black candidates for office in 1984 and they were all defeated, including U.S. Representative Katie Hall (Caitlin 1985). Hatcher's image as a political leader suffered a major defeat.

Hatcher had not been able (or necessarily willing, according to some) to establish ties with the Republican-dominated state legislature, and in early 1986, the state taxation board granted U.S. Steel of Gary a reduction of $16 million in its property tax assessments, leading to a 10 percent shortfall for the city of Gary and its school system. The state taxation board had previously refused to allow the city to raise taxes (*Post Tribune* 1/16/86). Hatcher was faulted by many for not seeking support from the state legislature until 1983, far into his mayoralty, when it was effectively too late. Others understood that Hatcher was very distrustful of whites in the state legislature and in the Gary suburban areas. Barnes, on the other hand, had worked to build support among whites in suburban areas and enjoyed considerable popularity among them. Hatcher was, in part, hampered by his record of insurgency-style politics and apparently by his own conception of the dictates of independent, insurgent black politics. Hatcher's primary support group of black voters had become ambivalent about his leadership. In 1987, he had great difficulty mobilizing his supporters and Barnes won the Gary mayoralty with 56 percent of the vote, carrying all but one of the city's voting districts.

In significant ways, the involuntary succession of long-term insurgents in Gary and Newark reflect the limitations and inflexibility of insurgent styles of political leadership at the level of city government, given the rather dependent nature of the city. We also get insights into the plight of black mayoral leadership in older northern cities with economies historically based on heavy industries, which have in recent years declined in concert with the declining status of the United States in world trade. However, Coleman Young's tenure in Detroit offers an interesting contrast in regard to the sustentation of insurgent-style leadership. Over the years, Young has engaged in an interesting mix of roles, as both social reformer concerned with social welfare issues, and as a fiscal conservative. He has also courted the local business community, including Republican businesspeople and politicians, while maintaining the loyalty of his primary support base among black voters. He used city funds to finance the acquisition of land for a new General Motors plant inside the city, rather than lose it to a suburban jurisdiction. These and many other actions taken by Young have been highly controversial for one reason or another (Hill 1983). However, Coleman Young's tenure has been distinguished by one major objective. He has held on to that which defined Detroit as an economic entity: its image and position as the center of the U.S. automobile industry. Depending on one's perspective, one might conclude that the black residents of Detroit have paid a very high price in shouldering the responsibilities of governance. Summing up the evolution of Detroit's politics under Coleman Young, Wilbur Rich offers a poignant statement of the apparent ineluctable nature of change in the new black politics: "Detroit's politics have changed. No longer black politics, they are the current politics of Detroit. People who were black leaders are now city leaders." (Rich 1989, 267).

SUMMARY: RACIAL RECONCILIATION AND THE PASSING OF THE OLD ORDER

The election and collective experience of black mayors have taken place within the context of currents of broader socio-political change. Black mayors were first elected in the wake of the civil rights movement and the period of major unrest of the late 1960s. The brief, but no less strident, period of the black power movement which followed also contributed to the context out of which emerged the new black politics. Thus, it was expected that those black mayors would be activists and strong social reform advocates. They could be no less.

However, time makes for change, and the era of the insurgent black mayor as social reformer seems to have passed. The passing of the old order seems to occur at the point of succession. Although there is significant overlapping of the old dynamics, the emergence of a new dynamic becomes evident at this stage. There are several reasons for this apparent change. Succession occurs at a point distant in time from the "fever pitch" of racial tensions attendant to the election of first black mayors. Thus, the racial appeals formula is sometimes not as potent in its effect. Also, many succession races frequently enjoy a solid black population majority, diminishing somewhat the importance and necessity of racial appeals. While racial voting persists, it persists with somewhat less passion. For blacks, there is probably the realization that the likely major changes, certainly the major particularistic benefits, have generally been reaped. Black mayors at that point also appear to have learned a very sobering lesson on the limits of local governmental power to transform the social order. Having learned the realities of political power, they are less strident in social reform advocacy. For some whites, the point of succession may become the strategic last stand in terms of retaining the mayoralty for the foreseeable future. However, whites, too, appear to have learned a sobering, but reassuring, lesson at the point of succession: that black mayoral leadership may well be the new political reality, and that new reality is not one of political, social, or economic doom for whites.

While the point of succession in many cases appears to be the benchmark of major change, to a substantial degree the impetus for change is simply a temporal factor; the passage of time and attendant broader currents of change. It is evident that change in perceptions, and self-definition of roles occur over time for long-term incumbent black mayors, though they attempt to sustain the rhetorical tempo of insurgency. Long-term incumbents have been overtaken by broader currents of change: declining economies in their respective cities, the declining fortunes of the national Democratic party, and the vulnerability these two factors created during a Republican regime which deemphasized cities and urban problems. Long-term incumbents who have thrived somewhat during this time period, Coleman Young of Detroit for example, have done so by embracing a more expansive definition of the role of mayor. For many black politicians, holding office has come to mean more or less than seeking social reforms, and has come to mean assuming responsibility for the full mantle of governance. That means assuming responsibility for the total social, political, and economic well-being of the city. The new or nascent ethos appears to be one of saving the city, as a civic duty and responsibility, and as a means of benefitting the entire electorate, and perhaps as a means of proving that black leaders can indeed take on the full mantle of governance. There are some indications as well that the black electorate is increasingly expecting or demanding a broader approach to governance. Although there were many overlapping and interrelated factors, these new demands appear to have been the central message of the involuntary successions in Gary and Newark.

Another aspect of the new normalcy is the forging of strong alliances between black mayors and the white business community. This has occurred in both succession mayoralties in Atlanta and in the New Orleans succession mayoralty as well, and the long-term incumbencies in Detroit and Washington, D.C. This is something of an ironic development because early black mayors actually ran against the white business community, who in many cases, had dominated city hall in a fashion which deliberately barred inclusion of blacks and accommodation of their interests. Perhaps this change is as much indicative of the ineluctable triumph of conservatism as anything else.

Although the element of race remains disproportionately a factor in black mayoral elections, the element of race has taken on varied dimensions over time. First, in many mayoral contests, race is the prime currency, a currency to be manipulated by black and white candidates. Race is more a currency in some locales where there is a sizable black population. In some contexts, the black population is not only accustomed and responsive to racial appeals in political mobilization efforts, but due to historical patterns of white-dominated exclusionary governance, many blacks expect sincere articulation and representation of their interests to be made within a racial context. Second, it is the case that race is manipulated by incumbent blacks to serve their own maintenance needs in office, sometimes in the absence of any clear racist threat. White candidates have manipulated the element of race in efforts to retain or establish a dominant political position. The element of race also gets manipulated by some black candidates seeking to mobilize the white voter against a black whose image can be "radicalized." Finally, race gets used in its traditional stigma, in which one black candidate depicts another as synonymous with stereotypical fears whites hold against blacks.

As major currents of socio-political change have spawned and defined black mayoralties, one might reasonably expect that they would be affected by the nascent national trends towards black crossover politics. Black crossover politics must be defined in relationship to the style of black politics that preceded it. The new black politics was a politics based on racial appeals, tied to a concentrated black population base, with candidates promising descriptive and substantive representation for their black constituents, supported by a relatively small contingent of white supporters. In contrast, black crossover politics is primarily race-neutral in its appeal, at most making an appeal for racial harmony, and crossover candidates may or may not seek election in predominantly black locales. Also, crossover candidates do not advocate an identifiably black agenda.

How then might the evolution or institutionalization of black mayoralties have permitted anticipation of the strategic changes embodied in the 1989 elections? The elections of 1989 have been variously referred to as black crossover politics, the politics of deracialization, and rather ominously as "the death of black politics." In their essence, the elections of 1989 were the crystallization of the black politics of racial reconciliation. Given what had been the emergent and defining characteristics of the new black politics, and the continuing racial order in American politics, black politicians seeking major crossover appeal had to adopt some variant of racial reconciliation. Thus, black crossover politics is primarily race-neutral. It is a politics in which the black candidate diminishes the significance of his race and proffers appeals based on partisanship, a modified populism, or other traditional, non-racial themes.

The major consequences of black crossover politics will likely be the total delegitimizing of insurgent-style politics. Insurgency has effectively long been dead, but its spirit has been kept alive by tactics of long-term black incumbents, the effective internalization of insurgency, and its embodiment as a social reform strategy (the collective and preferred conception of the new black politics). This preferred conception has been buttressed by a kind of obsession with scoring; with increasing the number of black elected officials nationwide, again assuming that descriptive representation is synonmous with substantive representation, or that somehow sufficient numbers of black representatives would pose an effective challenge against the system and make for a realization of the black agenda. However, scoring has been the proverbial, political double-edged sword.

While the black presence in American politics has traditionally been associated with the threat of system-challenging action, the new crossover politics significantly disassociates the black presence from system challenge and instead emphasizes the "positive symbolism" of race. In short, racial reconciliation in all its variations, was born of insurgency. It is the alternative to insurgent politics. In its latest manifestation, the politics of racial reconciliation is a strategically pristine, political counteroffer, with a lagniappe. For whites it provides an opportunity to embrace demonstrably the principles of full participatory equality for all Americans regardless of race; for blacks it provides major symbolic gratificaticn and necessary opportunities to take pride in the achievements of blacks to more and higher political offices. That this variant of racial reconciliation is apparently devoid even of a generalized black agenda is indeed a profound dilemma of black politics in the present era.

REFERENCES

Alkalimat, Abdul and Doug Gills. 1984. "*Black Power* v. *Racism:* Harold Washington Becomes Mayor." In *The New Black Vote.* Ed. Rod Bush. 53–179. San Francisco: Synthesis Publications.

Bayor, Ronald H. 1989. "Urban Renewal, Public Housing and the Racial Shaping of Atlanta." *Journal of Policy History* 1(4).

Bullock, Charles. 1984. "Racial Crossover Voting and the Election of Black Officials." *Journal of Politics* 46 (February): 238–51.

Caitlin, Robert. 1985. "Organizational Effectiveness and Black Political Participation: The Case of Katie Hall." *Phylon* 41(3): 179–92.

Eisinger, Peter K. 1980. *The Politics of Displacement: Racial and Ethnic Transition in Three American Cities.* New York: Academic Press.

Feemstra, L. Paul. 1969. "Black Control of Central Cities." *Journal of American Institute of Planners.* 4: 75–79.

Hahn, Harlan, David Klingman, and Harry Pachon. 1976. "Cleavages, Coalitions, and the Black Candidate: The Los Angeles Mayoralty Elections of 1969 and 1973." *Western Political Quarterly* 29 (December): 507–520.

Hill, Richard Child. 1983. "Crisis in the Motor City: The Politics of Economic Development in Detroit." In *Restructuring the City.* Susan Fainstein, et al. New York: Longman, 80–125.

Isadore, Chris. 1988. *The Post Tribune.* Personal Interview, May 31.

Keiser, Richard A. 1990. "The Rise of a Biracial Coalition in Philadelphia." In *Racial Politics in American Cities.* Eds. Rufus P. Browning et al. New York: Longman.

Lane, James. 1979. *City of the Century: Gary from 1900–1975.* Bloomington, IN: Indiana University Press.

Levine, Charles H. 1974. *Racial Politics and the American Mayor: Power, Polarization, and Performance.* Lexington, MA: Lexington Books.

Nelson, William E. 1982. "Cleveland: The Rise and Fall of the New Black Politics." In *The New Black Politics: The Search for Political Power.* 1st ed., eds. Michael Preston et al. 187–208. New York: Longman.

Nelson, William E. and Philip Meranto. 1977. *Electing Black Mayors: Political Action in the Black Community.* Columbus, OH: Ohio State University Press.

Nordlinger, Eric A. 1971. "Political Development: Time Sequences and Rates of Change." In *Political Development and Social Change.* 2nd ed., eds. Finkle and Richard W. Gable. New York: John Wiley & Sons.

Persons, Georgia A. 1985. "Reflections on Mayoral Leadership: The Impact of Changing Issues and Changing Times." *Phylon* 46(3) (September): 205–218.

Persons, Georgia A. and Lenneal Henderson, Jr. 1990. "Mayor of the Colony: Effective Mayoral Leadership as a Matter of Public Perception." *National Political Science Review* 2.

Pettigrew, Thomas F. 1976. "Black Mayoralty Campaigns." In *Urban Governance and Minorities.* Ed. Herrington Bryce. New York: Praeger.

Pitkin, Hanna F. 1967. *The Concept of Representation.* Berkeley: University of California Press.

Polsby, Nelson W. 1968. "Institutionalization of the U.S. House of Representatives" *American Political Science Review* 62(1): 144–68.

Preston, Michael B. 1990. "1990 Big City Black Mayors: Have They Made a Difference? A Symposium." *National Political Science Review,* 2: 129–195.

Preston, Michael, B., Lenneal J. Henderson, Jr., and Paul Puryear, eds. 1982. *The New Black Politics: The Search for Political Power,* 1st ed. New York: Longman.

Ransom, Bruce. 1987. "Black Independent Electoral Politics in Philadelphia: The Election of Mayor W. Wilson Goode." In *The New Black Politics: The Search for Political Power.* 2nd ed., eds. Michael B. Preston, Lenneal J. Henderson, Jr. New York: Longman.

Rich, Wilbur. 1989. *Coleman Young and Detroit Politics: From Social Activist to Power Broker.* Detroit, MI: Wayne State University Press.

Schexnider, Alvin J. 1982. "Political Mobilization in the South: The Election of a Black Mayor in New Orleans." In *The New Black Politics: The Search for Political Power.* 1st ed., eds. Michael B. Preston, Lenneal J. Henderson, Jr., and Paul Puryear. New York: Longman.

Stone, Clarence. 1989. *Regime Politics: Governing Atlanta 1946–1988.* Lawrence, KA: University Press of Kansas.

Walters, Ronald W. 1980. "The Challenge of Black Leadership: An Analysis of the Problem of Strategy Shift." *The Urban League Review* 5(1) (Summer): 77–88.

Watson, Sharon. 1984. "The Second Time Around: A Profile of Black Mayoral Reelection Campaigns." *Phylon* 45 (Fall): 166–178.

Wilson, William J. 1978. *The Declining Significance of Race: Blacks and Changing American Institutions.* Chicago: University of Chicago Press.

———. 1987. *The Truly Disadvantaged: The Inner City, the Underclass, and Public Policy.* Chicago: University of Chicago Press.

NOTES

1. The November 1989 elections were the focus of heated debate at the 1990 Annual Meeting of the National Conference of Black Political Scientists held in March, 1990, in Atlanta. The debate from the conference became the focus of a media-sponsored debate, with particular focus on Virginia Governor L. Douglas Wilder.
2. The District of Columbia's first black mayor, Walter Washington, was initially appointed by President Lyndon Baines Johnson (who also appointed the entire city council), when the city was being governed completely by the federal government. Washington subsequently sought and won election under the 1973 Home Rule Charter. In his bid for reelection, Washington lost in a three-way race to Marion Barry, who had formerly served as president of the D.C. School Board. Prior to the (limited) Home Rule Charter of 1973, the only local elective offices open to D.C. residents were seats on the school board.
3. New Orleans is characterized as an involuntary succession since the first black mayor, the late Earnest Morial, sought a change in the city charter to permit him to serve more than two, consecutive four-year terms. This proposal was defeated in a referendum vote, effectively forcing Morial from office.
4. Atlanta's mayoral elections are non-partisan. Therefore, the initial election is the general election with a runoff required by state law if no candidate receives more than 50 percent (plus 1) of the total vote.

Chapter
4

The Conceptualization of Deracialization:

Thinking Through the Dilemma

Joseph P. McCormick II
Charles E. Jones

As knowledge of a particular subject-matter grows, our conception of that subject-matter changes: as our concepts become more fitting, we learn more and more. . . . the better our concepts, the better the theory we can formulate with them, and in turn, the better concepts available for the next improved theory.

Abraham Kaplan
The Conduct of Inquiry, pp. 53–54.

INTRODUCTION

The electoral victories of African-American candidates across the nation on November 7, 1989, constituted a watershed event in American politics in general and African-American politics in particular. Individuals of African descent won unprecedented mayoral elections in New York City; New Haven, Connecticut; Seattle, Washington; and Durham, North Carolina. In addition, city hall in Cleveland, Ohio, was captured by an African-American candidate for the first time since Carl Stokes' election as mayor in 1967. Also on this day was the landmark election of L. Douglas Wilder as governor of Virginia. The Wilder victory marked the only occasion in the history of the country that an African-American has won a gubernatorial election.

A point of major significance of these elections was the ability of the victorious candidates—all chief executives—to attract a sufficient degree of voter support to win in what are predominantly white political jurisdictions. These African-American candidates were able to overcome one of the more formidable features of the race factor in American politics, *the reluctance of white voters to support African-American office seekers.*[1]

The central objectives of this chapter are to clarify and advance the use of an analytical concept that can be employed for explaining these landmark electoral victories in majority white districts by African-American candidates in November 1989. We call this concept *deracialization.* We assert that these victories suggest a potential trend toward the deemphasis on racially-specific issues by African-American candidates for public office. While this concept may prove to have some explanatory utility in the years ahead, as other African-Americans run for office in predominantly white political jurisdictions, such events may represent somewhat of an analytical dilemma for students of black politics. In a discussion of the implications associated with the electoral variant of deracialization found at the end of this chapter, we attempt to untangle this potential analytical dilemma.

Before attempting to explain the utility of this concept, however, we first examine some of the attempts that have recently been made to interpret and give meaning to the events of November 1989. This is followed by a review of literature that has given rise to at least two variations of our central analytical concept. The literature review is followed by a section focusing on the factors that, in our judgment, have influenced the adoption of the electoral variation of deracialization by African-American candidates who have run for office in predominantly white political jurisdictions. Our reformulated definition of deracialization and a discussion of its three components is presented in the next section. Finally, we close this chapter by examining the answers to three questions that yield some of the implications associated with the pursuit of a deracialized election strategy by African-American candidates who seek office in predominantly white jurisdictions.

INTERPRETATIONS OF "BLACK TUESDAY"

The reactions to and interpretations of what one scholar (McCormick 1989) called "Black Tuesday" have varied. The explanations of the November 1989 victories range from dismissing the outcomes of these elections as an emerging trend to pronouncements which proclaim either the maturation *or* deterioration of African-American politics. One category of interpretation contends that, minus the media attention—which suggests that these elections were artifacts of "black aggregated success"—during an off-presidential year election, *there is very little that is new about the political victories of November 1989* (Ruffins 1990; Smith 1990; Walters 1990). Smith (1990, 2) argues that ". . . to the extent that patterns are discernable . . . the 1989 elections are not all that new in terms of what we know about the post-civil rights pattern of black electoral coalitions and governance." This line of reasoning is further reinforced by Ronald Walters (1990, 3) who asserts,

> . . . it is possible to dismiss the fact that "mainstream/crossover" politics is a new phenomenon, since even a cursory look at the data . . . clearly shows that since at least 1968 Blacks have represented a variety of political jurisdictions where Blacks constituted a minority of the population.

While it is true that the first wave of African-American politicians, that is, those mayors and members of the U.S. Congress elected to office in the late 1960s and early to mid 1970s, did make overtures to the white electorate, that appeal was made with a "small net." More specifically, those appeals were made to a comparatively small portion of the white electorate, mainly liberal and high-income white voters (Nelson and Meranto 1977; Pettigrew 1976). A departure from the profile of white voter support in the first wave of African-American elected officials is evident in the 1989 victories. In these victories both the degree and breadth of white voter support for the African-American victors had changed. Previous research (Levine 1974; Hahn et al. 1976; Halley et al. 1976) has discerned an "invisible ceiling" of white support for African-American office seekers, in the first wave of African-American electoral victories, at or around 25 percent. In the case of the November 1989 elections however, all of the victorious black candidates received at least 40 percent of the white vote. Moreover, these candidates were more successful in attracting a wider range of white electoral support.

For example, of the 76 percent of the voters who supported L. Douglas Wilder in Virginia, twice as many of these voters identified themselves as "moderates" (50 percent) as those who identified themselves as "liberals" (26 percent). Surprisingly, 19 percent of Wilder's voter support came from voters who identified themselves as "conservatives."[2] Given the comparatively small proportion of black voters as a part of the total electorate in Virginia—approximately 15 percent—we can safely assume that these self-identifications largely apply to white voters.

A second interpretation identifies a potentially new phenomenon in these recent elections and proclaims this possible trend as *a sign of the maturation and sophistication of African-American politics* (Ardrey 1990; Williams 1990; Schexnider 1990). This view maintains that African-American success in November 1989, based largely on political pragmatism and the savvy of the candidates, constitutes a model worthy of emulation by future generations of politicians who happen to be African-American. Thus Schexnider (1990, 35–36) for example, in commenting on L. Douglas Wilder's gubernatorial victory in Virginia, writes, ". . . Wilder demonstrated that race can be overcome, . . . with a mainstream, centrist appeal that reaches out to all segments of the electorate."

In contrast to what could be labeled the "maturation/pragmatism" point of view, is a counter-thesis advocated by Smith (1990) and Walters (1990) which asserts that *these victories on Black Tuesday mark the "death of African-American politics."* Smith, for example, notes, "The elections of 1989 represent . . . not a new phenomenon but more of the same, not a maturing of Black politics but still further evidence of its degeneration" (Smith 1990, 8). Walters (1990, 39) brings a large dose of analytical clarity to this issue, however, when he points out that the election of a number of African-Americans to positions of leadership in majority white political jurisdictions ". . . is not properly speaking to be regarded as 'Black politics.' "

Before we can determine what these events portend for the future direction of African-American politics, we think it first appropriate to make the necessary distinction between *electoral strategies* connected with attempts to capture office in majority white political jurisdictions and *agenda-setting strategies* that are connected with governance after elections have been won. A review of the literature reveals such a distinction and thus two related variations of our central analytical concept.

A REVIEW OF THE LITERATURE: TWO ANALYTICAL THREADS

Our examination of the emerging body of literature on the concept "deracialization" (formally defined below) reveals two identifiable threads of analysis. The first thread of analysis involves the use of *deracialization as an agenda-setting strategy.* The second thread involves the use of *deracialization as an electoral strategy.* While it is the latter thread that receives most of our concern in this chapter, it is important to point out that it was an earlier use of this concept as an *agenda-setting strategy* that places it in our analytical lexicon and thus influences its use as an explanatory electoral strategy. We examine three waves of scholarship where these variations of the concept have been given various levels of attention and use.

The First Wave

In 1973 the National Urban League (NUL) assembled a group of scholars, activists, and public officials to discuss charting a course for the NUL in the aftermath of the "protest" phase of the civil rights movement.[3] Two major areas of concern of this assembly were with *strategies* (and tactics) that "minority groups (especially blacks)" should adopt to advance their interests in the 1970s and with the kind of *issues* around which political mobilization by these groups should be developed.

In his contribution to this assembly, political scientist Charles V. Hamilton prepared a short essay in which he addressed both of these concerns.[4] Hamilton discussed the limitations of "protest" as a vehicle for the maintenance of long-term support. Hamilton recognized that the political conditions of the 1970s (that is, many of the legislative objectives of the civil rights movements had been achieved), did not readily lend themselves to protest action. A change in conditions demanded a change in tactics. In Hamilton's view, what Martin Luther King, Jr., referred to as the "newer stages of struggle" necessitated a new set of issues around which to mobilize support. For Hamilton, such an issue was "full employment."[5] This was an issue in the 1970s that continues in the 1990s to be of major importance to African-Americans, given their comparatively worse unemployment statistical profile.[6]

If such an issue was to reach the formal issue agenda[7] of the federal government, Hamilton stressed the necessity of building a base of political support that stretches beyond the African-American community. In this regard he pointed out that the issue of full employment was one that affected the larger society:

> [Full employment] applies to the total society, not only to blacks and other traditionally stigmatized minorities, who are seen as wanting only hand-outs. It would, in other words, recognize the critical factor of race and racism, but it offers, a *"deracialized"* solution.

Unfortunately in this seminal essay, Professor Hamilton neither formally defines the concept *deracialization* nor does he spell out how the agenda-setting variant of this concept could be pursued by its practitioners.

In the spring of 1976, Hamilton offered a second effort in which the concept of deracialization was given greater attention (Hamilton 1977). In this effort, Hamilton discussed an approach that he felt the Democratic party's platform should stress toward issues of vital importance to African-Americans in the 1976 presidential campaign. Hamilton formally labeled this agenda-setting *qua* electoral strategy, deracialization. Essentially he advised the Democrats to pursue a deracialized electoral strategy, thereby denying their Republican opponents the opportunity of using race as a polarizing issue, as had occurred in the 1972 presidential contest. In effect, Hamilton called upon the Democratic party to emphasize those issues that would have an appeal *to broad segments of the electorate across racial lines,* for example, national health insurance and an income-maintenance program. These two papers by Hamilton constitute the first wave of scholarship where the concept of deracialization received some specific analytical attention and where the agenda-setting and electoral variants—albeit related—can be identified.

The Second Wave

Some fourteen years later, sociologist William Julius Wilson (W. Wilson 1990) took a position similar to the one Hamilton had taken in 1976. Wilson advised decision makers within the national Democratic party to support what he called "race-neutral" public policy programs as a means for winning presidential elections in the 1990s. In this regard Wilson writes (1990, 74):

In the 1990s the party needs to promote new policies to fight inequality that differ from court-ordered busing, affirmative action programs, and anti-discrimination lawsuits of the recent past. By stressing coalition politics and race-neutral programs such as full employment strategies, job skills training, comprehensive health care, reforms in the public schools, child care legislation, and prevention of crime and drug abuse, the Democrats can significantly strengthen their position.

Following the line of reasoning seen in the policy recommendations he advanced under the rubric "the hidden agenda" in his 1987 book *The Truly Disadvantaged* (W. Wilson 1987), Wilson proposes an agenda-building *qua* electoral strategy that bears striking similarity to the position advanced by Hamilton in 1976.

He states (1990, 81):

An emphasis on coalition politics that features progressive, race-neutral policies could have two positive effects. It could help the Democratic party to regain lost political support, and it could lead to programs that would especially benefit the more disadvantaged members of minority groups—without being minority [i.e., race-specific] policies.

While Wilson does not formally call this strategy deracialization, we feel that its similarity to the Hamilton position and the common set of concerns that shaped the sort of advice that both scholars have offered, justify the use of this label.[8] Wilson's work thus can be said to constitute the second wave of scholarship where deracialization as an agenda-building *qua* electoral strategy is given some major emphasis.

Both Hamilton and Wilson recognize the pivotal nature of race and racism in American politics and the extent to which: (1) the material conditions of African-Americans, as a group, and Euro-Americans, as a group, are objectively different (U.S. Bureau of the Census 1989; Reid 1982); (2) the extent to which the perceptions of citizens from these communities about the nature of such conditions are frequently different (Cavanagh 1985, 3–9); and (3) the extent to which policy proposals for addressing the material conditions of African-Americans (particularly those situated on the lower rungs of the economic ladder) are subject to intense national debate, controversy, and sometime outright opposition. Given these realities, Hamilton and Wilson recognize that if policy-related concerns of African-Americans are to be addressed by policy makers, strategically, these concerns will have to be linked to what Wilson (1987, 155) calls ". . . programs to which the more advantaged groups of all races and class backgrounds can positively relate."

The Hamilton/Wilson position suggests that in an attempt to get a given set of issues on the formal or institutional agenda of government (Cobb and Elder 1972, 86), for example, issues of particular—though not exclusive—concern to African-Americans, it is important to identify those issues that are likely to gain formal agenda status. Their position also implies that it is important to deracialize these issues as a means for generating support from other actors inside and outside of the public policy-making system. In order to address effectively any set of issues in the American public policy process, the advocates of such issues must secure support from those charged with legitimating policy options— elected officials (Jones 1984, 57–73; Anderson 1990, 82–93). Issue advocates must have the support of elected officials and these individuals must first be elected. Consequently, deracialization not only manifests itself as an agenda-setting strategy, but as the third wave of scholarship indicates, it also has a much broader application as an electoral strategy.

The Third Wave

Application of the electoral variant of deracialization was seen in two papers presented by political scientists at a symposium sponsored by the Joint Center for Political Studies in December 1989. This symposium assembled a group of political activists and scholars to discuss the similarities and differences of the November 1989 elections and their implications (racial and otherwise) for the future. In one paper, Professor Charles Jones (Jones 1989) advanced deracialization as a multidimensional *electoral strategy* focusing on mobilization tactics, issues, and the political style of the candidate. L. Douglas Wilder's gubernatorial victory in Virginia served as the case material in this paper.

The second paper, by Professor Joseph McCormick, examined both the Wilder contest and six local-level, large city (population greater than 100,000), electoral contests where blacks either retained or won office as mayor. Here McCormick utilized the concept of deracialization to say the following about its use as an election strategy: "The essence of this political strategy is that its proponents would seek *to deemphasize* those issues that may be viewed *in explicitly racial terms* . . . while emphasizing those issues that appear to transcend the racial question. . . ." (emphasis added) (McCormick 1989, 7).

These papers by Jones and McCormick constituted the front end of the third wave of scholarship where the electoral variant of this concept was advanced. These papers were followed by the contributions of other political scientists who presented papers on the November 1989 elections at a conference in March 1990, sponsored by the National Conference of Black Political Scientists (NCOBPS).

At the annual meeting of NCOBPS in March 1990, the November 1989 election results were given a great deal of analytical attention. For example, Professors Charles Jones and Michael L. Clemons presented a paper in which they advanced a model of racial crossover voting where the concept of deracialization was a fundamental explanatory component used in a discussion of the Wilder gubernatorial victory in Virginia. Through this model, Jones and Clemons sought to explain the prospects for electoral success by African-American candidates running for office in majority white political jurisdictions. Jones and Clemons offered the following definition of deracialization *as an electoral strategy:* "Conducting a campaign in a manner which diffuses the polarizing effects of the race factor in an election" (Jones and Clemons 1990, 12).

In addition to this paper by Jones and Clemons, papers cited in the previous section of this chapter by Ardrey, Schexnider, Smith, and Walters were also presented at this conference. Collectively, these papers fueled a fiery debate that took place during the course of the conference over the various meanings and interpretations of the November 1989 elections, summarized herein. Proponents of the use of the electoral variant of deracialization bore a significant brunt of the "attack" with one scholar labeling the concept an "oxymoron," with another throwing his hands up in frustration and exclaiming, "I'm not sure what this all means." Quite clearly, as this conference came to a close, the gauntlet had been dropped at the feet of the proponents of this analytical construct to go back to the "drawing board" and reconsider its meaning and the electoral conditions under which its use as a descriptive tool was most applicable.

FACTORS THAT INFLUENCE THE ADOPTION OF A DERACIALIZED ELECTORAL STRATEGY

In our reformulation of the concept of deracialization we reemphasize the distinction between deracialization as *an agenda-setting strategy* and its use as *an electoral strategy.* Given our concern, however, with explaining the potential of African-Americans capturing electoral office *in predominantly white political jurisdictions,* we will restrict our focus in this section of the chapter to the electoral variant of this analytical construct. In our judgment, at least three factors have contributed to the potential trend where African-American politicians seek to capture office in white political jurisdictions and, as such, tend to utilize a deracialized election strategy.

The "Saturation Thesis/Counter-Thesis"

Some scholars have begun to argue that limits have been reached in terms of the number of African-American elected officials who have been elected in predominantly black election districts (Barone and Ujifusa 1986; Swain 1989). Therefore, as the proponents of the saturation thesis argue, African-Americans who aspire for office are most likely to do so in those areas that are majority white.

A counter-argument to the saturation thesis maintains that a saturation point of majority black political jurisdictions having reached their limits in terms of their potential yield of black elected officials (BEOs), has yet to be reached. This is particularly the case in the South where, in 1988, almost six out of ten African-Americans lived (U.S. Bureau of Census 1989, Table B, 3) and where two-thirds of all black elected officials in the United

States could be found. In this regard, available data (Darden 1984) indicate that there remains significant potential for more African-Americans to be elected to office, even though there are various impediments—*particularly in majority black political jurisdictions of the South*—that dilute the impact of African-American bloc voting, for example, the power of incumbency, intraracial factionalism, at-large districts, multimember districts, and so on.[9]

These are the sort of structural constraints that dictate short-range and long-range strategic planning on the part of the African-American community, increased political mobilization, and the pursuit of appropriate legal challenges available under Section 5 of the Voting Rights Act of 1965 (Days and Guinier 1984). This state of affairs also suggests that until the sort of constraints found in many predominantly black political jurisdictions in the South, not now represented by African-American officials, are removed, the potential for more BEOs in predominantly white political jurisdictions appears to be greater. The utilization of a deracialized electoral strategy may strengthen such prospects.[10]

The "Ambition" Factor

As one seeks to move up the electoral ladder from the local level, through the state to the national electoral arena, a candidate has to expand the composition of one's base of support. What we refer to here as the "ambition factor" (Anderson 1989) refers not only to a focus on the personal political aspirations of the African-American political candidate, but *a fundamental recognition on the candidate's part that a vital part of the means to the desired electoral end, in a predominantly white political jurisdiction, is the need not only to appeal to black voters—the "natural" constituent base—but to also generate sufficient white support.* If the candidacy is what McLemore (Cavanagh 1983, 3) has called a "serious bid for office" (where winning votes is a paramount concern) and not a "protest" campaign (where procedural and/or substantive reform are deemed most important), then the necessity on the part of the African-American candidate running for office in the predominantly white jurisdiction to make an appeal to white voters becomes that much more important.

The clearest example of this proposition is seen in the shift in campaign style between Jesse Jackson's 1984 (see McCormick and Smith 1989) and 1988 attempts to win the Democratic presidential nomination. The 1984 nomination bid was an "insurgent protest" (Smith and McCormick 1984) while the 1988 effort was far more serious in the sense that Jackson appeared less concerned with restructuring the Democratic party's nomination process and its formal agenda and was more concerned with winning delegates. Jackson's base of white support expanded in his 1988 effort as he made more direct appeals to white voters and avoided the sort of issues perceived as racially confrontational (Taylor 1988a; Taylor 1988b;

Taylor 1988c). This crucial difference of whether the electoral attempt by the African-American candidate is a "protest" effort or a "serious" one has major implications regarding the extent to which a deracialized electoral strategy on the part of the African-American candidate can be properly anticipated.

The "Subtle Racism" Factor

Our discussion on this potential trend in American electoral politics has indicated that the logic of a deracialized electoral strategy, as pursued by African-American political candidates who run for office in predominantly white political jurisdictions, precludes a strong and explicit emphasis on race-specific policy options during the course of the campaign. We should point out, however, that a propensity to deemphasize racially-specific policy options by African-American candidates for public office in such jurisdictions is not necessarily born of a politically naive notion that some sort of racial millennium has arrived. Quite the contrary. Racism is one of the more insidious cognitive demons in the psyches of Americans that all too often comes to the fore when skillfully summoned.[11]

In this regard, the likelihood of an African-American candidate in a predominantly white political jurisdiction utilizing a deracialized electoral strategy is reinforced where he or she may face a white opponent who *may* inject elements of subtle racism into the campaign. Thomas Pettigrew (Cavanagh 1983, 27–28) has pointed out that the use of "somewhat ambiguous code words and slogans," or the attempt ". . . to identify [an African-American candidate] with the far left or with militant black figures who are known to frighten other blacks and most whites" are two of the more frequent practices of subtle racism that he has uncovered in his research on campaign techniques.[12] Pettigrew goes on to say (Pettigrew 1983, 28):

> . . . for those whites who may miss the subtleties, you have parts of your campaign use old-fashioned racist techniques. You can do this in small sectors. Anywhere it looks like it would be a good idea, you send out racist literature. If this is exposed, the central campaign can always say we don't know anything about this, we're outraged by this and we will stop it immediately. . . .

This scholar (Cavanagh 1983, 28) argues that, ". . . white candidates wittingly or unwittingly are likely to fall into this pattern under the pressures of campaigning and maximizing the white vote." These fairly well established tendencies on the part of white candidates, where there are either perceived "liberal" white opponents or opponents who are African-American, therefore may reinforce the utilization of a deracialized electoral strategy by the African-American candidate.

DERACIALIZATION: A DEFINITION

It is with the above factors in mind that we advance the following definition of deracialization *as an electoral strategy:*

> Conducting a campaign in a stylistic fashion that defuses the polarizing effects of race by avoiding explicit reference to race-specific issues, while at the same time emphasizing those issues that are perceived as racially transcendent, thus mobilizing a broad segment of the electorate for purposes of capturing or maintaining public office.

From this definition, we derive three components, all of which are needed to enhance effectively the likelihood of white electoral support in predominantly white political jurisdictions where African-American candidates seek to be elected. These components are *political style, mobilization tactics,* and *issues.*

Political Style

One of the most important components of a deracialized electoral strategy is the political style of the African-American candidate. A black candidate's success in attracting support from the white electorate is very much linked to projecting *a nonthreatening image* (J. Wilson 1980, 214–254; Goldstein 1981, 144). White voters appear to be uncomfortable with the fiery confrontational political style that tended to characterize many of the first wave of black politicians elected immediately after the passage of the Voting Rights Act (Walton 1976, 87). Needless to say, an image which is perceived as threatening by the white electorate would constitute a serious impediment to an African-American candidate's success in predominantly white political jurisdictions.

Mobilization Tactics

The manner in which the African-American candidate mobilizes the electorate is another key factor in a deracialized electoral strategy. A deracialized electoral strategy would dictate that African-American candidates in majority white political jurisdictions, who are running to win, should avoid employing direct racial appeals in organizing the black community (Pettigrew and Alston, 1988). The 1983 mayoral bid by Harold Washington provides us with a useful illustration of the use of racially focused mobilization tactics resulting in a decline of white support (Pettigrew and Alston, 1988: 86–87).

Issues

The final component of a deracialized election strategy requires that African-American office seekers adopt issues which appeal to a broad segment of the electorate in order to maximize the likelihood of receiving white support. As such, *black candidates should avoid emphasis of a racially specific issue agenda.* The essence of this electoral strategy is that its proponents would seek to deemphasize those issues that may be viewed in explicitly racial terms, for example, minority set-asides, affirmative action, or the plight of the black urban underclass, while emphasizing those issues that appear to transcend the racial question. There is little doubt that a black candidate's platform plays an important role in building the biracial or multiethnic coalition needed to win in a majority white political jurisdiction.

In effect, deracialization as an electoral strategy requires attentiveness to political style, mobilization tactics, and issues. We should add that the degree to which an African-American candidate attempts to deracialize a campaign is also dictated by the political context of the interracial contest. What type of elected office is being sought—legislative, executive, judicial? What level of office is being sought—local, state-wide, national? Is the contest occurring during a presidential election year? In what region of the country does the contest occur? What is the nature of the larger political culture—liberal, conservative, and/or single-issue tendencies? All of these forces—in addition to those that we discussed above—will shape the decision to pursue a deracialized electoral strategy as well as the content and tactics of such a strategy. What then are the implications of this electoral strategy for the course of African-American politics in the years ahead? We now turn to a discussion of three implications that are associated with this political strategy.

IMPLICATIONS OF THE PURSUIT OF A DERACIALIZED ELECTORAL STRATEGY

In this chapter we have attempted to clarify and advance the use of an analytical concept that can be employed for explaining the landmark electoral victories by African-American candidates in majority white districts in November 1989. At least three sets of implications emerge from our analysis, which we address in answers to the following three questions:

1. *What is it about this electoral strategy that evokes some serious reservations among African-Americans?* A dominant material reality and concern within the African-American community is the widening chasm between those on the lower and upper rungs of the economic ladder. For example, a recent study by the National Research Council (Jaynes and Williams, 1989, 275) notes that in "... 1970, 15.7 percent of black families had incomes over $35,000; by 1986 this proportion had grown to 21.1 percent (in 1986 constant dollars).... During the same years, the proportion of black families with incomes of less than $10,000 also grew, from 26.8 percent to 30.2 percent."

This widening chasm and the perception that the opportunities for those on the lower rungs of this economic ladder are increasingly shrinking has led many African-Americans to look legitimately to public policy makers to address these problems. Those expectations are particularly evident where these public policy makers are African-American.

Matthew Holden reminds us that "cynicism and fear" is a long-standing component of African-American culture (Holden 1973, 24–25). Historically, within the African-American community there has been a relatively low level of mass trust in the leadership of this community and an ever present fear of a "sellout." As such, some African-Americans are worried about the consequences of a deracialized electoral strategy when a victorious African-American candidate acquires the reins of formal legal authority. It is too soon to tell if the logic of a deracialized electoral strategy will carry over as a post-election strategy of governance. In our judgment, the extent to which African-American elected officials pursue a deracialized strategy of governance will be significantly influenced by the racial composition of the electorate where they have won office and the nature of the larger political culture where these officials are found. An important determinant in this political equation will be the extent to which the African-American community is politically organized and prepared to make race-specific demands on these officials. In the absence of such demands from a politically organized African-American community, there is little reason to expect African-American elected officials who capture office in predominantly white political jurisdictions to be in the vanguard of articulating racially-specific policy issues.

2. *To what extent should African-American elected officials who are elected in predominantly white political jurisdictions openly pursue race-specific public policy options after winning office?* The analysis we have offered here offers no ready answers to this difficult question. Support from white voters and other elected officials is a crucial factor as the political feasibility of any race-specific policy option is considered by an African-American elected official. That white support is necessary to make such options become reality, however, should not necessarily preclude the advocacy of race-specific policy options by African-American elected officials. As Harold Cruse has recently argued (Cruse 1990), given the nature of the African-American predicament, race-specific policies are needed to mitigate the impact of racism on both the African-American middle class and the urban underclass. The racial "balance of power" in such political jurisdictions may be a key variable in dictating how politically aggressive an African-American elected official can be in initiating such policy options. While we consider it politically improbable for these politicians in predominantly white jurisdictions to be constantly at the vanguard on race-specific policy issues, their failure to address such issues periodically and send appropriate signals to the black community could undoubtedly cost them crucial support within that community that could prove to be damaging when reelection is sought.[13]

3. *To what extent can we characterize this recent wave of electoral victories by African-Americans in predominantly white political jurisdictions as an expression of black politics?* Professor Mack Jones reminds us that it is useful theoretically to think of "Black Politics" as a power struggle between whites bent on maintaining their position cf superordinate power and blacks struggling to escape this dominance (Jones cited in Smith, 1988a). In this same theoretical vein, Ron Walters (Walters 1990, 28–29) has recently argued that, characteristically, black politics in its electoral form, entails: a challenging of the practices of institutional racism; a development of institutionalized political power; a strong, progressive, change-oriented posture; a forging of interracial political alliances and coalitions that are deemed to meet the material needs of the black community; and adopting a manner of governance that seeks to benefit all citizens within its legitimate purview.

In our judgment, these scholars do not see black politics merely as an expression, *by those who happen to be black,* to capture public office electorally and exercise formal legal authority. For them, in its electoral form, black politics involves efforts by blacks to capture public office for the express purpose of using the policy tools of government to improve the material conditions of black constituents in a way that is sensitive to the historical role and continuing impact of white racism in American political life.[14] It is in this regard that the Jones/Walters view of black politics is instrumentally connected with that view of black politics implicit in Charles Hamilton's view of deracialization as an electoral strategy (commented on earlier in this chapter). All of these perspectives share the notion of using the electorally acquired, formal legal authority of government for the expressed purpose of improving the material conditions of African-Americans, which in the course of so doing, may entail confrontation with extant practices of institutional racism.

This line of reasoning may initially lead one to conclude that the very nature of deracialization—as an electoral strategy with its explicit de-emphasis on racially specific issues—forecloses consideration of including its African-American practitioners, who have won public office in predominantly white political jurisdictions within the theoretical orbit of black politics outlined herein. To do otherwise, it could be argued, would be to speak of a true oxymoron, *deracialized black politics.* Yet we can begin to untangle this analytical dilemma by reemphasizing the following point: we will be better able to determine whether the political behavior of these African-American politicians elected in predominantly white jurisdictions merits inclusion within the analytical parameters of black politics, when we examine what they have done while in office to address the policy-oriented concerns of African-Americans. If deracialization as a successful electoral strategy leads its practitioners to ignore the policy-oriented concerns of African-Americans, then we should rightfully dismiss their political behavior as nonlegitimate expressions of black politics. As the historian John Hope Franklin observed on a recent television documentary on this new wave of "crossover politicians" (Williams 1990), "One hopes they will not lose focus on the problems that black people face, for if they do, they will have gained the prize, but will have lost their souls."

REFERENCES

Anderson, James E. 1990. *Public Policymaking: An Introduction.* Boston: Houghton Mifflin Company.

Anderson, Susan. "Eyes on the Prizes, Not the People." *The Nation,* 16 October 1989, 405–407.

Ardrey, Sandra C. "The Maturation of Black Political Power: The Case of Cleveland, Ohio." Paper delivered at the annual meeting of the National Conference of Black Political Scientists, Atlanta, GA, March 15–17, 1990.

Barone, Michael, and Grant Ujifusa. 1986. *The Almanac of American Politics.* Washington, D.C.: The National Journal.

Benedetto, Richard, and Paul Clancy. "Victory's Thrill Put Aside for the Uphill Battle." *USA Today,* 14 June 1990, 1Aff.

Carmichael, Stokely, and Charles Hamilton. 1967. *Black Power: The Politics of Liberation in America.* New York: Vintage Books.

Cavanagh, Thomas E., ed. 1983. *Race and Political Strategy: A JCPS Roundtable.* Washington, D.C.: The Joint Center for Political Studies.

————. 1985. *Inside Black America: The Message of the Black Vote in the 1984 Elections.* Washington, D.C.: The Joint Center for Political Studies.

Cobb, R.W., and C.D. Elder. 1972. *Participation in American Politics: The Dynamics of Agenda-Building.* Boston: Allyn & Bacon.

Cruse, Harold. 1990. "New Black Leadership Required." *New Politics* 2(4): 43–47.

Darden, Joe T. 1984. "Black Political Under-representation in Majority Black Places." *Journal of Black Studies* 15 (September): 101–116.

Days, Drew S., III, and Lani Guinier. 1984. "Enforcement of Section 5 of the Voting Rights Act." In *Minority Vote Dilution.* Ed. Chandler Davidson. Washington, D.C.: Howard University Press, 167–180.

Edsall, Thomas B. 1988. "Race: Still a Force in Politics." *The Washington Post,* 31 July 1988, A1.

Goldstein, Michael. 1981. "The Political Careers of Fred Roberts and Tom Bradley: Political Style and Black Politics in Los Angeles." *The Western Journal of Black Studies* 5(2): 139–146.

Hahn, Harlan, David Klingman, and Harry Pachon. 1976. "Cleavage, Coalitions, and the Black Candidate: The Los Angeles Mayoralty Elections of 1969 and 1973." *Western Political Quarterly* 29 (December): 507–520.

Halley, Robert M., Alan Acock, and Thomas Green. 1976. "Ethnicity and Social Class: Voting in the 1973 Los Angeles Municipal Elections." *Western Political Quarterly* 29 (December): 521–530.

Hamilton, Charles V. 1973. "Full Employment as a Viable Issue." In *When the Marching Stopped: An Analysis of Black Issues in the '70s.* New York: The National Urban League, 87–91.

——. 1977. "Deracialization: Examination of a Political Strategy." *First World* 1 (2): 3–5.

Hawkins, Augustus F. 1986. "Whatever Happened to Full Employment?" *The Urban League Review* 10 (1): 9–12.

Holden, Matthew Jr. 1973. *The Politics of the Black 'Nation'.* San Francisco: Chandler Publishing Co.

Jaynes, Gerald D., and R.M. Williams, Jr., eds. 1989. *Common Destiny: Blacks and American Society.* Washington, D.C.: National Academy Press.

Jones, Charles E. "The Virginia Gubernatorial Race: How Wilder Won." Paper delivered at a symposium, Blacks in the November '89 Elections: What Is Changing. Sponsored by the Joint Center for Political Studies, Washington, D.C., December 5, 1989.

Jones, C.E., and M.L. Clemons. "Black Gubernatorial Success: An Analysis of the Wilder Victory." A paper prepared for delivery at the annual meeting of the National Conference of Black Political Scientists, Atlanta, GA, March 15–17, 1990.

Jones, Charles O. 1984. *An Introduction to the Study of Public Policy.* 3rd ed., Monterey, CA: Brooks/Cole Publishing Co.

Kaplan, Abraham. 1964. *The Conduct of Inquiry: Methodology for Behavioral Social Science.* San Francisco: Chandler Publishing Co.

Levine, Charles H. 1974. *Racial Conflict and the American Mayor.* Lexington, MA: Heath.

Maraniss, David. "Campaigning in Code." *The Washington Post,* 1 July 1990, A1ff.

McCormick, J.P., II. "Black Tuesday and the Politics of Deracialization." Paper delivered at a symposium, Blacks in the November '89 Elections: What Is Changing. Sponsored by the Joint Center for Political Studies, Washington, D.C., December 5, 1989.

McCormick, J.P., II, and Robert C. Smith. 1989. "Through the Prism of African-American Culture: An Interpretation of the Jackson Campaign Style." In *Jesse Jackson's 1984 Presidential Campaign: Challenge and Change in American Politics.* Ed. L. Barker and R. Walters. Urbana: University of Illinois Press, 96–107.

Nelson, William E., Jr., and Philip Meranto. 1977. *Electing Black Mayors: Political Action in the Black Community.* Columbus: Ohio State University Press.

Pettigrew, Thomas F. 1976. "Black Mayoralty Campaigns." In *Urban Governance and Minorities.* Ed. Herrington Bryce. New York: Praeger.

Pettigrew, Thomas F., and Denise A. Alston. 1988. "Tom Bradley's Campaigns for Governor." Washington, D.C.: Joint Center for Political Studies.

Reid, John. 1982. *Black America in the 1980s.* Washington, D.C.: Joint Center for Political Studies.

Ruffins, Paul. 1990. "Interracial Coalitions." *The Atlantic* 265 (6): 28–34.

Schexnider, Alvin J. "The Politics of Pragmatism: An Analysis of the 1989 Gubernatorial Election in Virginia." Paper delivered at the annual meeting of the National Conference of Black Political Scientists, Atlanta, GA, March 15–17, 1990.

Smith, Robert C. 1988a. "Politics Is Not Enough: A Study in the Institutionalization of the Afro-American Freedom Movement." (an unpublished paper), 1.

———. 1988b. "Liberal Jurisprudence and the Quest for Racial Representation." *Southern University Law Review* 15(1): 1–50.

———. "The Death of Black Politics?" Paper prepared for delivered at the annual meeting of the National Conference of Black Political Scientists, Atlanta, GA, March 15–17, 1990.

Smith, Robert C., and J.P. McCormick II. 1984. "The Challenge of a Black Presidential Candidacy." *New Directions: The Howard University Magazine* 11(2): 38–43.

Swain, Carol M. "The Politics of Black Representation in U.S. Congressional Districts." Paper presented at the annual meeting of the Southern Political Science Association, Memphis, TN, 1989.

Taylor, Paul. Jackson Triumphs With Landslide Over Dukakis in Michigan. *The Washington Post*, 28 March 1988a: A1ff.

———. Jackson Stirs the White Underdogs. *The Washington Post*, 16 July 1988b: A1.

———. Jackson Tones Down Rhetoric, Speaks of Healing and Unity. *The Washington Post*, 16 July 1988c:A1.

U.S. Bureau of the Census, 1989. Current Population Reports, Series P-20, No. 442, *The Black Population in the United States: March 1988.* Washington, D.C.: U.S. Government Printing Office.

Walters, Ronald W. 1980. "The Challenge of Black Leadership: An Analysis of the Problem of Strategy Shift." *The Urban League Review* 5(1): 77–88.

———. "Fording the New Mainstream: The Death of Black Politics?" Paper delivered at the annual meeting of the National Conference of Black Political Scientists, Atlanta, GA, March 15–17, 1990.

Walton, Hanes, Jr. 1976. "Black Politics in the South: Projections for the Coming Decade." In *Public Policy for the Black Community.* Ed. Marguerite Ross Barnett and James A. Hefner. New York: Alfred Publishing Co., 77–100.

Williams, Juan. Narrator of "Politics: The New Black Power." WETA-TV, channel 26, Washington, D.C., 26 February 1990.

———. "The New Mosiac of Race." *The Washington Post*, 19 November 1989, D1ff.

Wilson, James Q. 1980. Reprinted. *Negro Politics: The Search for Leadership.* New York: Octagon Books.

Wilson, William J. 1987. *The Truly Disadvantaged: The Inner City, the Underclass, and Public Policy.* Chicago: University of Chicago Press.

———. 1990. "Race-Neutral Programs and the Democratic Coalition." *The American Prospect* (Spring) 1: 74–81.

NOTES

1. The interest of scholars and practitioners in the issue of the strategic choices confronting African-American candidates who run for elective office in majority white political jurisdictions predates the November 1989 elections. See Cavanagh 1983, 1–26.

2. *New York Times*-CBS News, "1989 Virginia Election Poll." *New York Times*-CBS News, 1–3. Data were obtained directly from this source.

3. Papers from this symposium were assembled in a volume entitled, *When the Marching Stopped: An Analysis of Black Issues in the 1970s* (New York: National Urban League, 1973), 87–91.

4. See Charles V. Hamilton, "Full Employment as a Viable Issue." In *When the Marching Stopped: An Analysis of Black Issues in the '70s* (New York: National Urban League, 1973), 87–91.

5. The topic of "full employment" as a major public policy issue has been on the formal agenda of the federal government since the enactment of the Employment Act of 1946. The original intent of this legislation was to guarantee the right to a job for everyone willing to work. Neither this legislation not its statutory offspring, the Full Employment and Balanced Growth Act of 1978 (the Humphrey-Hawkins bill), succeeded in gaining any national compliance with, or fiscal support of, the notion of "the right to a job." See Augustus F. Hawkins, "Whatever Happened to Full Employment." *The Urban League Review* 10 (Summer 1986), 9–12, and other essays in this volume.

6. In 1988, the unemployment rate for blacks was 2½ times that for whites (11.7 percent versus 4.7 percent). In the post-recession period of 1983, the unemployment rate for black teenagers (16 to 19 years of age) reached 48.5 percent—29.2 percentage points higher than that for white teenagers (19.3 percent). By 1988, however, the unemployment rate for black teenagers had declined to 32.4 percent—19.3 points higher, but still 2½ times that of white teenagers (13.1 percent). See U.S. Bureau of the Census, current Population Reports, Series P-20, No. 442, *The Black Population in the United States: March 1988* (Washington, D.C.: U.S. Government Printing Office, 1989), 9.

7. Here we rely on the definition of "formal" or "institutional agenda" as used by Cobb and Elder: ". . . that set of items explicitly up for the active and serious consideration of authoritative decision makers." See R.W. Cobb and C.D. Elder, *Participation in American Politics: The Dynamics of Agenda-Building* (Boston, MA: Allyn and Bacon, Inc., 1972), 86.

8. We should point out that Wilson uses the term "deracialization" in his 1987 book *The Truly Disadvantaged* but not in the strategic sense that we use it here. In two instances (Wilson 1987, 122 and 134), the concept of deracialization is used by Wilson to refer to the "removal of racial barriers" as they stand as impediments to the upward mobility of African-Americans. This removal of racial barriers, Wilson implies (1987, 122), is facilitated through the use of equal employment legislation, e.g., Title VII of the 1964 Civil Rights Act.

9. A proponent of the counter-argument to the "saturation thesis" points out in his own research on this issue: ". . . a recent investigation of this phenomenon at the congressional level . . . found that the advantages of incumbency (especially money) and factionalism in the black community are important explanations of the failure of majority black districts to elect black representatives.

10. A published journalistic account on the recent electoral fortunes of some black political aspirants in the South validates our interpretation of events. This account points to black candidates moderating their views in an attempt to appeal to more conservative white voters and a down playing of racial issues. The latter point is a hallmark of a deracialized electoral strategy. See Benedetto and Clancy 1990, 1Aff.

11. Though it did not occur in an electoral contest where an African-American candidate was involved, surely one of the most poignant instances of racist "dirty tricks" and code words could be seen in the Willie Horton furlough issue in the 1988 presidential campaign. See Edsall 1988 for a useful journalistic account of these issues.

12. The most recent (and perhaps most shameful) display of such code words, apparently being used to mobilized disaffected white voters, can be seen in the senatorial bid by David Duke in Louisiana. See Maraniss 1990.

13. As an illustrative case, we would encourage students of black electoral politics to watch closely the first term of Mayor Michael White in Cleveland, Ohio. White, an African-American, won only about 30 percent of the black vote in his November 1989 victory over George Forbes, while carrying 76 percent of the white vote. Given the comparatively poor socio-economic conditions of Cleveland's black community, it is likely that leaders from that community will make demands on the white administration for some public policy grounded relief. The relevant electoral question becomes, how will whites respond to such demands?

14. The literature that informs this theoretical line of argument is too broad to cite here. We think it fair to say, however, that this view of black politics is philosophically linked with the concept of black power as discussed by Carmichael and Hamilton (1967).

Part
Two

DERACIALIZATION AND THE STRATEGIC CALCULUS OF BLACK POLITICS

Chapter
5

Richmond and the Politics of Calculated Cooperation

W. Avon Drake
Robert D. Holsworth

INTRODUCTION

The Supreme Court's decision in *Richmond* v. *Croson* generated a new round of concern and commentary about the legal status of affirmative action. Public officials in American cities conferred to discuss the potential impact of *Croson* on their own affirmative action programs. Editorial writers in papers around the country praised and denounced the Court's decision. And scholars quickly produced essays that placed *Croson* in historical perspective and evaluated its implications. At first, a number of analysts downplayed the importance of *Croson* and suggested that the Court was simply overruling an ill-conceived plan by the Richmond City Council that would not directly influence the legality of most existing affirmative action programs. But when *Croson* was followed by three other major opinions on civil rights cases that articulated a similar outlook, it became harder to deny that the Court had moved rightward and had significantly altered the American political terrain.

Discussions about the implications of *Richmond* v *Croson* are extremely significant for evaluating the legacy of the Reagan administration and the manner in which the Supreme Court has redefined the meaning of civil rights. In an earlier article, we explored these issues and the challenges that the Court's decisions posed for African-American politicians.[1] But we also think that it is important to understand the political context in which set-aside policies such as the one challenged in *Croson* arose. The affirmative action program in Richmond was part of a broader strategy of economic advancement pursued by black leaders in a city where, like most American urban areas, the business sector was dominated by whites. The strategy of calculated cooperation pursued by African-American political officials accepted the priority of downtown revitalization, but attempted to ensure that the benefits of city-directed economic growth were channelled, at least in part, to the black community.

This essay begins by outlining the emergence of black political power in Richmond. We pay special attention to the relationship between black elected officials and the white economic establishment. The essay describes the tensions that developed and the manner in which an accommodation was pursued. We show how African-American political leaders attempted to shape economic development policies to advance black interests and how various affirmative action policies ultimately served in the 1980s as instruments of elite racial reconciliation. In the remainder of the essay, we explore the limitations of the manner in which black interests were advanced in Richmond and investigate some of the dilemmas that our case study raises for African-American urban politics more generally.

THE EMERGENCE OF BLACK POLITICAL POWER

Although the population of Richmond was nearly 50 percent black by the end of the 1960s, political power remained firmly in the hands of whites until 1977. The election that year which brought a black majority to power on the city council was the culmination of an arduous struggle that had, in retrospect, three clearly defined stages. First, in the late 1950s and early 1960s under the leadership of an organization called the Crusade for Voters, black Richmonders developed the capacity to wield the balance of power among competing white candidates in councilmanic elections. The Crusade had its origins in the Committee to Save Public Schools, a group formed in response to a statewide referendum in 1956 that proposed to give localities the power to close schools rather than desegregate. When fewer than 4000 blacks in the city of Richmond voted on the issue, many younger members of the committee believed that it was imperative to establish an organization devoted exclusively to voter registration and political campaigns.[2]

Prior to this time, blacks who held the franchise typically voted in a "single shot" fashion for African-American candidates who stood little chance of winning or for the rare white aspirant who articulated sympathy with black goals. The Crusade worked to change this pattern and it quickly became the preeminent black political organization in Virginia. Its leaders developed a program of "calculated cooperation" with white leaders.[3] The Crusade endorsed a slate of candidates that included members of the white establishment and presented these to rank and file blacks on the Sunday preceding the election during church services and afternoon meetings of fraternal organizations. Stressing the imperative of black political unity, the Crusade developed a reputation for delivering the vote.

Crusade leaders believed that the strategy of demonstrating the power of the black vote would be more effective than moral suasion. They felt that black voting behavior would eventually compel white politicians who were acting in their own self-interests to address black concerns and direct more benefits from city government to the African-American community. Crusade officials could point in the early 1960s to the formation of a city commission on race relations and the appointment of African-Americans to a number of city boards and commissions as concrete outcomes that justified their strategy.

The second stage in the struggle for black political power began in 1966 when the combination of the elimination of the poll tax and the Crusade's successful effort at voter registration gave black Richmonders a measure of independent political power. At that time, a young black civil rights lawyer endorsed by the Crusade, Henry L. Marsh III, was able to get elected to city council primarily on the strength of the black vote. More importantly, during his campaign Marsh articulated an assertive vision of black politics and spent his time on the stump attacking Richmond Forward, the political voice of corporate Richmond. Calling himself a "candidate of the people, the grassroots people," Marsh contrasted his human rights agenda to the downtown revitalization priorities of Richmond Forward with his slogan "build people, not things."[4] As A. J. Dickinson noted in a Yale honors thesis in 1967, Marsh's "election heralded the arrival of potent black ballot power to Richmond. No longer did the Negro voter hold just the balance of power; he had become a power in his own right, able to choose and elect his own candidates for public office. No longer was an alliance with Richmond Forward a practical political necessity."[5]

Marsh's election and the recognition that demographic trends would soon lead to a black majority in the city frightened those who wished to retain white dominance. In the late 1960s, city leaders attempted to annex part of adjacent Chesterfield County that was predominantly white. The ostensible reason for the annexation was that the city was in desperate need for land that could be utilized for industrial development. This had been an ongoing concern of Richmond's leaders for more than a decade. But many observers believed that the urgency surrounding the attempt proceeded from a desire to block the ascent of an emerging black majority.[6] In fact, white leaders held secret meetings about the annexation, which deliberately excluded Henry L. Marsh III, and other black spokespersons. The resulting litigation led to a court order that prevented the city from holding councilmanic elections for almost seven years. At that time, the United States Supreme Court approved a compromise solution that allowed the annexation to stand, but coupled it with the replacement of the at-large method for selecting council with a ward-based system.

The special election of 1977 marked the third stage in the emergence of black political power in Richmond. The voting resulted in blacks' gaining control of the city council by a five to four majority. Since Richmond's council-manager form of government calls for the mayor to be elected from the council by its members, the election also resulted in the selection of Richmond's first black mayor, Henry L. Marsh III. In many ways, Marsh was a logical choice for the job. Not only had he been on the city council for more than a decade, but he was also generally acknowledged as the guiding intellectual force behind black political efforts in the city. The black majority's power was solidified as it was returned to office in the regularly scheduled councilmanic elections in 1978.

CONFLICT, ACCOMMODATION, AND DIVISION

Conflict

The emergence of a black-dominated council immediately raised the question of what stance the new majority would adopt toward the white power structure. Would it update the old Crusade strategy of calculated cooperation, or would it stake out the kind of boldly independent program that Marsh had touched upon in his 1966 campaign with his "build people not things" slogan? In the days following the election, Marsh sent out mixed signals. He served notice that a human rights agenda focusing on the alleviation of poverty would be a high priority of the new majority. He also spoke about the necessity to channel more resources into the school system. But Marsh carefully took steps to assure the business community that a revolution was not coming to the city. He engineered the selection of a white businessman, who was a partner at one of the city's preeminent brokerage houses, as vice-mayor. He spoke about his recognition that the continuation of a good business climate was critical to the city's future. Indeed, two months after his election it appeared to reporters for the Richmond newspapers that Marsh was running another campaign, a "campaign of reassurance" in which the business community was informed of his readiness to work with them. In fact, the major complaint voiced by white council members during the first months following Marsh's election was that he had not developed a visible agenda for the future.[7]

In 1978, white complaints about the new majority became more pronounced. The discontent no longer focused on the presumed inactivity of the mayor, but on the priorities established and the actions taken by the Marsh faction. The most volatile issue centered on the black majority's dismissal of the white city manager, William Leidinger, after the 1978 elections, which returned to office all members of the black majority. Marsh claimed that Leidinger had failed to give proper attention to the stated policy concerns and priorities of the city council, particularly affirmative action, funding recommendations for the schools, and neighborhood improvement programs. In addition, he contended that Leidinger had exploited the city manager's power to "interfere with the council's policy making role." In particular, Marsh maintained that Leidinger "estimated revenue projections consistently low and expenditures consistently high."[8]

Marsh's rationale for Leidinger's removal was not accepted by spokespersons for the white establishment. Members of the white elite generally believed that Leidinger was an intelligent city manager who performed his job competently. When Leidinger made public a conversation in which Marsh gave him the opportunity to resign instead of being dismissed, a number of business leaders summoned the black members of the council to a meeting in a Main Street office and threatened that "blood might flow in the streets" if the council did not revoke its decision. On one level, the white power structure saw the firing of the city manager as an ugly manifestation of race-based decision making. From this perspective, Leidinger was removed simply because he happened to be white. The conservative editorial pages of the *Richmond Times-Dispatch* argued that "if a white majority were trying to do what council's black majority is doing, the NAACP would be at the courthouse before breakfast to file a suit. And Henry Marsh would be among the first to cry 'racism.' "[9]

But what was even more distressing to the white elite was that the decision to fire Leidinger appeared to be an attack on the role of business in the city. Indeed, blacks on the council and others who supported the termination spoke about the necessity of reigning in business' prerogatives. Councilwoman Claudette McDaniel, for instance, explained her vote to fire the city manager by stating that "big businesses must take their rightful place" in the new ordering of priorities.[10] Norvell Robinson, president of the Crusade for Voters, expressed his approval of Leidinger's removal with the statement that "it is imperative to the agenda of this council in order that it is able to expedite the mandate of all the people and not just a dozen downtown businesses."[11] And while Henry Marsh reiterated his belief in a partnership between business and government, he also insisted that "we have to share in the relationship."[12]

The rhetoric in 1978 was much less reassuring to whites than the statements that they heard in 1977. To some businesspeople, the city council was declaring war on the corporate elite. They believed that the firing of Leidinger might be merely a prelude to a wholesale reordering of policy initiatives. They feared that the council would attempt to extract more revenue in order to finance its newly declared social agenda. The editorial pages of the daily papers voiced this opinion in the sharpest terms, intimating that corporate departures and white middle-class flight to the surrounding counties would result from such policies.

> Leidinger is to go not because the black council members consider him to be an incompetent administrator . . . but primarily because the black council

members consider him to be "pro-business." They wish to replace him, they say, with someone who is "pro-people." This antibusiness attitude, if it prevails, could be the ruin of Richmond.[13]

To the black majority, the white establishment had overreacted to what was a perfectly reasonable use of the council's prerogative. They attributed this to the establishment's reluctance to recognize the reality of black political power in Richmond. In an interview with reporter and author Margaret Edds, Henry Marsh III, noted that the very fact that the council had retained Leidinger for fifteen months was a sign of its goodwill.

> We went out of our way to accommodate the concerns of whites. The normal thing to have done would have been to change city managers immediately. The city manager that the whites had at the time had led the fight in the courts (on the annexation issue). He had testified against me and the other blacks. He had led the fight to keep us from getting there. We felt it would be a good way of assuring the whites that we weren't trying to castrate them.[14]

One study suggests that commencing with Leidinger's removal as city manager in 1978, Richmond politics became defined by a "series of conflicts that saw council votes sharply divided along racial lines."[15] From 1978 forward, votes on a number of important appointments and budget issues were decided by a five to four breakdown in which patterns were established by race. The white minority on the council repeatedly claimed that Marsh had decimated the official committee system and that he had effectively excluded the council minority from participation in decision making. And the editorial pages of the daily newspapers were relentless in their criticism of both the process by which the black majority ruled and the substance of their policies. In essence, white critics of city government viewed Marsh as a racialist intent on balkanizing local politics.

In 1980, Teams for Progress, the successor to Richmond Forward, backed the campaign of a local white businessman, Andrew Gillespie, who attempted to unseat Claudette McDaniel in the councilmanic elections. Charges made during the campaign further exacerbated racial bitterness in the city. The editorial pages of the afternoon daily, *The Richmond News Leader,* ran a series of columns that accused McDaniel of using city funds to conduct a survey that was the basis for her master's thesis at Virginia Commonwealth University (VCU). The editorial page went even further and ridiculed McDaniel's intelligence by quoting, with apparent agreement, a charge levelled by a white councilman that McDaniel probably did not write the master's thesis herself and was aided by someone at VCU. Despite these efforts, McDaniel was returned to office and the black majority remained intact.

The controversy that erupted in 1981 over the council's passage of an ordinance that effectively prohibited the construction of a Hilton Hotel adjacent to the Main Street banking district rivalled the Leidinger removal in its bitterness. Earlier that year, the Hilton chain announced its desire to build a $24.5 million hotel project in the city just south of the downtown banking center. The black majority on the council worried that the Hilton complex might make it impossible to find funding for the proposed hotel in the city's downtown revitalization plan, Project One, which had been on the drawing board since the 1970s. The council majority refused to approve the relocation of sewage lines that would have permitted construction to begin, and passed an ordinance that required economic development projects to be compatible with the priorities of Project One.

The white minority on the council and the city's business establishment attacked the council's decision. They argued that it was restraint of trade and that the vagueness of the ordinance would mire the city in potentially costly litigation. Former city manager and now councilman William Leidinger noted that the "litigation might be far more damaging to Project One than the Hilton's competition. . . . We're playing very dangerous and I think that we're going to come out on the short end of the stick."[16] When the city's ordinance became the subject of an article in *The Wall Street Journal,* the corporate establishment concluded that the climate for doing business in Richmond had been seriously damaged.

Henry L. Marsh III and the black majority did not accept the perspective that Leidinger and the editorial pages had used to frame the controversy. Marsh argued that Richmond had already agreed that government could be used to guide and promote downtown redevelopment. He did not believe that the ordinance hindering the construction of the Hilton was qualitatively different from any other action the council might take to shape the direction of economic development downtown. Marsh noted that Project One, which the white community largely supported, required the city to put 40 or 50 people out of business. Far from being a fight over free enterprise principles, Marsh believed that the Hilton controversy was inflamed by the newspaper editorial writers who wanted to "stir up the community against the black leadership." In Marsh's mind, the real objection was that it was black leaders who were now making the decisions guiding the development of the city's retail core.

Accommodation

The racial and ideological divisions on the council were genuine and the personal bitterness was palpable. But this does not mean that Henry Marsh III and the black majority had completely abandoned the old Crusade strategy of calculated cooperation. Although the Leidinger firing in 1978 provoked speculation among whites that it was the beginning of an antibusiness crusade on the part of the council's black majority, these fears were never fully justified. The antibusiness rhetoric that was voiced during the controversy did not presage a fully articulated policy agenda that threatened corporate Richmond, or even challenged its notion of the most appropriate economic development strategy for the city. In reality, antibusiness rhetoric expressed the resentment of the African-American population about black exclusion from the process of formulating priorities and from the benefits of growth. It did not signify the emergence of a political philosophy inherently opposed to center city revitalization.

The turmoil that accompanied Leidinger's removal in 1978 obviously lowered the comfort level of corporate Richmond with the council and it probably permanently scarred Henry Marsh's reputation in the broader white community. But it soon became evident that Marsh and his supporters were not attempting to revolutionize city government. Manuel Deese, the black city manager who was hired to replace Leidinger a few months later, was a professional public administrator who was not visibly committed to a definable political ideology. In fact, Deese had been deputy city manager in Richmond and was originally hired by William Leidinger.

The belief in the necessity of a partnership with business was reflected most visibly in the economic development strategy adopted by the black majority. For all the rhetoric about neighborhood improvements and the desirability of combatting business dominance, their plan was remarkably similar to that which had been articulated long before their own political ascendancy. The proposal which Henry L. Marsh III, and his supporters eventually endorsed, Project One, was a modified version of a master plan for downtown that had been drawn up in the 1960s when whites firmly controlled city government. In sum, the black majority also emphasized downtown redevelopment as the key to the future of Richmond, albeit the reasons for endorsing this emphasis may have differed from those put forward by the business community. The council thus threw its weight behind a hotel-convention center complex which it hoped would draw people back to the central city and increase the tax revenues that could be used to fund educational and social initiatives.[17]

Perhaps it could be argued that the antibusiness ethos of the black majority was demonstrated more through the Hilton controversy than it was in the removal of Leidinger. But such a claim would also be much too simplistic. In the first place, the alternative to the Hilton was the Project One development where city funds were being spent to support business growth. The Richmond City Council never developed the kind of populist orientation that was seen, for example, in Dennis Kucinich's Cleveland. Second, the persistent conflict on council and the heated exchanges over the Hilton decision did not lead Henry L. Marsh III to reject the possibility of continued cooperation with the corporate elite. Indeed, in the aftermath of the Hilton controversy, Marsh approached one of the business community's most respected leaders, T. Justin Moore, CEO of Virginia Power, with a plan for reinvigorating and ultimately formalizing the partnership between the black majority and the white business establishment.

Marsh recognized that there were powerful elements in the business community that had an interest in a more cooperative relationship. By the early 1980s, many corporate leaders had come to believe that the highly publicized wars on the council could only undermine Richmond's reputation as a city hospitable to business. They were more committed to keeping and enhancing Richmond's appeal as a location for corporate headquarters than they were in obtaining a Pyrrhic victory in the local political struggle. For this reason, they were able to look beyond the divisiveness that characterized the council and see how their own long-term interests were best served by a less conflictive relationship with the black majority. At the same time, the Richmond arts community (which had substantial ties to corporate leadership) began to view a revitalized downtown as critical to its plans for preserving the city's architectural distinctiveness and enhancing the visibility of its cultural offerings.[18]

The result was the formation of the public-private partnership called Richmond Renaissance less than five months after the battle over the Hilton development. For its part, the city agreed to put up its half of the $2.4 million seed money by using more than 20 percent of its Community Development Block Grant money for the year.[19] T. Justin Moore of Virginia Power observed, "[T]he business community is excited and enthusiastic over entering into partnership with the city in accelerating economic development (and that) it wouldn't have happened without Mayor Marsh as the catalyst." City Manager Manuel Deese called it "the greatest damn thing in years" and speculated that it could "make this town explode" with economic development. And the editorial page of *The Richmond News Leader* commended the effort, noting that "the formation of Richmond Renaissance for the city's economic revitalization comes as good news. It may even be great news."[20]

By the early 1980s, black-white political relationships were simultaneously cooperative and antagonistic. On one hand, the public-private partnership for downtown redevelopment—Richmond Renaissance—was everywhere hailed as an example of interracial cooperation that would work for the good of all Richmonders and could even be a model for other cities. It represented the desire of both the black political elite and white corporate leadership to set aside their traditional distrust and develop a better working relationship. As the newspaper report on its formation mentioned, both "Moore and Marsh emphasized that, besides promoting growth, this is a means of bringing the Richmond community together and of ending the political and racial polarization that has seemed to divide the black-governed city and the white-dominated business community."[21] At the same time, the racial division that existed on the council did not disappear. Agreement about downtown development did not diminish the personal bitterness that had developed between the two factions. Nor did it cause the editorial pages of the daily papers to believe that the Marsh faction should be entrusted with directing the future of the city.

Division

The city council election of 1982 resulted in a surprising and dramatic configuration of Richmond politics. In this election, Roy West, a relatively conservative black high school principal, defeated a member of the Marsh faction, Willie Dell, who was clearly identified as an ideological progressive. West had campaigned in his ward on the themes that the Marsh faction was unnecessarily divisive, and that Ms. Dell had not provided the benefits for the ward that it needed. Professing that he would be politically independent, West succeeded in garnering significant support among black middle-class voters in his ward and he received near unanimous support among the 31 percent of the ward that was white. In an unexpected and stunning maneuver, West accepted an overture from the white minority and was selected as mayor when he added his own vote to the four which they provided.[22]

West's victory in 1982 changed the nature of politics in Richmond for the remainder of the decade. West's election eclipsed Marsh's and the black majority's monopoly on council decision making. On a number of issues, West voted with the four white members of the council to thwart the agenda of the African-American members of the 1977 majority. A year after his installation as mayor, the *Richmond Times-Dispatch* was reporting that the council "is as deeply divided as it has been at any time since ward elections brought blacks to power in 1977."[23] Much of the division occurred on issues affecting education, especially West's repeated criticisms of the superintendent, who had been supported by the Marsh faction, and conflicts over school board appointees. But this division was also evident in appointments to city boards and commissions and in the annual budgetary battles about which wards should be the recipients of city-sponsored projects.

Marsh claimed that West's tendency to vote with whites on the council on a number of issues had ceded control of the city back to the white establishment. For his part, West asserted that he was merely a new kind of black leader, a consensus builder and a man of substance who "represents a new path for black politics in Richmond away from the messianic kind of process in black leadership in which a messiah arrives on the scene and is entrenched forever."[24] Although West did not receive a majority of the black vote in his ward in the 1982 election, his outlook and style did have a measure of appeal in the black community. First, his criticisms of Marsh's divisiveness did strike a chord in a segment of the black middle class, who believed that the mayor ought to have pursued a more conciliatory policy. Second, there was an element to West centering on his call for a return to basics and more discipline in the schools that appealed to the self-help traditions embraced by many rank and file black citizens.

In 1984, the traditional black leadership made a determined effort to unseat West and elect Willie Dell once again. Henry L. Marsh III, the Crusade for Voters, and the Black Ministers Conference all threw their weight behind Ms. Dell. Criticizing West for selling out to whites, they conducted a campaign that emphasized the need for black people in the district to punish West for his transgressions. Antibusiness rhetoric surfaced once again as Ms. Dell noted that the election would determine

... who's going to set the priority for the city and who gets to set the direction for the city—whether it's going to be Main Street folks or whether it's going to be grass roots folks or whether the leadership is going to be back in the hands of black people.[25]

West responded by pointing to his record as a "bridge builder," by claiming that he really got the important things done for black Richmonders and by denouncing the traditional organizations as unrepresentative of actual black sentiments.[26] When West won by an even greater margin than he had in 1982, it was clear that the era of black solidarity had ended in Richmond.

CALCULATED COOPERATION AND ELITE RACIAL RECONCILIATION

Our discussion of the conflict and the accommodation that accompanied the emergence of black political power in Richmond has maintained that even prior to the election of Roy West, the black majority on the council did not formulate and stand behind an economic development strategy fundamentally different than that which preceded their election. But it did attempt to shape this process to guarantee that black Richmonders would receive identifiable benefits and have, in Marsh's words, a "share in the relationship." To a large degree, this strategy simply applied the old Crusade theme of calculated cooperation to the new circumstances in which blacks had obtained significant political representation. The conflicts that developed on the council in the 1970s and early 1980s were related to ideology and personality. But these were also, at least in part, the natural consequence of negotiating what the terms of the compromise would be.

It is worth noting that the disputes that developed in the 1980s between Roy West and Henry L. Marsh III, rarely focused on issues concerned with the general economic development policy of the city and the manner in which black interests were advanced within it. West's abandonment of the Marsh faction certainly hindered the quest for black political empowerment in Richmond. But West's conservatism did not mean that he embraced the free market critique of black leadership that had been advanced by a scholar such as Thomas Sowell, who maintains that programs such as set-asides and affirmative action policies in employment are immoral and impractical infringements on the workings of the market. West endorsed city divestiture policies toward South Africa, he was a strong supporter of the set-aside programs, and he joined with other black members of the council in supporting affirmative action guidelines. Indeed, he frequently pointed to this as an indication that he worked for substantive benefits for black citizens and was not merely a symbolic leader. In fact, he occasionally chided the Marsh faction for taking so long to make affirmative action a regular part of city policy.

The council attempted to pursue identifiable black economic interests in a number of ways during the 1970s and 1980s. First, it attempted to ensure that black Richmonders were seriously considered for high-level appointments in city government as well as being adequately represented in the city work force. From our position, the Leidinger removal was perhaps more symbolic of the council's commitment to African-American representation in high-level city positions than it was of an antibusiness ethos. Initially, the council maintained a controversial residency requirement in the hope of utilizing this to increase black representation in the work force. But even when the residency requirement was removed, the council attempted to ensure that more key positions in the city government were filled by African-Americans. By the end of the 1980s, the racial composition of the city work force had been considerably changed. Forty-five percent of the managerial and professional positions and 86 percent of the service/maintenance positions were held by African-Americans.[27]

The council majority attempted to shape economic development in the city to benefit black Richmond in two principal ways. First, the Marsh faction attempted to locate these projects in places that were accessible to the African-American community. Marsh's commitment to Project One and his willingness to block the Hilton complex were related to the planned location of the respective sites. Simply put, Project One was located in the north core of downtown, an area much closer to where black Richmonders lived and owned property than was the proposed site of the Hilton, at the southern end of the banking district. Second, Marsh was instrumental in ensuring that a planned festival mall was erected on Broad Street adjacent to the Project One development rather than on the James River, six or eight blocks south of the traditional locus for black shopping. Broad Street had been the traditional dividing line between black and white Richmond and the walkway over it connecting the principal sections of the mall was named "The Bridge" for its connotations of racial reconciliation.

The council majority also attempted to write set-aside goals into bills when city government decided to use public funds for economic development projects. During the initial phase of Project One, the council passed a set-aside ordinance calling for 25 percent of the construction jobs to be given to black Richmonders. And, when the festival mall, Sixth Street Marketplace, was built, the city manager negotiated a series of agreements requiring minority participation in the project. Although Marsh was unable to pass an ordinance calling for 33 percent minority ownership and ultimately was compelled to accept a 15 percent ownership quota, substantial provision for minority involvement remained. According to the agreement negotiated with the developer, 20 percent of all architectural and engineering services, 30 percent of all construction subcontracts, 30 percent of construction workers, 30 percent of professionals employed by the partnership, and 20 percent of all service contracts had to be reserved for minorities.[28]

City construction contracts were another instrument by which the council majority attempted to advance black interests. Almost five years after the black majority was elected, a study in 1982 determined that black contractors were receiving less than 1 percent of the monies in city construction contracts. The council convened a special working group of council members, city officials (including its legal office), and outside consultants such as the director of the Metropolitan Business League, to examine the manner in which other cities had responded to the problem, and to formulate a program for Richmond. The council eventually passed the group's recommendation that a set-aside program be established. The key provision of the council's ordinance was the requirement that, absent a waiver, majority contractors use minority subcontractors for at least 30 percent of the total dollar value in all city construction contracts.[29] It was this part of the city's affirmative action agenda which was the basis of the historic *Croson* challenge.

The manner in which Marsh attempted to protect black interests was not always applauded by whites. As we have seen, his decision to block the development of the Hilton through the use of a constitutionally questionable city ordinance was widely criticized. Even many businesspeople who professed to support Project One could not justify what they believed was a heavy-handed method for protecting the city's investment. In addition, some of the percentage goals for employment and minority ownership voiced by the Marsh regime were criticized as unrealistically high.

But at the same time, much of corporate Richmond appeared to accept the affirmative action features of the city development strategy as an acceptable price of doing business. Indeed, many companies came to see a public commitment to affirmative action as a method for pursuing their self-interests. Philip Morris, the city's largest private employer, was under increasing attack in the 1980s by antismoking groups in the state and around the nation. One instrument for parrying the assaults was to become a model corporate citizen. The company thus became a major patron of the arts. It also developed a program to utilize minority suppliers that would help to remind Richmonders of the company's contribution to the city's economic well-being.

Besides Philip Morris, other large businesses located in Richmond were developing an increasingly national and international presence. A number of executives from these companies had little emotional attachment to the old order. They wanted Richmond to develop a reputation as a city hospitable to business so that other corporate headquarters could be attracted to the city. They had no desire for their home base to be identified as a cauldron of racial conflict, for this would only make Richmond less attractive to companies contemplating relocation. Given these concerns, it was not surprising that in the Richmond of the 1980s, major banks and corporations proudly pointed to their own affirmative action programs as an example of their commitment to the black community. These self-avowedly "progressive" businesses were not about to jeopardize their standing in the community on behalf of pure free-market principles that did not serve their immediate or long-term interests.

Affirmative action policies have often been criticized for the resentment they have engendered in the white community, and public opinion polls have continually shown that white Americans do not support programs that establish numerical quotas based on race. But we have to be careful to distinguish rank and file opinion from elite behavior. In Richmond, affirmative action became an instrument of racial reconciliation among the city's business and governing elite as it served to cement the partnership between black officials and white business leaders. It was a method for managing racial conflict and for ensuring that the existing latent tensions were not easily inflamed. Affirmative action policies enabled black leaders to claim that they were meeting the needs of the community and that they had successfully extracted concessions from white business as the price of cooperation. For white leaders, acceptance of affirmative action permitted them to pursue their chosen strategy of economic redevelopment with strong support from the black elite. Moreover, the partnership arrangement was a public relations boon for the city, as it allowed the political and corporate leadership to market Richmond as an example of interracial cooperation where "good things were happening."[30]

To be sure, there was white business opposition to the economic development policies of the city, but only part of this was related to initiatives that promoted black interests. Business opposition to city policy was located primarily in pockets of the white small business community. In the 1970s small businesspeople did not want the convention center built at its proposed site (as they were the people being displaced), and opposed increased taxes to pay for the development. A racial component was sometimes exhibited in these struggles. But small business had also resisted the convention center plans when these were formulated under the auspices of white leadership as well. In the 1980s, opposition to the affirmative actions plans of the city was primarily confined to the construction industry, which felt that it was directly harmed by the programs. The historic challenge of *Croson* emerged from the periphery and not the center of the Richmond corporate community. The ordinance which had established the set-aside program had been passed by a six to two vote. At no time did the opposition to the ordinance reach the level that had been present during the Leidinger firing or the Hilton controversy.

Evaluating Calculated Cooperation

It is not a simple task to analyze the effects of the strategy of calculated cooperation that black political leaders employed in Richmond. There is neither a scholarly consensus on what constitutes successful urban leadership in the late twentieth-century United States, nor agreement on the most appropriate criteria for evaluating African-American political officials. Indeed, much of the literature furnishes a detailed accounting of the obstacles that stand in the way of autonomous action. In addition, the peculiar situation in Richmond where a black mayor, Roy West, was elected by the white members of the council makes it even more difficult to argue that African-American leadership could have pursued an entirely different policy agenda. But it is possible to illuminate the issues involved in furnishing an assessment by examining the results of the policies designed to promote black economic advancement on which the position of Roy West did not differ substantially from the other members of the council.

The results of city efforts to link its economic development issues to an explicit African-American interest were mixed. The council was able to promote the 15 percent level of minority participation and nine local black-owned businesses were among the original group of mall proprietors. Locating the marketplace adjacent to the downtown shopping district with a substantial black patronage was symbolic of the city's commitment not to exclude African-Americans from Richmond's future. By most accounts, the marketplace and its adjacent festival park were places where Richmonders of both races mingled comfortably. On a number of special occasions, such as New Year's Eve and the June Jubilee music festival, the marketplace complex appeared to be literally fulfilling its symbolic meaning of racial reconciliation.

However, the economics of the marketplace was another matter altogether. By 1990, it had yet to turn the corner and continually required substantial infusions of city funds. The marketplace's developer projected that the mall would make a profit after a single year of operation. But the original sales estimates were more than twice as high as what actually developed. It was generally acknowledged that the retail mix that emphasized specialty stores catering to conventioneers was catastrophically misdirected and that a major reorientation was necessary. In 1987, the developer bowed out of the project and the city of Richmond, in effect, went into the mall business. By 1989, the city had already paid out more than $15 million in construction and operating costs and was planning to continue paying about $4 million per year for various costs at least through 1991. In early 1990, one of its anchor department stores had closed its doors and, among those which remained, only a few had developed a steady and loyal clientele.[31] In 1991, consultants from the Urban Land Institute recommended that the city demolish half the marketplace and turn it into an urban park.

Minority participation in the mall had experienced similar problems. In the first place, the 15 percent set-aside figure applied to the percentage of businesses in the complex and not to square footage of business space. Minority businesses tended to be the smaller, more precarious operations in the complex along with kiosk operations.[32] Indeed, of the nine original minority businesses, only one was still located in the marketplace in 1990.[33] And as the city attempted to alter the retail mix by subsidizing the entry costs of national chains, it became even more difficult to predict how the original vision of minority involvement could be implemented. By 1990, defenders of the marketplace were justifying it on the grounds that downtown would have been worse off without it. And there were more than a few Richmonders using 20-20 hindsight to suggest that it should have been put on the James River in the first place.

If we turn to the affirmative action agenda, our analysis suggests that it furnished limited benefits for African-American citizens. It is evident that city employment has become more open to blacks and that progress has been made at all levels, including senior management positions. Data compiled by the Department of Personnel and the Department of Human Resources and Employee Relations indicate that there has been an increase in the percentage of the city government's work force comprised by African-Americans at almost all levels. In 1978, 36 percent of the managerial and professional positions were held by blacks. In 1988, that figure had risen to 45 percent. At the other end of the scale, African-Americans held 66 percent of the service and maintenance worker positions in 1978 and a decade later the figure had risen to 86 percent.

But such advances have to be placed in a broader context, namely the decline in total city employment. The number of employees in the city work force peaked in 1978 and has decreased since then. Richmond city managers have continually pointed to the elimination of city positions as an indication of their administrative skills. Moreover, these cutbacks have had a differential impact on working and middle-class blacks. For example, between 1978 and 1982, there were 49 more African-Americans in managerial and professional jobs. But there were 125 fewer African-Americans working for the city in service and maintenance positions. This decline occurred despite an increase in the percentage of African-Americans employed in the service/maintenace job category. In Richmond, government employment became most accessible to African-Americans during the very period that the suburbanization of the society and the changing political economy made the promotion of economic advances through urban patronage more difficult for rank and file blacks.

The set-aside program in construction that was the object of controversy in the *Richmond* v. *Croson* case lends itself to a similar interpretation. In the first full year after the Minority Utilization Plan went into effect, minority participation in city construction contracts increased to 40 percent. In fiscal year 1985–1986, minority participation dipped slightly to 37.8 percent, and then increased again in 1986–1987 to 39.27 percent. A city official acknowledged to us that during the first eighteen months of the program, the city had not instituted a mechanism for checking whether the minority firms were legitimate businesses or merely fronts established by the majority contractors. By 1985, however, the city had formulated a compliance program which required that firms had to be certifiably 51 percent minority-owned to be eligible for set-aside approval. Participants still registered occasional complaints about the process, but it was generally acknowledged that the legitimacy of the firms was more likely to be checked.

We examined the distribution of set-asides monies for the years 1985 and 1986 before the circuit court's decision terminated the program. Approximately 47 companies received construction monies for a mean total of $248,786 per firm in the two-year period. But these funds were not evenly distributed. Perhaps the most interesting feature of the distribution was that in 1985, and again in 1986, two contractors received a majority of the money that went to minority firms. In 1985, Dwight Snead earned $1,971,000 and the Quail Oak Company $828,000 out of a sum total of $5,446,291 obtained by minority contractors. In 1986, Quail Oak received $1,731,297 and Dwight Snead $1,529,833 out of a pool of $6,246,667 that went to minority construction companies.[34]

The operation of the set-aside program thus did function, to a limited degree, to furnish opportunities for black entrepreneurs. The Dwight Snead and the Quail Oak companies were able to take advantage of the policy to become successful and independent contractors in the city. Even after the set-aside program was vacated by the circuit court, these two firms performed well in the new environment. But they attributed their capacity to do so, in large part, to the opportunity provided by the council. As Curtis Harris, one of the owners of Quail Oak, told us in an interview, "I couldn't honestly tell you what I would be doing today without the set-aside program."[35]

The set-aside program may also have been important in a less tangible way. Our interviews with minority businesspersons, with city officials connected to the set-aside program, and with the director of the Metropolitan Business League, all evoked the assertion that the program helped to create a psychological climate more favorable to the entrepreneurial spirit among minorities. Institutions such as the Metropolitan Business League used the existence of the set-aside program to increase minority interest in its seminars on business plan preparation, financial accounting, and opportunities available in the local area. The combination of success stories such as Quail Oak and a guaranteed window of opportunity made it possible for others to consider ventures that they might have ignored without the policy.

At the same time, the success of the program was undeniably limited. Only two companies prospered appreciably before the circuit court's decision overturning the order went into effect. As one city official who supports the program himself told us, it was "very effective" for the "chosen few" as the benefits of the policy were relatively restricted and did not filter throughout the black community. One indication of the limited effect the program had on allowing black contractors to become competitive is what occurred after the circuit court's decision. City records indicate that minority contractors' share of city construction dollars plummeted from more than 30 percent to less than 5 percent in the two years thereafter.

Our final argument about the nature of calculated cooperation in Richmond is a theoretical point. We would contend that the practice of elite reconciliation did not necessarily strengthen the quality of democracy in the city. In the black community, the strategy employed to promote economic progress ultimately served to widen the gap between development-oriented elites and rank and file African-Americans. Indeed, we would contend that there has been a significant political demobilization during the past decade in Richmond. This is a complicated argument developed more fully elsewhere in the chapter. We think it is related to such factors as the resource limitations of neighborhood organizations, the social bases of groups such as the Crusade for Voters, the structure of electoral politics in the city, and the energy that was expended on controversies involving Roy West. For the purposes of this essay, we might simply note that our own study of the concerns expressed by African-American citizens in the neighborhoods revealed a substantial distance between what they viewed as the most pressing development needs, and the priorities expressed in the downtown revitalization plans and the recommendations of various consultants.

A gap was also developing in the white community between the development-oriented elites and rank and file citizens. Business leaders were key players in the downtown revitalization plans and willing supporters of city initiatives to channel some benefits to the black community. But they did not make a very visible effort to guide public sentiment about the necessity of downtown redevelopment or the wisdom of the city's affirmative action policies. By the end of the 1980s, the key concern to many white Richmonders was property tax assessments. They wanted Richmond to remain, as the popular saying went, a nice place to live, but they had little commitment to solving public problems through the use of government. Reconciliation at the elite level had not resulted in a popular mobilization to attack the social and economic problems that Richmond shared with other urban locations.

DILEMMAS OF AFRICAN-AMERICAN POLITICS IN THE POST-*CROSON* ERA

In the year since the *Croson* decision was handed down, African-American urban political officials have been dealing with its implications. A recent account noted that almost 50 affirmative action programs have been halted and almost 200 are facing upcoming legal challenges. City officials in Richmond responded to the *Croson* decision by convening a special working committee to examine the historical record and discover whether adequate documentation of discrimination in the construction industry exists that could meet the court's standards of proof. Nationally, African-American politicians have been lobbying Congress on behalf of legislation which might mitigate the impact of the court's decision and enable set-aside programs to remain intact.

We have maintained that the program that *Croson* overturned in Richmond was part of a larger strategy to promote black economic progress by African-American political leaders. Our examination of this broader context in Richmond has suggested that the entire strategy (and not just the set-aside feature of it) may be in need of fundamental reconsideration. At the very least, we believe that the following questions ought to be raised about both the practice and the study of black politics today.

1. *What are the range of options that are available to black elected officials?* Supporters of the strategy that officials in Richmond and other urban areas have pursued to achieve black economic progress frequently claim that it represents the best possible use of the limited power that elected officials hold. By pointing to the importance for government of decisions made in other arenas and the possibility of a backlash if an accommodation is not reached with corporate leaders, they suggest that no other development policy is practical. In Richmond, the acrimony that marked the Leidinger and Hilton controversies could be said to show how costly it was for the black majority to exercise autonomous power.

In recent years, a number of social-democratic and nationalist critics of black leadership have argued to the contrary, contending that the range of options is not constricted this tightly. Authors as diverse as Adolph Reed, Jr. and Harold Cruse have contended that black elected officials could have followed different policies that might have addressed the economic conditions of the black community more appropriately and enhanced African-American political empowerment. Reed suggests that black leaders could produce more benefits for their constituency by aggressively pursuing an agenda of grassroots mobilization and pressure politics. Reed believes that this option would allow African-Americans to expand the boundaries of calculated cooperation by extracting a larger share of urban resources.[36] Cruse also calls for a new vision of socio-economic change by black elites. Cruse argues that the civil rights vision of black advancement only weds African-Americans more tightly to a model of economic progress that increases their dependency. He proposes a strategy grounded in the notion of ethnic group pluralism which endorses the formation of an independent black political party and the creation of a contemporary version of Du Bois' inner black economy.[37] A detailed assessment of this debate will be critical to understanding and evaluating the policies of African-American leadership.

2. *To what extent have affirmative action programs such as the set-aside ordinance in Richmond helped to empower the black community?* Defenders of affirmative action might argue that even if the benefits of the set-aside program are limited, these do bring more African-Americans into the arenas where power and money are distributed. In the long term, the black community in general will be helped by this development. Social-democratic and nationalist critics of affirmative action dissent from

this perspective. They argue that initiatives such as the set-aside policy are part of an economic development strategy that not only has negligible impact on the material prospects of the majority of blacks, but that also has prevented their genuine needs and grievances from being politically articulated. In this respect, the issue for scholars seems to be whether the limited benefits provided by set-aside policies within the context of elite reconciliation are an instrument of long-term empowerment or a sophisticated mechanism for political demobilization.

3. *What criteria should scholars use to evaluate the practice of black elected officials?* The debate about the economic policies pursued by black elected officials is really intertwined with the broader discussion about the extent to which the "civil rights vision" is still relevant. In Richmond, for instance, black leaders have often portrayed their activities as a logical extension of the civil rights movement. In their minds, they have developed pragmatic instruments such as the public-private partnership, and various set-aside programs as pragmatic steps for achieving desirable ends. But free market conservative, social-democratic, and nationalist critics find this vision, albeit for different reasons, of limited applicability to the condition of African-Americans today. They believe that "pragmatism" is merely a screen for the lack of a well thought out intellectual framework. Case studies of black leadership such as our analysis of Richmond inevitably raise the question of what is the most appropriate stance for analyzing African-American politics. As Marguerite Ross Barnet wrote in 1982, "[M]uch of the literature on black politics has neatly ignored the lack of a general, commonly accepted framework for an analysis of black political life. Without such a framework, a multitude of nagging methodological and policy questions remain unresolved, and even more serious, often unrecognized."[38] Our study of politics and policy making in Richmond has revealed that the relevance of Barnet's comment has not diminished today.

NOTES

1. See W. Avon Drake and Robert D. Holsworth, "Electoral Politics, Affirmative Action and the Supreme Court: The Case of *Richmond* v. *Croson*," *National Political Science Review* 2(1): 65–91.
2. See A. J. Dickinson, "Myth and Manipulation: The Story of the Crusade for Voters in Richmond, Virginia," Yale University Honors Thesis, 1967. Our description of the Crusade in the 1950s and 1960s is heavily indebted to Dickinson's work.
3. *Ibid.*, 32–34.
4. *Ibid.*, 69.
5. *Ibid.*, 97
6. See John Moeser and Rutledge Dennis, *The Politics of Annexation* (Cambridge: Schenkman Publishing Company, 1982).
7. Bill Miller, "Marsh Continues to Run Campaign of Reassurance," *Richmond Times-Dispatch*, 17 April 1977, B-1.

8. "Text of Marsh's Statement on Leidinger," *Richmond Times-Dispatch*, 15 August 1978, B-1.

9. "Still a Bad Move," *Richmond Times-Dispatch*, 16 August 1978, A-6.

10. Bill Miller, "5–4 Vote Sets Date of September 11," *Richmond Times-Dispatch*, 29 August 1978, 1.

11. See Miller, "Firing Plans Termed Months Old," *Richmond Times-Dispatch*, 28 August 1978, A-11.

12. See Miller, "5–4 Vote Sets Date of September 11," 5.

13. Editorial, "A Sham, A Shame," *Richmond Times-Dispatch*, 27 August 1978, G-6.

14. Margaret Edds, "Interview with Henry L. Marsh III," 21 February 1985. Edds furnished the authors with a transcript of the interviews.

15. See Moeser and Dennis, *The Politics of Annexation*, 183.

16. Tom Campbell, "Council Minority, Hilton Lawyer Says Project One Actions Illegal," *Richmond Times-Dispatch*, 10 November 1980, A-1.

17. This is discussed in Christopher Silver, *Twentieth Century Richmond: Planning, Politics, and Race* (Knoxville: University of Tennessee Press, 1984), 315–320.

18. A good description of the genesis of the project was presented by Clarence Townes in a speech "Richmond Renaissance" presented at a conference in Gainesville, Florida, May 4, 1988. An interesting study of the role of the arts community in revitalization plans is J. Allen Whitt, "The Arts Coalition in Strategies of Urban Development," in *The Politics of Urban Development*, ed. C. N. Stone and H. T. Sanders (Lawrence, KA: University Press of Kansas, 1987), 144–156.

19. Tom Campbell, "City Renaissance Plan Unveiled," *Richmond Times-Dispatch*, 25 March 1982, 1.

20. "Renaissance," *The Richmond News Leader*, 25 March 1982, 10.

21. Tom Campbell, "City Renaissance Plan Unveiled," *Richmond Times-Dispatch*, 25 March 1982, 6.

22. Before casting his vote, West conferred with State Senator and now Governor L. Douglas Wilder. Henry L. Marsh III, was Wilder's law school roommate at Howard University. According to many observers, Wilder and Marsh were rivals at the time for the unofficial position of the most powerful African-American politician in Virginia. Marsh stated to us that Wilder has denied any complicity in West's maneuver. But other sources, including a biography of the current governor, note that Wilder did nothing to discourage West from unseating his former roommate. For a recounting of Wilder's role in the events, see Donald P. Baker, *Wilder: Hold Fast to Dreams* (Washington, D.C.: Seven Locks Press, 1989).

23. Tom Campbell, "Marsh-West Split Widens Council Rift," *Richmond Times-Dispatch*, 18 July 1983, 1.

24. *Ibid.*

25. Tom Campbell, "West's Race Is for More Than Council Seat," *Richmond Times-Dispatch*, 19 July 1983, 1.

26. *Ibid.*

27. Our information here comes from the "Affirmative Action Summary," supplied by the Department of Employee Relations, Richmond, Virginia, 1988.

28. Tom Campbell, "Minority Role Pact Reached by City, House," *Richmond Times-Dispatch*, 15 November 1983, p. A-1; Monte Young, "Marsh Reduces Minority Request," *Richmond Times-Dispatch*, 15 November 1983, p. A-1;

and Monte Young, "Marsh Reduces Minority Request," *Richmond Times-Dispatch,* 2 December 1983, p. B-1.

29. For a more extensive analysis, see W. Avon Drake and Robert D. Holsworth, "Affirmative Action, Set Asides and Black Progress." Paper presented at the American Political Science Association Annual Meeting, September 1989.

30. For an interesting comparison that contains a number of features similar to our analysis, see Clarence Stone, *Regime Politics: Governing Atlanta, 1946–1988.* (Lawrence, KA: University Press of Kansas, 1989), especially Chapters 5 and 7.

31. Phil Murray and Randy Hallman, "Marketplace Targeted by Council Challengers," *The Richmond News Leader,* 16 April 1990, 1.

32. *Ibid.*

33. Hazel Trice Edney, "Marketplace Lacks Black Businesses," *Richmond Afro-American,* 14 April 1990, A-1.

34. Our discussion of the set-aside program is drawn from our more complete analysis in "Affirmative Action, Set Asides and Black Progress."

35. *Ibid.,* 35.

36. Adolph Reed, Jr., "A Critique of Neo-Progressivism in Theorizing About Local Development Policy: A Case from Atlanta," in *The Politics of Urban Development,* eds. Clarence N. Stone and H. Sanders (Lawrence, KA: University of Kansas Press, 1987).

37. Harold Cruse, *Plural But Equal: A Critical Study of Blacks and Minorities in America's Plural Society.* (New York: Quill Press, 1987), 25–69.

38. Marguerite Ross Barnet, "The Congressional Black Caucus: Illusions and Realities of Power," in *The New Black Politics: The Search for Political Power,* eds. Michael B. Preston, Lenneal J. Henderson, Jr., and Paul Puryear (New York and London: Longman, 1982), 29.

Chapter
6

Cleveland and the Politics of Resurgence:

The Search for Effective Political Control

Saundra C. Ardrey

*R*ecent research in African-American politics has focused on the search for effective political control that can be used to transform existing sociopolitical and economic institutions (especially in urban areas) into mechanisms that distribute benefits to the African-American community. This phenomenon, "new black politics," has been defined as an effort by black activists to make the transition from protest to politics. In a very real sense it is an attempt by black elected officials to capture the decision-making process to make government more responsive to the needs of its black citizenry.

In an article outlining the fundamental objectives of the new black politics, William E. Nelson, Jr. (1987, 1) writes, "In this sense, the new black politics would become an instrument of social change, permanently eradicating obstacles to the upward mobility and continuing progress of the entire black community." This search for political control, one that began in the 1960s with the civil rights movement, has continued into the 1990s. It is a search being made by many who believe that the electoral arena holds the key to the unlocking of black economic and social entrapment.

STYLES AND APPROACHES

After passage of the 1965 Voting Rights Act, the first wave of black elected officials were representatives of predominantly black political jurisdictions. The style and approach to politics of this first group, nurtured and shaped by their involvement in the civil rights movement, was often confrontational and critical of the system. These messages were guaranteed to appeal to their majority black constituency—a black constituency that was often in need of very basic municipal services. This need within the black community spurred politicians to articulate a black agenda which included such issues as affirmative action, increased spending on social programs, and an emphasis on minority set-aside programs in the workplace.

One of the most controversial and powerful politicians to emerge from this environment was George Forbes of Cleveland, Ohio. Considered by many to be the most powerful black politician in Cleveland, he was defeated in 1989 for mayor by former state senator Mike White. Forbes had been able to secure his position within the black community through an articulation of the black agenda—demanding that affirmative action requirements be written into city ordinances and speaking out against racial discrimination in areas such as law enforcement and housing. According to Nelson (1987, 183), Forbes (during his tenure as city council president) routinely delayed approval of the city's budget to force the police department to accept hiring quotas and called for a reexamination of the city's redevelopment plan and its impact on the black community.

For 26 years, Forbes used a confrontational, often abusive style to consolidate his power. He used race and charges of racism to discredit his opponents.[1] While this combative style worked for Forbes, as well as for other black politicians, it is not one that appeals to the white community, nor is the message of racial polarization a message that attracts white voters.

Political jurisdictions in which blacks are not the numerical majority more often than not dictate a change in style and approach. To win an election, black candidates must attract not only black support but white voters as well. This variation in political style made necessary by political reality has its theoretical roots in the "political strategy of deracialization," advocated some 13 years ago by Charles Hamilton (1977). Professor Hamilton advised candidates (speaking specifically to Democratic presidential hopefuls) to emphasize issues that would appeal to broad segments of the electorate across racial lines.

The intent of this political strategy is

> . . . to deemphasize those issues that may be viewed in explicitly racial terms, e.g., minority set-asides, affirmative action, or the plight of the urban underclass, while emphasizing those issues that appear to transcend the racial question . . . (McCormick 1990, 26).

One of the first examples of this strategy of deracialization (which predates the theory itself) is seen in the 1967 campaign of the first black mayor of Cleveland, Ohio, Carl Stokes. (I return to a more detailed discussion of this election later.) Additionally, there is some evidence (even though the numbers are small) that this strategy was adopted by many blacks who sought office in majority white districts in the November 1989 elections. Chester Jenkins, mayor of Durham, North Carolina, emphasized his ability to handle fiscal responsibilities; John Daniels, mayor of New Haven, Connecticut, campaigned on issues of crime and drugs. Both Mayor Dinkins of New York and Governor Wilder of Virginia benefited from their pro-choice stance on abortion, and Mayor Mike White of Cleveland, Ohio, led a campaign for neighborhood cooperation and racial harmony. Black politics is growing and maturing with the realization that different situations call for a different kind of campaign.

THE SEARCH BEGINS

The search for effective political control by blacks in Cleveland, Ohio, began in 1965 with the decision by Congressman Carl Stokes to run for mayor of that city. It was a political decision made possible by the growing number of blacks in the metropolitan area. From 1940 to 1965 the black population in Cuyahoga County had grown from 9.7 percent of the total population to 34.4 percent. Further examination of this statistic suggests that the black population was heavily concentrated (86 percent) in the inner-city area of Cleveland.[2] Voter registration in the predominantly black wards had also increased, especially between the years 1963 and 1965. This increase in black voter registration was greater than the voter registration numbers in the majority white wards; therefore, blacks represented close to 40 percent of the registered voters, compared to their 30 percent of the population. The political climate, thus, seemed ripe for the candidacy of a black mayoral hopeful.

Nelson and Meranto (1977, 322) have argued that

. . . a large numerical concentration of blacks within a governmental jurisdiction is at best only a potential political resource in the quest for electoral black power. Numerical concentration is a resource that must be supplemented by other political resources. . . .

The need for other political resources is a political condition, *ceteris paribus,* which says that the large numerical concentration can only be effective when "all other factors are equal." For the minority community this means that turnout must be high; the vote must be cohesive; black must vote as a bloc; and that the majority electorates' turnout must be low and/or the vote must split itself fairly equally between two or more whi candidates. Nowhere is this political dilemma more apparent than in t Cleveland elections of 1965 and 1967. Cleveland blacks constituted ab 40 percent of the voters and were concentrated in neighborhoods ea the Cuyahoga River. But this 40 percent was still not a large en number to elect Stokes without *ceteris paribus.*

An analysis of the 1965 general election (Stokes ran as an indepe nt and therefore did not participate in a primary election) shows that kes did indeed receive a substantial bloc vote from blacks (85 percent support from predominantly black wards)[3] but still not in the 90 percent range that the campaign had expected. White voters split their vote among three candidates, but not evenly enough. Stokes polled only 3 percent of the white vote, far short of the needed support from liberal-minded whites. So, in 1965 the Stokes campaign efforts were narrowly defeated. But in losing, Stokes energized the black community and made the impossible now seem possible.[4]

In the 1967 primary and general elections, Carl Stokes ran a "dual strategy" campaign (one for the black community and quite another for the white wards) to address the shortcomings evident in the previous election. The strategy in the black community was to capitalize on the growing sense of racial pride—a sense of group consciousness inculcated by the civil rights movement that had moved north during the late 1960s. Selling "blackness" and support for a brother became the key to guaranteeing a high turnout and to securing the goal of increasing that 85 percent bloc vote to the 90 percent range. Stokes' campaign workers organized and energized the neighborhoods with what have become classic techniques of political motivation in the black community.[5]

The objectives and tasks in the white neighborhoods on the west side were a bit more complicated and the environment substantially more hostile. Basically, Stokes' theme was one of assurance: assurance that he would be a mayor for *all* the people and that he was the only man who could resolve major conflicts facing the city—the least of which were the worsening relationships between racial and ethnic groups.

How effective was this strategy? Primary election results saw a record-high 73 percent voter turnout among registered black voters.[6] Of these votes Stokes received 96 percent support, an increase of 11 percent from 1965! This unprecedented turnout and vote solidarity stand as a testament to the success and effectiveness of the campaign's mobilization strategies. Turnout in the predominantly white districts was only 58 percent; however, Stokes was able to garner 15 percent of this vote, an increase from the 3 percent white support in 1965. With this solid black base and respectable white support Stokes won the primary, beating the incumbent mayor and one other candidate by some 10,000 votes.[7]

The momentum of the campaign continued into the general election. Strong organization with dedicated, energetic workers kept black voters united and politically attuned. Stokes spent most of his time in the white community (some of his workers complained that too much of his time was spent there) spreading the message of "assurance" and "conciliation," assuaging fears that a black mayor would be a black power advocate. He emphasized his experience with solving urban fiscal problems and concentrated on "populist" issues that would appeal to voters across racial/ethnic divisions. Such issues included, but were not limited to, labor and employment benefits, neighborhood enrichment, small business development, and housing shortages.[8]

In an appeal to the business sector, Carl Stokes emphasized why he was the only candidate who could improve the Cleveland "climate" and thereby revitalize the economic life of the city. These were the issues deliberately selected to present Stokes as a "mayor for all the people" *and* to downplay the issue of race. One example of this effort to "deracialize" the campaign and the issues was the reluctance on the part of Carl Stokes to publicly meet with or to acknowledge the aid of SCLC or Dr. Martin Luther King, Jr., because, ". . . it threatened his image of being a mayor of all the people, and it would scare the white community" (Nelson and Meranto 1977, 123). With much maneuvering and some blunders[9] Carl Stokes became the first black mayor of a major urban center. His support in the black wards was a solid 95 percent and 20 percent in the white neighborhoods (see Table 6.1).

Stokes' success in emphasizing "blackness" and raising the specter of racial solidarity, that is, black power in the black community while concomitantly seeking to deemphasize race, to address issues that transcend the racial question for the white community, makes poignant the differences between the two electorates and attests to the political necessity of running very different kinds of campaigns.

Carl Stokes, a "new black politician," firmly believed that with consolidated support in the black community, his administration could begin to transform existing socio-economic municipal institutions into instruments more responsive to the needs of the African-American community. According to Nelson (1987, 176) this would entail

> . . . the creation of a suitable political organization capable of mobilizing broad scale support for the implementation of the social reform agenda put forward in both the public and private sector by his administration.

The Twenty-first District Democratic Caucus was created just after the 1969 election to meet this objective. For two years the Caucus wielded considerable influence in local politics, mobilizing critical black support behind candidates of both parties and electing its own slate of candidates.

Table 6.1 CLEVELAND'S 1967 MAYORAL GENERAL ELECTION VOTE DISTRIBUTION

	Overall totals	Black wards	White wards	Transitional wards
Number of Registered Voters	326,003	99,884	173,469	52,378
Turnout	257,113	81,645	135,827	41,416
% Turnout	78	82	78	79
% Votes for Stokes	50	93	20	61

Predominantly black wards in 1967 included 10 wards east of the Cuyahoga River. Predominantly white wards numbered at 18 and wards in transition from predominantly white to black were 5.

Source: Cuyahoga County Board of Elections

Most importantly, Mayor Stokes used the political clout of the Caucus to halt opposition to his social reforms in the city council.[10] This was black power, black control. It was independent, concentrated, and consolidated.

The period between 1965 and 1971 was the heyday of black political participation and mobilization in the greater Cleveland area. Carl Stokes' decision to not seek reelection in 1971 forewarned the demise of the Caucus and effectively ended this era.

TWENTY YEARS IN THE DESERT

Until the election of Mike White as mayor of Cleveland in November 1989, there had been no other black mayor since Carl Stokes' administration. There have been, however, black aspirants for the mayor's office, the most notable being Arnold Pinkney, who waged unsuccessful campaigns in 1971 and 1975. How can we account for this noticeable hiatus in black control? What happened to the idealism and high levels of political participation that were so evident during the Stokes years? There are several factors that allow us to analyze and explain "twenty years in the desert." First and foremost was the passing of the protest activities of the civil rights and black power movements both at the national and local levels during the 1970s and 1980s. Stokes' campaign efforts had been fueled by feelings of racial pride, ideals of black control, and group solidarity. In other words, there was a growing sense of group consciousness and a realization that group action was needed to improve conditions that generated political awareness and feelings of political efficacy. This enthusiasm, which existed because of the movements of the 1960s, was harnessed and organized by Stokes' workers, which made their job of mobilization— if not easier—less tedious. Leaders in Cleveland agree that the influence and activism of local civil rights groups such as the NAACP and the Urban League have been less than satisfactory over the last twenty years; for all practical purposes, there was no visible civil rights movement in Cleveland during this interim. This loss of stimuli that had once galvanized the black community fed a growing sense of alienation/apathy and precipitated the dismantling of organizational mechanisms in which to support a viable black political candidate for mayor.

A second explanation, or factor, that led to the demise of "new black politics" in Cleveland was the lack of the institutionalization of black politics. Carl Stokes had envisioned an independent political power base that extended beyond the vestiges of the mayor's office and beyond the magnetism of Stokes himself. Leaders of this political organization (the Twenty-first District Caucus) would be able to win major concessions from the white power structure and then distribute health care, jobs (patronage), and the benefits to their followers. It was to be an organizational foundation on which not only current black leaders, but future leaders as well, would use to transform urban structures. The Caucus was never quite able to live up to Stokes' expectations, was never to become the political foundation so needed for the institutionalization of political achievements. Stokes' departure from the political scene, the loss of his magnetism, and his personal control seriously weakened the effectiveness of the Caucus. It was for all practical purposes a "Stokes machine" unable to function without Stokes. Conflict and dissension among the Caucus's three key leaders, Councilman George Forbes, Carl Stokes' brother, Congressman Louis Stokes, and Arnold Pinkney, further exacerbated the situation.[11] This internal conflict coupled with the loss of the mayoral races sealed the fate of not only the Caucus but also of "new black politics."

Perhaps the third and final explanation for a 20-year hiatus between black mayors is a testament to what one might call "success-itis." Stokes and the black community were fighting for a "piece of the action," fighting for a chance to become part of the decision-making polity of the city. And to some extent this objective was achieved. Stokes was very skillful in recruiting African-Americans into major positions in municipal government. He was able to channel city contracts into many minority businesses, thereby encouraging black enterprise. Many blacks, most especially those from the middle-income level, became part of the political and economic system. Leaders of the "outsiders," the protesters, achieved their goal of inclusion and became "insiders"; they joined the establishment. And as all too often happens these new players became "protective" of that system, and accommodationist. Political leadership in black politics was refocused into a style that lacked the kind of aggressiveness, "militancy," or urgency that was so characteristic of the earlier style of leadership.

Nelson (1987, 178) writes that during the decades of the 1970s

> Black political leaders . . . ceased to champion programs of social reform and community redevelopment, but embraced more pragmatic programs that would enhance their access to high levels of material benefits. This style of politics continued to grow in magnitude and influence in the decade of the 1970s; in the 1980s the basic pillars of traditional machine politics have remained firmly in place.

THE CASE OF MIKE WHITE

It is reported that at age 14, Mike White vowed "to become mayor of Cleveland."[12] Some 24 years later White stunned many political observers by fulfilling that promise. Michael White, without much money or name recognition, declared his candidacy for mayor in January 1989. Not many gave the one-time protégé of George Forbes, former city council member and state senator, much of a chance. In fact, *The Cleveland Plain Dealer* routinely described him in the early months of the campaign as a "second tier" candidate. Conventional wisdom has it that the die was cast for a mayoral victory by Mike White in the primary election held on October 3.

Voter registration in the city of Cleveland at the time of the primary was 292,192. The black community in wards one through ten represented 51 percent of that total, an increase of about 11 percent from the 1965–1969 days of Carl Stokes. The black community was thus in a position to elect a mayoral candidate in both the primary and general elections without *ceteris paribus* existing in the white electorate. But as it was an accomplishment that could be achieved *only if* turnout in the black wards was high (90 percent or more) and politically cohesive, that is, a bloc vote for one candidate. Group solidarity was essential since the gap separating the two groups was a thin one of about 4000 votes.

According to political analysts familiar with the Forbes campaign, the realization that blacks were the numerical majority in voter registration was one factor that persuaded George Forbes to enter the mayoral race.[13] His campaign strategists theorized that with 26 years of political experience came not only name recognition but political clout and a certain amount of patronage that could be bartered for support and votes, especially in his east-side base.

In the primary race, George Forbes was joined by Mike White and three white candidates, Municipal Court Clerk Benny Bonanno, Cuyahoga County Commissioner Timothy Hagan, and Board of Election President Ralph Perk. Throughout the campaign City Council President George Forbes was considered a certainty to get enough votes to capture one of the two positions needed to get into the general election. Bonanno, with his base in the ethnic community, was considered a favorite for the number two spot. Second tier candidates included Hagan, Perk, and White. Political analysts had given White little chance of winning because he shared an east-side political base with Forbes, who was better financed and had greater name recognition. But what White lacked in money he made up in high energy and effective organization. With a cadre of young and dedicated workers, White simply out-campaigned his challengers. Throughout the primary (and general election) White portrayed himself as a new breed of politician; he offered "new leadership" that broke from the racially divisive politics endemic to the Cleveland political scene.[14] His conciliatory style and willingness to campaign on the issues and to run hard on both the east (predominantly black) and west (mostly white) sides of town hit a responsive chord—especially among white voters. The campaign theme, "Rebuild our Neighborhoods," was a message deliberately selected to attract residents—both black and white—who had not benefited from the economic growth and redevelopment in the downtown area. With 40 percent of Clevelanders living below the poverty line and in areas plagued by crime, drug abuse, and an ineffectual school system, Mike White's vision of a city government that worked for the people commanded attention.

Attention came with an endorsement by *The Plain Dealer* just before the election. In endorsing Mike White over George Forbes and the other white candidates, the newspaper[15] cited a need for "new leadership that makes a clear break with the racially divisive politics of the past." The editorial lauded White for "sticking to the issues and running hard on all sides of town." It urged Cleveland voters to send a message that they wanted to be led by a "mayor who has their interests, not special interests, at heart." White was said to have "vision, youth, enthusiasm and a commitment to his hometown." This "calming" message to the white community, this "seal of approval" by an instrument of the WASP establishment was similar in tone to the endorsement given by *The Plain Dealer*[16] on September 3, 1967, to Carl Stokes. The editorial stressed Stokes' "qualifications to be mayor," his "professional skills," and hometown roots. For both Stokes and Michael White, the newspaper played the role of assuaging the fears of the white community and touting them as candidates for *all* the people. As with the Stokes' organization in 1967, the endorsement stimulated the Mike White campaign and gave it much needed credibility and momentum. Reverend Marvin MacMickle, a Mike White campaign advisor and president of the Cleveland NAACP, believes that that endorsement was *the* deciding factor in the primary,

> . . . despite how long he had been running and campaigning still he had not really emerge as a really recognizable candidate until he was endorsed by *The Plain Dealer*. . . . That was a decisive event in the primary. Everybody was expecting a two-person general election of Forbes and Benny Bonanno and Michael emerged in large measure on the strength of that *Plain Dealer* endorsement.[17]

Evidence of this momentum was apparent in a poll conducted by *The Plain Dealer* (September 26–28) that surveyed 759 Cleveland voters on several issues from the campaign. On their mayoral preference, Forbes led the contenders with 23 percent. The biggest surprise was White's strong showing of 16 percent in a close race for second place. Closer examination of these overall figures gives an indication of the final outcome of the primary (and foreshadows the outcome of the general election). While Forbes was the clear leader, his well-known temper and outbursts prompted a large number of respondents to say they were less likely to vote for him. The negative response was especially pronounced among whites; 60 percent of the white respondents said they were less likely to vote for Forbes because of his tantrums. Only 20 percent of the blacks said his behavior would cause them not to vote for him. Forbes' "tough guy," combative image also seemed to worry whites; he received only 5 percent support from white respondents. Most of Forbes' support came solidly from the black community (43 percent). On the other hand, Mike White was the only candidate to poll support from both black and white respondents. Table 6.2 shows that Mike White was supported by 18 percent of the black and 14 percent of the white respondents. Hagan and Bonanno split the white respondents (20 percent and 23 percent, respectively), and received no more than 2 percent of the black supporters.

The October primary was not without its controversies.[18] Hagan lam-

Table 6.2   CANDIDATE RATINGS WITH VOTER GROUPS*

	Forbes	Bonanno	Hagan	White	Perk	Not sure
Race						
white	5	23	20	14	8	27
black	43	1	2	18	0	32
Age						
18–34	22	15	14	25	3	19
35–55	25	12	10	16	3	28
55–over	21	13	9	9	5	38
Income						
under $15,000	30	12	9	13	2	31
$15–30,000	19	11	14	16	7	31
$30–50,000	23	17	10	22	3	21
over $50,000	27	15	14	19	2	18

*Reading across, percent of preference for each candidate among registered voters surveyed in each category.

Source: "PD Poll," *The Plain Dealer,* 1 October 1989. Reprinted from The Plain Dealer.

basted Bonanno for a letter he had written in 1983 in support of a Mafia figure, and he accused Forbes of using Forbes' position on the city council to enrich himself and his friends. Hagan's taunting of Forbes prompted an outburst in which he called Hagan a racist and uttered the infamous "at least I don't pimp my wife" quote. Mike White and Ralph Perk may have escaped much of this bruising because they were perceived as nonthreatening.

On a cold and windy October 3, the primary turnout was 44 percent for the general electorate. In the black community turnout mirrored that figure with 44 percent, and in the white community turnout was only slightly less at 43 percent. This turnout is disappointingly low for both communities considering the "high-stimulus" nature of the campaign. The low turnout also attests to the absence of, or perhaps the low priority given to, mobilization efforts in the black community. Compare the 43 percent turnout in this primary with the 73 percent turnout in the 1967 primary. Gone were the days of mass appeals to racial pride and group consciousness to motivate voters to the polls. Mike White's campaign, while active in voter registration, did not focus on a mass mobilization of the black electorate. In fact, the campaign spent most of its efforts in the white community conceding the east side to George Forbes. However, Forbes' efforts in the black community pales in comparison to Stokes; weak organizational structures and neighborhood coordination were endemic to his campaign.[19] Rather than stimulating the black grass roots, Forbes concentrated on winning endorsements from political and economic elites.

When all the votes were counted, Council President Forbes won 38 percent of the vote and State Senator Michael White finished second with 25 percent. Forbes carried the predominantly black wards on the east side but picked up very little support from west of the Cuyahoga. Table 6.3 gives a breakdown by wards of the primary election. Forbes received 67 percent of the total vote in the predominantly black wards (1 through 10); but 91 percent of his support came from these 10 wards. Just 9 percent of Forbes' total came from the 11 predominantly white wards (11 through 21).

The table also shows that Mike White, the only candidate to receive substantial votes from both the black and white wards, received 52 percent of his vote on the east side and 48 percent on the west side. This is a statistic that did not go unnoticed by the White campaign. Speaking just after the primary election, Mike White credited his second place finish to his west-side supporters "who looked beyond racial politics" (*The Plain Dealer*, 4 October 1989, p. 12-A).

Political analyst James Kweder believes that ". . . the white candidates divided their vote and eliminated each other. Mike got lucky with the numbers. The arithmetic was perfect for Mike." Professor Kweder asserts that the presence of Ralph Perk on the ballot may have drawn enough of the ethnic vote away from Bonanno to deny him that second place.[20] Perk's 5,891 votes added to Bonanno's 28,268 would have given the latter enough votes for that coveted second place.

The finish by Forbes and White ensured for Cleveland its first black mayor since Carl Stokes' tenure. The black community was in a "can't lose situation."

REFERENDUM ON FORBES

During the interim between the primary and general election, Board of Election statistics show that voter registration in the city had increased three percent, by 8,244 votes. Predominantly black wards 1 through 10 had 152,723 registered voters for 51 percent, while wards 11 through 21 had 49 percent, or 147,413 registered voters. There were 5,310 more registered in the black wards than in wards on the west side. So, again the black electorate found itself in an enviable position. Not only did they constitute a majority of the voting population, albeit by a thin margin, but there were also two black candidates. This majority in the black electorate should have given George Forbes (with his political base in the black neighborhoods) an advantage. Political mobilization of his grass-roots constituency that would both stimulate interest and ensure a high turnout would have been the strategy for electoral success. But, alas, the political realities are not always so certain.

Political analysts familiar with Cleveland politics view the general election as a "referendum on Forbes." In more than 16 years as city

Table 6.3 PRIMARY ELECTION RESULTS BY WARDS

Predominantly black wards

	Ballots Cast	Benny Bonanno	George L. Forbes	Timothy F. Hagan	Ralph J. Perk, Jr.	Michael White
Ward 1	9736	154	6483	127	41	2545
Ward 2	6495	322	3997	190	105	1640
Ward 3	8239	106	5632	89	69	2019
Ward 4	6966	249	3894	286	290	1985
Ward 5	4452	66	2950	215	195	1100
Ward 6	5661	453	3136	215	195	1388
Ward 7	5692	101	4057	95	70	1115
Ward 8	7041	75	4288	109	47	2257
Ward 9	6380	74	4673	75	25	1316
Ward 10	5027	222	3176	143	65	1255

Predominantly white wards

	Ballots Cast	Benny Bonanno	George L. Forbes	Timothy F. Hagan	Ralph J. Perk, Jr.	Michael White
Ward 11	6573	2911	470	1117	517	1363
Ward 12	4896	2228	153	787	819	777
Ward 13	4342	1281	720	659	371	1167
Ward 14	4466	1593	478	753	237	1248
Ward 15	5650	2797	210	767	478	1260
Ward 16	7705	3837	293	767	547	1673
Ward 17	3565	1324	164	783	240	935
Ward 18	4196	1925	177	657	307	1012
Ward 19	6245	2520	674	940	412	1510
Ward 20	6171	2877	330	943	421	1458
Ward 21	8729	3153	538	1801	600	2417
Absentee Ballot	6303	1907	1650	809	600	2417
TOTAL	128,277	28,268	46,493	11,799	5,891	31,440

Source: The Plain Dealer, 5 October 1989, p. 7-A. Reprinted from The Plain Dealer.

120

council president, George Forbes created a record; he amassed a personal fortune and wielded influence aggressively and often with a heavy hand. During these years a long list of charges, public temper tantrums, and revelations only served to vilify him not only with the white electorate but also with some black voters. According to a political activist, "there were a lot of people out there waiting—had been waiting for years to get George."[21]

The Forbes camp was well aware of the negative image of their candidate but may not have realized the depth and breadth of that perception. Forbes' original campaign theme—"Forbes, Tough Man for a Tough Job"—was changed after the primary because of voter reaction. What ensued for the next five weeks between the primary and the general election was an attempt to change his style, to create a new, softer image, that is, to become more conciliatory. Commercials now featured a "warmer" Forbes playing with his grandson; his theme became "He gets the job done." In this new mood of conciliation, Forbes also adopted issue stances[22] that focused on his commitment to "ensure that Cleveland grows together, not apart." He stressed his experience and knowledge of city government that he had used for the people. ("For 10 years, I've been a full partner engaged in making our economy viable. My goals have been jobs, new housing, hotels, . . .") But it was a case of too little too late. The "make-over" was an almost impossible task made even more difficult by a barrage of negative campaign ads run by Mike White in the closing days of the race.[23]

To say that the general election was a referendum on Forbes is to take nothing away from the zeal and tenacity with which Mike White attacked his race. The high energy and idealism exhibited by White and his staffers during the primary season continued into the general election. White campaigned on "people" issues on both sides of the river in a style that depicted him as a consensus builder. As alluded to in the previous section, Mike White selected issues that deemphasized the issue of race. Upon closer examination these issues, which transcended race, seem to fit with a more populist agenda, an agenda that would attract grass-roots working class whites. Setting the tone of his agenda was the campaign slogan, "Rebuild Our Neighborhoods," the purpose of which, according to political analyst Marvin MacMickle, was to focus attention on the booming downtown area that had benefitted from the revitalization efforts of Forbes and Mayor Voinovoch—efforts that had largely benefitted the corporate community without much precipitation into other neighborhoods. White proposed, in a sense, to redistribute the wealth, to refocus city coffers outward from downtown, to rebuild Cleveland communities. To do this, White campaigned on the promise to create a small-business division directly assisting small businesses, to develop a housing foundation to build new homes and make large tracts of land available for home construction rather than for corporate building.[24] White promised not to raise taxes, to reduce busing, and to provide schools of choice. In general, his was a campaign to reform Cleveland politics, to take the politics out of city government and to do that in the name of the "little people." This was a message that appealed to both the grass-roots populace, especially in white wards, *and* it had a special attraction to young, educated reform-minded Clevelanders.

Mike White's campaign during the general election did not go unscathed. Not long after his primary victory, his candidacy was rocked by allegations that he abused his first two wives and owned several rental properties that had been cited for more than 200 housing code violations. Polls taken by *The Plain Dealer*[25] just days before the election showed that these accusations did indeed hurt White: Forbes narrowed the gap to 8 percentage points down from 19 percentage points.[26]

Much has been made of the endorsements and coalitions that were formed during the campaign. Several reports published just after the general election credited Mike White's victory to the formation of biracial coalitions. But upon closer examination it is evident that both Forbes and White practiced multiracial coalition building. The lists of groups that joined forces with Forbes reads like a *Who's Who* of the Cleveland establishment. The unions representing city employees provided volunteers, money, and in the case of the Cleveland Police Patrolmen's Association, a background check on Mike White. The white business establishment was also solidly in the Forbes camp.

The endorsements by council members reflected their political relations with Forbes during his tenure as council president. All but one of the black councilmen supported Forbes; Jeffrey Johnson, a longtime Forbes opponent, was the only black to endorse White. Political standouts such as U.S. Representative Louis Stokes, former Cleveland mayor Ralph Perk, and U.S. Representative Mary Oaker, endorsed and made commercials for Forbes. All in all the politically prominent business establishment and organized labor bankrolled the Forbes campaign to the tune of about one million dollars. This was certainly coalition building—multiracial and elitist. And perhaps as Reverend Marvin MacMickle suggests, too much time was spent "amassing prestigious endorsements" from unions, individuals, and organizations that either could not vote for him, or that could not/would not deliver votes to the polls. Not enough energy or concern was given to his black constituency.

The list of endorsements for Mike White is not so long. There were few members from the business world, only two unions, and a handful of politicians. Johnson and six white councilmen (mostly representing westside wards) supported White. Two of these councilmen opened Mike White for mayor campaign offices in their wards, which turned out to be a most effective way in which to reach grass-roots voters. Mike White and his supporters shared their agenda and vision for a better Cleveland with white and black voters, walked the streets, and forged an effective coalition with the common folk of Cleveland. This, too, was coalition building—

multiracial, pluralistic, and inclusive. On the strength of this grass-roots support, Mike White went into the general election with a solid lead—especially in the white community.

On election day, voter turnout was 53 percent.[27] Turnout in wards 1 through 10 was 52 percent, or 80,166 voters (out of 152,723 registered), and in wards 11 through 21 turnout was 79,950 (out of 147,413), or 54 percent. Michael R. White commanded a 56 percent to 44 percent lead over George Forbes. White had been able to reach white voters with his message and to capitalize on a deep-seated dislike of Forbes on the west side. White carried these wards with 81 percent of the votes while Forbes received only 19 percent. Forbes' support remained in the black community and on the east side; he received 70 percent of the vote in wards 1 through 10. Mike White received 30 percent (see Table 6.4 for a breakdown of votes by wards).

Pollmet, Inc., a black Cleveland-based polling company, conducted a post-electoral analysis of key black precincts in wards 1 through 10 and found that Forbes received an average of 75 percent of the black vote.[28] This percentage is lower than political pundits expected given the experience, power, and clout Forbes had amassed in the black community. Reverend MacMickle stated, ". . . it is surprising that George did not receive more support. The question to ask is, why George *only got* 75 percent of the vote and not 80, 90?" Perhaps the answer lies in the fact that some black voters were dissatisfied with Forbes' style of leadership and agreed with Mike White's assertion that Forbes had not done enough to ensure economic advancement and community revitalization in the areas surrounding the downtown area—most notably in black neighborhoods. Evidence of support for Mike White's agenda and/or dislike for George Forbes is evident in the 25 percent support garnered by White in the black community.

The less-than-expected voter turnout (52 percent) in the black wards (especially low when compared to the Stokes turnout figures of 82 percent in 1967) was due to at least two facts. A different kind of political climate existed in Cleveland; there was no active civil rights movement or grassroots mobilization efforts which could serve to excite and galvanize the community. Another fact that explains the attenuated turnout rate (in both communities) lies in the perception that existed among many blacks that regardless of the winner, the city would have a black man as mayor. As Larry Brisker, founder of Pollmet, Inc., explained, "Blacks were in a win-win situation and whites found themselves in a predicament so often experienced by blacks—a choice of choosing between the 'lesser of two evils.' "[29]

The election outcome can be summarized with two observations. Reverend MacMickle said of Forbes' defeat:

He had been so blatant in his use of power. George does not try to decoy you. . . . He's going to use the force that he has to get what he's after.

Table 6.4   CLEVELAND'S 1989 GENERAL ELECTION VOTE DISTRIBUTION

Black wards	Total	George Forbes	Percent for Forbes	Mike White	Percent for White
1	11,266	8,081	71.73%	3,185	28.27%
2	7,910	5,304	67.05	2,606	32.95
3	9,684	7,089	73.20	2,595	26.80
4	7,799	4,990	63.98	2,809	36.02
5	5,479	3,864	70.52	1,615	29.48
6	6,632	4,282	64.57	2,350	35.43
7	6,685	5,030	75.24	1,655	24.76
8	8,040	5,280	65.67	2,760	34.33
9	7,236	5,598	77.36	1,638	22.64
10	6,371	4,304	67.56	2,067	32.44
Totals	77,102	53,822		23,280	
Average	7,710	5,382	69.69%	2,328	30.31%

White wards	Total	George Forbes	Percent for Forbes	Mike White	Percent for White
11	7,678	1,545	20.12%	6,133	79.88%
12	6,173	742	12.02	5,431	87.98
13	5,066	1,399	27.62	3,667	72.38
14	5,473	1,122	20.50	4,351	79.50
15	7,268	992	13.65	6,276	86.35
16	9,333	1,428	15.30	7,905	84.70
17	4,732	786	16.61	3,946	83.39
18	5,569	835	14.99	4,734	85.01
19	7,540	1,721	22.82	5,819	77.18
20	7,732	1,297	16.77	6,435	83.23
21	10,330	2,478	23.99	7,852	76.01
Totals	76,894	14,345		62,549	
Average	6,990	1,304	18.58%	5,686	81.42%
Cleveland	153,996	68,167		85,829	
Average	7,333	3,246	44.14%	4,087	55.86%

Source: Pollmet, Inc.

And obviously white America is not accustomed to a black man fully exercising the power that is available to him and to do that on behalf of black people.[30]

And on the nature of White's victory, Chandler Davidson (1972, 219) theorized that whites will vote for a black candidate if that candidate downplays social and racial issues and appeals to whites' economic interests and to their sense of justice.

CONCLUSION

To understand the election of Mike White as mayor of Cleveland is to understand the uniqueness of that city's political terrain. In a city infamous for racial divisions and conflictive politics it is indeed remarkable that two black mayoral candidates could square off in the general election.

Mike White's decision to campaign on "citywide issues," to present himself as the conciliatory candidate, places him firmly in that school of politicians who know how to address a variety of issues, and who feel comfortable maneuvering in a multiracial environment. White's showing in the primary (he ran second in every majority white ward except one) is a testament to his ability to turn potentially divisive issues into "people issues" that transcend race. Problems such as drug abuse, crime, deteriorating infrastructures, and vanishing federal funds are problems that plague all residents of inner cities. And for blacks to be successful in heterogeneous districts there must be a redefining, a broadening of scope.

The primary election, too, saw the change in the political perspective of the white voter. Conventional wisdom predicted that black voters would select a black candidate with white voters electing a white. But as demonstrated, Mike White received enough crossover votes to catapult him past his challengers.

In the general election, racial polarization was not a factor. But this is not to say that racially divisive politics will not resurface in future elections, especially if (as some have predicted) Bonanno decides to challenge White in the 1993 elections. To survive such a contest, Mike White must solidify his base in the white community by continuing to focus on the populist themes of his campaign. Delivering on these promises will, no doubt, strengthen his position on both sides of the river, especially the west side. Mike White must increase his level of support within the black community by addressing (and delivering on) concerns on the black agenda. He must satisfy two constituencies. This will not be an easy task, for Mike White must walk a political tightrope. The establishment, the white community, clearly expects their new mayor to declare that his "first loyalty is to Cleveland" and that he must continue " . . . its downtown renaissance but have that prosperity spread throughout the city."[31] In an editorial the day after the election, Mary Sharkey stated in *The Plain Dealer* that, "White must reach out to the business community, whose participation is essential to a thriving city." Mike White won the election with support from the white community and it is evident that they fully expect him to practice "the politics of inclusion."[32]

Turning this vision into reality and delivering on the black agenda, while a political tightrope, is by no means an impossible task. Mary Sharkey further stated, "Community leaders must [work] to heal the ills that afflict Cleveland: joblessness, crime, homelessness and drugs."[33] Working to alleviate these social ills will benefit both communities. A populist agenda, in the hands of a skilled politician, can be an effective tool in a city plagued by poverty and racial tensions.

We began this paper by defining new black politics as an effort to gain effective political power that would be used to distribute benefits in the African-American community and to eradicate obstacles to the upward mobility of that community. That, then, stands as the ultimate test of the success or failure of the newly elected "Mike Whites" across the country.

REFERENCES

Davidson, Chandler. 1972. *Biracial Politics*. Baton Rouge, LA: Louisiana State University Press.

Hamilton, Charles. 1977. "Deracialization: Examination of a Political Strategy." *First World*. 1(2): 3–5.

McCormick, Joseph. 1990. "The November Elections and The Politics of Deracialization." *New Directions: The Howard University Magazine*. 17(1): 22–27.

———. "The Continuing Significance of Race: Electoral Politics in Cleveland, Ohio, 1961–1979." Unpublished paper delivered at the annual meeting of the National Conference of Black Political Scientists, Atlanta, GA, March 4–16, 1980.

Nelson, William E. 1987. "Cleveland: The Evolution of Black Political Power." In *The New Black Politics: The Search for Political Power*. Ed. Michael Preston, Lenneal Henderson, and Paul Puryear. New York: Longman.

Nelson, William and Phillip Meranto. 1977. *Electing Black Mayors: Political Action in the Black Community*. Columbus, OH: The Ohio State University Press.

NOTES

1. This information is taken from an interview of Cleveland political activists conducted by the author in January 1990.
2. Statistics taken from Census Data provided by the Urban Center, The College of Urban Affairs, Cleveland State University.
3. Cuyahoga Board of Elections returns.
4. For a complete analysis of the 1965 Cleveland mayoral race, see Nelson and Meranto 1977.
5. See Nelson and Meranto, a detailed discussion of the techniques used so effectively to galvanize the black community.
6. Cuyahoga Board of Elections returns.
7. Nelson and Meranto, 140.
8. Information on Stokes' campaign issues and agenda is taken from numerous articles in *The Plain Dealer* and *Call and Post*, October–November 1967.
9. Carl Stokes committed a major gaffe in a campaign debate with Republican opponent Seth Taft, in which he (Stokes) accused Taft and his supporters of being racist.

10. Nelson, 1987, 177.
11. *Ibid.*
12. Information provided by Professor James Kweder, Cleveland State University, Department of Political Science, in a telephone interview on 25 January 1990. Michael White is a graduate of The Ohio State University with a master's degree in Public Administration.
13. Cleveland interview of political activists, January 1990.
14. See, for example, Joseph McCormick's unpublished article, "The Continuing Significance of Race . . ." March 1980.
15. The noted quotes are taken from "Once More: Mike White," *The Plain Dealer*, 2 October 1989, Editorial Page.
16. See front page editorial, *The Plain Dealer*, 3 September 1967.
17. Interview with Reverend Marvin MacMickle, president of the Cleveland branch of the National Association for the Advancement of Colored People, in January 1990.
18. Reported controversies are taken from "Politicos Doubt Forbes Can Beat White," *The Plain Dealer*, 4 October 1989.
19. Kweder 1990.
20. *Ibid.*
21. Forbes only appeared once on a ballot outside his Glenville ward when he unsuccessfully ran for Congress against Carl Stokes in the 1960s.
22. Quotes are from "Issues, Candidates Rated in Citizen's League Report," *The Plain Dealer*, 5 November 1989.
23. See, for example, White's campaign ad, "Does He Think We've Forgotten?" *The Plain Dealer*, 5 November 1989, p. 16-A.
24. "Issues, Candidates, . . ." *op. cit.*
25. "White's Lead Tightens in PD Poll," *The Plain Dealer*, 5 November 1989.
26. The housing code violation seemed to hurt White more than the allegations of wife beating. Eighty percent of those interviewed in *The Plain Dealer* poll reported that the wife beating charges made no difference in their mayoral preference. That's unbelievable, but, alas, the subject for another paper.
27. General election statistics provided by the Cuyahoga Board of Elections.
28. Survey conducted after the general election by Pollmet, Inc., one of the few black polling companies in the country that can conduct a nationwide survey.
29. Telephone interview with Larry Brisker, dean at Cuyahoga Community College, Metro Campus, and president of Pollmet, Inc.
30. MacMickle 1990.
31. Mary Sharkey, "Mayor White's Challenge," *The Plain Dealer*, 8 November 1990 p. 6-B.
32. *Ibid.*
33. *Ibid.*

Chapter 7

A Model of Racial Crossover Voting:

An Assessment of the Wilder Victory

Charles E. Jones
Michael L. Clemons

INTRODUCTION

The high concentration of blacks in major urban centers, and the fruits derived from redistricting initiatives have fueled unprecedented growth in the number of black elected officials (BEOs) throughout the nation, especially in the South. However, previous research indicates that the vast majority of BEOs have relied on majority black constituent bases (O'Hare 1986; Williams 1987). O'Hare (1986, 6) has asserted, "The extent to which blacks are elected primarily in black majority jurisdictions will have direct bearing on the likely growth of black elected officials in the near future, since the number of black majority jurisdictions is not likely to increase significantly in the next few years."

With this new political challenge now at the front door of black office seekers, a reassessment of traditional political campaign strategies and tactics employed by black candidates is imperative. Consequently, the future fortunes of black candidates seeking statewide elective office hinge upon their ability to stimulate racial crossover voting.

The purpose of this study is twofold: (1) to construct a theoretical model to explain black political success in majority white districts; and (2) to apply this model to analyze the political victory of L. Douglas Wilder, the first black elected governor in the history of the United States. The election of Wilder is of enormous theoretical import, given the paucity of black candidates who are elected to statewide positions.

THEORETICAL FRAMEWORK

Since the 1960s the growth in the number of black elected officials has been phenomenal. In 1964, BEOs numbered a mere 103. By 1989 that number had risen to 7226 (JCPS 1989, 3). However, significant future gains require that black office seekers capture seats in majority white electoral jurisdictions. Currently, only eight of 7226 BEOs hold statewide elective offices. We seek to construct a model which embodies those factors critical to the stimulation of racial crossover voting.

The components of our model are drawn from several subsets of American politics literature including (but not limited to) state politics, political parties, campaigns and elections, and the media. Elements of the framework were also gleaned from previous studies of black electoral politics.

The overarching assumption of the model is that race has been, and continues to be, a preeminent factor in the American electoral process (Alkalimat and Gills 1984; Lowen 1987; Carmines and Stimson 1989). Pettigrew and Alston (1988, 92) contend that "race continues to play a significant negative role when black candidates run for high office." They (Pettigrew and Alston 1988, 32) further observe that "race in America still serves as a political lightning rod that attracts political energy whether the candidates intend it or not."

One manifestation of the racial factor in American politics has been the reluctance of the white electorate to support black office seekers. Henry (1987, 77) examined selected mayoral elections between 1967 and 1983 and found that white electoral support for black candidates ranged from 9 to 23 percent. There have been but few recent exceptions to this pattern. Both Tom Bradley, in his unsuccessful bid for the office of governor in California, and Wilder, who was elected to the lieutenant governorship in 1985 (Sabato 1987), received over 40 percent of the white vote. Overall however, racial crossover voting among the white electorate has not been commensurate with that accorded white political candidates by black voters. Suffice it to say (Piliawsky 1989, 6), "black electoral success has been limited by the unwillingness of whites to vote for blacks running against whites."

A second premise of the proposed framework is that the black candidate's natural base of support, the black electorate, lacks the numerical strength to elect independently black office seekers to statewide positions. Therefore, it is essential that black candidates broaden their electoral base due to the substantial importance of white votes. Thus, we suggest that the ability of black office seekers to build biracial coalitions is, to a large extent, contingent upon the adroitness with which the racial factor is neutralized.

Depicted in Figure 7.1, our model of racial crossover voting consists of five major components: (1) political apprenticeship; (2) party apparatus; (3) a media/racial ombudsman role; (4) a deracialized political strategy;

(−)   (+)

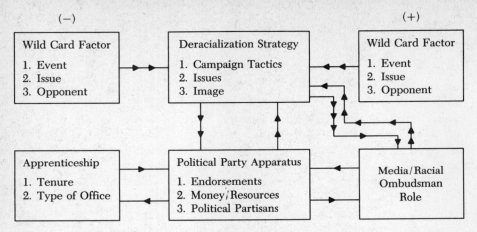

Figure 7.1 A model for the enhancement of racial crossover voting

NOTE: The directional flow arrows indicate the interconnectivity of each component of the model.

and (5) the "wild card" factor. The critical importance of these variables lies in their potential to mitigate the impact of race. The analytic utility of our model rests in its capacity to explain black political success, or the lack thereof, in majority white localities.

Political Apprenticeship

Individuals vying for statewide elected positions are expected to possess the requisite political qualifications. The premium on political experience is virtually inescapable for positions at the statewide level, particularly the governorship. According to Dye (1988, 186), " 'Promotion' from a state-wide elective office—lieutenant governor and attorney general, espe-cially—is the most well-worn path to the governorship." Political appren-ticeship acquired along these paths is generally viewed as fundamental to the capture of the gubernatorial prize (Sabato 1983).

The racial factor in elections accentuates the need for black political contenders to have prior experience in an elective office. The absence of an appropriate apprenticeship may provide a convenient rationale for some segments of the white electorate not to cast their ballots for the black candidate. Moreover, the black office seeker who lacks this important credential may be doomed to criticism by the opponent and the media throughout the campaign. The 1984 and 1988 presidential campaigns of Jesse Jackson are cases in point. Although Jackson ably presented himself as an articulate and knowledgeable problem solver with an extensive career in the field of civil rights, he was plagued by the criticism that he was not qualified to hold the office of the presidency (Barker 1987, 34).

Party Apparatus

Also pivotal to the success of black office seekers in majority white political jurisdictions is the ability to operate inside the party apparatus. Although there has been a relative decline in the significance of American political parties due to the increasing cost of campaigns, the rise of political action committees (PACs), and the growing role of political consultants, for black candidates, functioning within the party remains a crucial condition for winning.

Genuine party support yields three major advantages to the campaigns of black office seekers: (1) key political endorsements; (2) money and resources; and (3) mobilization of party partisans. The primary benefit of these services is the lessening of the race factor in the political contest.

The political endorsement of prominent party leaders can enhance the legitimacy and credibility of a black candidate. The public support of major white party officials helps to assuage the concerns white voters may have about supporting a black office seeker. In addition, white party leaders provide critical assistance in shielding black candidates from negative campaign tactics of a racial nature (Pettigrew and Alston 1988).

State party organizations perform such vital services as fund-raising, voter registration and mobilization (Dye 1988). Thus, the black candidate who operates within the party apparatus stands to gain access to such indispensable resources. This is particularly important given that the campaigns of black candidates seeking elective office are often underfinanced (Wilhite and Theilman 1986).

The statewide bid of the black candidate who has the support of party machinery may also benefit from the backing of traditional political allies who can assist in mobilizing the electorate. Support of this kind partially compensates for a shortage of campaign finances and facilitates the formation of a unified constituent base. Although there has been a decrease in party identification among the electorate (Merrin 1979), the party label remains an important cue for voters (LeBlanc 1982, 144–146). Reliance on the party label as a cue for voting helps to undercut the liability of the black office seeker's race. This is not to suggest that a black party nominee will not cause some defection among white party supporters (Henry 1987, 84–88), but rather that strong party attachment will help to limit this consequence.

Racial Ombudsman

Political observers (Patterson 1980; Dye and Zeigler 1989) have documented the emergence of the media as a major actor in the electoral process. Notwithstanding their tendency to trivialize the campaign process, one of the media's most important functions is to cover and promote an issue-oriented campaign. With the prevalence of negative campaigning in recent elections, this role is a valued contribution to the electoral process. Within this broad context, we suggest that a crucial determinant of black political success in majority white districts is the media's assumption of the role of racial ombudsman.

Under the role of racial ombudsman, the media acts to prevent the successful exploitation of divisive racial symbols in an interracial political contest (Jones 1987, 14–15). Incidents of race-baiting and the interjection of racially tainted campaign tactics are met with strong condemnation by the media. In essence, the media operates as a racial referee.

It is important to note that the notion of racial ombudsman does not imply a media double standard. Instead, the assumption is that the media will move in a fairly precise and deliberate fashion to blunt the manipulation of racially laden campaign tactics.

Deracialized Political Strategy

The essential task of black office seekers in majority white jurisdictions is to maintain the delicate balance between solidifying their natural electoral base and not alienating the white constituency (Cavanagh 1983). If properly executed, the application of a multifaceted, deracialized strategy can help to overcome this hurdle.

The notion of a "deracialized political strategy" was first advanced by Hamilton in 1973 during an assemblage of scholars, activists, and public officials brought together by the National Urban League to explore potential avenues for organizational action. At this meeting, Hamilton stressed the need to identify a set of issues which could effectively promote a progressive agenda. A new issue agenda, according to Hamilton, would promote the formation of a political base that extended beyond the black community. For Hamilton, full employment was one such issue.

In 1976 Hamilton revisited the idea of agenda setting, this time placing it within a broader strategic context. In a position paper commissioned by the national Democratic party, Hamilton argued that certain tangible political benefits may be derived from the utilization of a deracialized strategy. He elaborated:

> . . . there were certain clear political advantages to be derived from emphasizing issues that lent themselves to what I called 'deracialized solutions.' By this I meant that certain issues, such as full employment, a meaningful national health-insurance law, and a sound income-maintenance program, would (or at least ought to) appeal to broad segments of the electorate across racial lines. (Hamilton 1977, 3)

This conception of deracialization places the emphasis on advocating those issues which transcend race (Hamilton 1977; McCormick 1990).

Our utilization of the deracialization concept builds upon the work of Charles Hamilton by taking into account the need to deemphasize race in order to garner the necessary degree of white electoral support to win in predominantly white jurisdictions. However, we view a deracialized political strategy as a multidimensional approach which moves beyond the singular focus on issues. We define a deracialized political strategy as conducting a campaign in such a way as to diffuse the polarizing effects of the race factor in an election. From this definition we derive the following three elements, all of which are needed to diffuse racial discord effectively: issues, campaign tactics, and political style.

One facet of deracialization requires black candidates to adopt issues which appeal to a broad segment of the electorate to maximize the likelihood of receiving white support. Black candidates should therefore avoid advocating a racially specific issue agenda. McCormick (1990, 26) comments that "the essence of this political strategy is that its proponents would seek to deemphasize those issues that may be viewed in explicitly racial terms, for example, minority set-asides, affirmative action, or the plight of the urban underclass, while emphasizing those issues that appear to transcend the racial question." However, an exclusive focus on issues is insufficient as a means of stimulating racial crossover voting.

Of equal importance to the proper execution of a deracialized political strategy are the campaign tactics employed by the black candidate to mobilize the electorate. Specifically, black office seekers in predominantly white districts should avoid employing overt racial appeals in organizing their primary support base—the black community (Cavanagh 1983). Black political candidates risk alienating the white electorate with the use of race-based campaign tactics. The 1984 presidential bid of Jesse Jackson is one example of a contest in which campaign tactics based on racial appeals led to the polarization of the white electorate (Reed 1986, 25).

The final aspect of deracialization is political style. A black candidate's success at attracting support from the white electorate is linked to projecting a nonthreatening image (Goldstein 1981, 144). White voters are uncomfortable with the fiery confrontational political style that tended to characterize many among the first wave of black politicians. Suffice it to say, an image perceived as threatening would constitute a serious impediment to a black candidate's success in predominantly white localities (Citrin, Green, and Sears 1990). Congressman Charles Rangel, a Democrat from New York elected to office in 1970, suggests that "it is going to take a different kind of politician to win a majority or largely white district than in a majority black district" (Donovan 1989, 3099). It is therefore necessary for black contenders to project a reassuring image to the white electorate.

In short, the notion of deracialization involves a multifaceted political strategy that focuses on issues, campaign tactics, and political style. Its implementation is affected by the racial composition of the electorate, the nature of the elective office, and the political culture of the locality. However, even when black candidates adeptly employ the deracialization strategy, they still may have to contend with the wild card factor.

Wild Card Factor

The wild card factor, the final component of our model, involves the intrusion of an unanticipated issue or event into a political campaign. Its presence may be attributed to forces external to, and independent of, the black candidate's campaign organization. Manifestations of the wild card include a salient issue (Bloice 1982), the quality of the political opponent (Jones 1987), or an event (Dye 1988, 187).

The wild card factor has important substantive implications, particularly for the black office seeker. Its impact is double-edged (see Figure 7.1) in that it can either siphon off critical support or provide the electoral cushion needed for a victory.

The 1982 California gubernatorial election provides an example that illustrates the effects of the wild card factor in a biracial campaign. Bloice (1982) suggests that the presence of the handgun control proposition prompted a larger conservative voter turnout which contributed to the defeat of Tom Bradley. Thus, interracial political contests in majority white jurisdictions are likely to be more sensitive to the volatility of the wild card factor. The black candidate's ability to manage or counter the wild card, depending on the political circumstances, is critical.

V.O. Key, Jr.'s (1966) classification scheme of the electorate helps bring into focus the dynamics of the wild card factor in interracial political contests. According to Key (1966) and other students (Broh 1973, 6) of American politics, three major groups are present within the electorate in any given election: "standpatters," "switchers," and "new voters." The manifestation of the wild card as an issue may cause the attraction or defection of vital electoral support. In Key's schema, "switchers" represent that segment of the electorate which may be the most sensitive to a candidate's position on the issues. Clearly then, the manner in which the black candidate approaches, manages, and diffuses this unanticipated force in relation to "switchers" can have overwhelming implications for the outcome of interracial political contests.

Thus far, the components of the proposed model have been described discretely. However, this format should not obfuscate the interconnectivity of each element (see Figure 7.1). An environment of probable dynamic interaction among factors exists, and is an inherent feature of the framework. Principally, the successful execution of a deracialized political strategy is a necessary prerequisite to a black candidate's receipt of substantive party support. Moreover, the utilization of a deracialized political strategy can serve to trigger the adoption of the racial ombudsman role by the media. Similarly, without a strong apprenticeship tenure, it is unlikely that black candidates seeking statewide political office will receive the level of party support required to win.

In the following section, the foregoing model is applied to the 1989 gubernatorial campaign in the Commonwealth of Virginia. Application of the model to this case enhances our understanding of the dynamics of black political success at the statewide level. We recognize that an application to a single case may preclude definitive generalizations. However, the usefulness of such an exploratory exercise permits one to establish the parameters of the model until additional cases are available for more systematic testing.

APPLICATION OF THE MODEL: THE 1989 WILDER ELECTION

The data utilized in the analysis were obtained from a variety of sources including personal interviews, official election results, campaign documents, and exit poll results. Exit poll data were collected from *The New York Times (NYT)*-CBS News Virginia Election Poll (N=1, 153), and Mason-Dixon Opinion Research results were derived from random exit poll interviews (N=4, 738) at 60 key precincts around the state.

In the 1989 gubernatorial race in Virginia, Wilder emerged as the victor, garnering slightly over 50 percent of the total votes cast. The final election tally (available after the state-mandated automatic recount of ballots when preliminary election results indicate a winner by a margin of 1 percent or less) revealed that he had won by .37 of 1 percent, the most narrow margin in the history of gubernatorial elections in the state (Virginia State Board of Elections 1989a). Consistent with the results of the 1985 races for statewide positions, the percentage of the total vote received by Wilder was significantly smaller than that received by his Democratic running mates Donald S. Beyers for the lieutenant governorship, and Mary Sue Terry for the office of attorney general (52 percent and 57 percent, respectively). Although Terry's strong showing can be attributed to incumbency, political stature, and popularity, Beyers' significantly stronger performance relative to that of Wilder's is perplexing in light of his low name recognition and lack of political apprenticeship. It is noteworthy that both Beyers and Terry are white.

Wilder managed to carry five out of ten Congressional districts (see Table 7.1). His strongest performances were in the tenth (59.3 percent) and eighth (55.4 percent) districts, both of which are located in the Northern Virginia corridor. The performances of both Beyers and Terry at the district level stand in stark contrast to that of Wilder. Beyers carried eight districts while Terry won by comfortable margins in all ten districts.

Table 7.2 shows that slightly less than half (49 percent) of those who voted for Wilder were college graduates or individuals who had done post-graduate work. Seventy-one percent (71 percent) of those who voted for Wilder had attended college. Nearly 60 percent of his supporters earned incomes below $50,000.

Wilder received substantial support from females (perhaps intensified by the interjection of abortion as a prominent and timely issue). Fifty-four

Table 7.1   ELECTORAL SUPPORT BY CONGRESSIONAL DISTRICTS FOR
DEMOCRATIC CANDIDATES IN THE 1989 VIRGINIA STATEWIDE
ELECTION

Congressional district	Wilder (Governor)		Beyers (Lt. Governor)		Terry (Attorney General)	
1	97,445	(51.1%)	95,662	(52.9%)	123,124	(67.8%)
2	79,685	(55.4%)	79,179	(57.0%)	99,261	(70.8%)
3	104,949	(48.2%)	113,154	(53.3%)	120,561	(56.3%)
4	95,278	(52.2%)	94,992	(55.4%)	125,254	(72.0%)
5	72,228	(42.1%)	76,503	(48.0%)	102,849	(63.0%)
6	77,189	(45.9%)	81,877	(50.1%)	99,135	(60.3%)
7	77,962	(42.7%)	84,972	(47.9%)	98,064	(55.4%)
8	102,225	(55.5%)	107,694	(59.2%)	111,607	(61.8%)
9	70,997	(48.2%)	77,658	(54.5%)	90,509	(63.6%)
10	119,208	(59.3%)	122,686	(61.8%)	125,731	(63.8%)
Totals	897,139	(50.1%)	934,377	(54.1%)	1,096,095	(63.2%)

Source: Official Election Results 1989, Virginia State Board of Elections.

percent of the women voted for Wilder compared to a 45 percent male vote (see Table 7.2).

Apprenticeship

Wilder's ascent to the governorship coincides with the traditional political career path to the office. Dye (1988, 186) found that nearly 90 percent of all individuals elected to this office held prior elective office. Both George Brown (Colorado) and Mervyn Dymally (California), for example, served in their respective state legislatures before being elected to the office of lieutenant governor in 1974. Similarly, former Republican Senator Edward Brooke of Massachusetts held the state's attorney general position before being elected to the United States Senate (Becker and Heaton 1967).

Wilder was elected to the Virginia Senate in 1970. At the time of his 1985 election to the lieutenant governor's office, he was a fifteen-year veteran who had amassed the seniority to chair three standing committees. He also headed the party organ responsible for committee assignments in the senate.

Wilder's senatorial experience coupled with his tenure as lieutenant governor helped to allay doubts among the white electorate about his qualifications to hold the governor's office. His prior elective experience also furnished him with a public record to offset character attacks launched by J. Marshall Coleman, the Republican contender. For example, during the campaign, Coleman constantly reminded voters of Wilder's 1978 state Supreme Court reprimand for failing to provide

Table 7.2   DEMOGRAPHIC CHARACTERISTICS OF THE
            WILDER VOTE IN THE 1989 VIRGINIA
            GUBERNATORIAL ELECTION

Characteristic	Percent votes cast
Age	
18–29	17%
30–44	38%
45–59	24%
60+	20%
Gender	
Men	45%
Women	54%
*Race**	
White	79%
Black	19%
Education	
Did not graduate from high school	5%
High school graduate	20%
Some college, but not four years	22%
College graduate	24%
Postgraduate study	25%
Annual income	
Under $12,500	7%
$12,500–$24,999	15%
$25,000–$34,999	14%
$35,000–$49,999	22%
$50,000–$100,000	31%
Over $100,000	5%

*These figures reflect the racial distribution of total support, rather than the racial proportion of the vote received by Wilder.

Source: *The New York Times*/CBS News Virginia Election Poll.

"proper and adequate" legal representation, suggesting that Wilder lacked the integrity and competence needed to hold the governor's post. However, Wilder's twenty years of public service provided the voters with a basis upon which to make an independent assessment.

Party Apparatus

A second pivotal factor underlying the Wilder victory was the support of the Democratic party apparatus. By operating within the party structure Wilder obtained invaluable campaign assistance. He received the public support of respected Democratic party leaders. All three major Democratic elected officials—United States Senator Charles Robb, Governor

Gerald L. Baliles, Attorney General Mary Sue Terry—and a host of state party leaders were on the podium at the Wilder campaign kickoff rally.

Other party officials also assumed an active role in the campaign. For example, Joseph W. McLean, the former executive director of the state Democratic party, was Wilder's campaign manager, and Lawrence H. Framme provided invaluable fund-raising assistance. The campaign support of Watkins M. Abbitt, a former segregationist from the conservative south side of the state, reflected the broad-based support that the black contender enjoyed from state Democratic officials.

The political backing and public endorsements of popular Democratic leaders enhanced Wilder's credibility among the white electorate. A major television campaign advertisement featured Senator Robb extolling the virtues of the Wilder candidacy. The influence of party leaders is seen in survey results that indicate that 21 percent of the white voters who cast ballots for Wilder were influenced by Robb's and Baliles' support (*NYT-CBS News* 1989, 3).

Wilder was able to cultivate the support of Charles Robb despite past political differences. The reconciliation between Robb and Wilder was mutually beneficial. Wilder needed Robb's assistance to bolster the confidence of white voters. Correspondingly, Robb's future presidential aspirations hinged on his support of the Wilder campaign in light of the vital importance of the black vote in the fragile national Democratic coalition. Axelrod (1972, 15) found that the black contribution to the Democratic party's total vote substantially increased "from 5 to 7 percent in 1952–1960 to 12 percent in 1964 and 19 percent in 1968."

Wilder's access to key party fund-raisers and resources helped him to overcome a major obstacle for black candidates seeking high political offices—a shortage of campaign funds. The 1989 gubernatorial election was the most expensive contest in the history of the state (Sabato 1989, 65). Combined, the two candidates raised $16,224,569 (Virginia State Board of Elections 1989b). Wilder was able to offset the funding discrepancy, customary in biracial political contests, by raising over seven million dollars ($7,056,268.78). Coleman, however, retained the edge by raising more than nine million dollars ($9,168,300.40) (Virginia Board of Elections 1989b).

Wilder received substantial contributions from the Democratic party apparatus. For example, the state party made a $750,000 donation while the Democratic Governors Association contributed $50,000. Party backing also helped encourage support from several major Democratic sources. Among these were a $100,000 contribution from Albert Dwoskin, a Northern Virginia real estate developer, and John Kluge, a Charlottesville billionaire, who donated $200,000 (Virginia State Board of Elections 1989b). Wilder's fund-raising ability provided the campaign with the financial resources to marshal a timely and effective response to Coleman's negative campaign tactics.

The final benefit derived from working within the party structure was access to a base of established partisan supporters, which included voters, political allies, and a cadre of campaign volunteers. Exit poll data indicate that Wilder successfully prevented a mass defection by Democratic party voters, who were to constitute 55 percent of the Wilder vote. This compares favorably to the degree of partisan support received by Coleman (50 percent) (*NYT*-CBS News 1989, 3). Surprisingly, Coleman suffered a larger party crossover vote than did Wilder. Thirteen percent of Republican voters supported Wilder compared to a 10 percent Democratic crossover vote for the Republican candidate (*NYT*-CBS News 1989, 3).

Wilder also secured the endorsement and campaign assistance of several traditional Democratic party allies. The state chapter of the National Education Association, and Clean Water Action, the state's leading environmental organization, are two such examples. Democratic party activists also formed Virginians United, an informal coalition of labor, health, minority, environmental, education, and women's organizations, to work on behalf of the Wilder candidacy. Virginians United conducted a number of specific activities including coalition building, voter mobilization, and campaign skills workshops (Mack 1990). In short, the campaign assistance provided by the state party apparatus was instrumental to the Wilder victory.

Racial Ombudsman

The relative absence of divisive racial politics characterized the 1989 gubernatorial election in Virginia. In general, both candidates steered clear of racially polarizing campaign tactics, in keeping with the political culture of Virginia, where race-baiting contests are not pervasive (Black 1976, 113–118). Furthermore, Wilder's successful bid for the office of lieutenant governor in 1985 helped to set the tone for the 1990 gubernatorial contest (Jones 1987).

The absence of racially divisive campaign tactics in the Virginia election stands in stark contrast to the 1982 Bradley-Deukmejian race. Pettigrew and Alston (1988, 30–37) detail a litany of racially tinged campaign tactics in the California gubernatorial race. While the media cannot prevent the manipulation of racial symbols, it can set the tone and monitor the election to help offset their impact.

Wilder was clearly successful in achieving the support of the print media, an important variable in racial crossover voting (Bullock 1984). An investigation of candidate endorsements by the newspaper with the largest circulation in each of 136 voting districts revealed that Wilder received 44 endorsements while Coleman obtained 24.[1] The balance of the newspapers had a policy of "no endorsement." These findings suggest that the print media, by and large, viewed Wilder as the "best candidate."

When a newspaper decides to support a black candidate on the basis of merit it is often interpreted as favoritism by that candidate's opponent and segments of the white electorate. This, coupled with the media's racial sensitivity in the role of "ombudsman," often leads to opponent claims that the media is protecting the black candidate.

Indeed, Coleman raised the racial specter during a press conference held on the Friday preceding the general election. He complained that the media was guilty of applying a double standard in favor of the black candidate. Coleman's complaint was reinforced by the ombudsman of the *Washington Post*. Richard Harwood asserted that Wilder "may have benefitted from some debatable news judgments" (Harwood 1989, D6). Notwithstanding the implication of biased coverage, it is important to note that in all political contests one candidate stands to benefit over another from "debatable news judgments." It is arguable, however, that the political utility of such assertions in biracial contests is much greater.

Deracialized Political Strategy

Wilder's stance on the issues, his mobilization tactics, and political style exemplified the multidimensional nature of the deracialized political strategy. Effective utilization of this approach helps to account for the extraordinary level of white support (39 percent) he received (see Table 7.2).

Throughout the campaign Wilder presented himself as a social moderate and fiscal conservative who represented the "New Virginia Mainstream"—a major theme of the campaign. A second thematic emphasis was "law and order," a focus consistent with his campaign position in 1985. He promised vigorous governmental action against the drug trade and proposed to create a drug czar position which he would occupy. Wilder also favored the death penalty for drug kingpins.

Nonetheless, the candidate failed to win the endorsement of the Fraternal Order of Police (FOP), a nearly 6000-member association of local law enforcement officers. The endorsement of this organization in the 1985 lieutenant governor's race had lent credibility to Wilder's staunch "law and order" focus. The defection of the FOP from the Wilder camp in 1989, however, did not prove to be a decisive factor.

Other issues, which permitted Wilder to broaden his electoral base, included a pro-choice stance on abortion, a commitment to tougher environmental laws pertaining to drilling on the Chesapeake Bay, and opposition to the "freedom of choice" plan in education. Wilder's moderate views on these issues and others boded well with the notably conservative Virginia electorate, thereby diminishing the divisive impact of race.

The second aspect of the deracialization strategy was Wilder's approach to mobilizing the electorate. He did not overtly activate the black community and avoided making direct racial appeals to his natural electoral base, black voters. Empirical support for this observation is found in an examination of Wilder's campaign scheduling calendar. Between June 19 and September 4, 1989, Wilder made 84 public appearances; only 10 were before black organizations (Wilder 1989a). Furthermore, Jesse Jackson, as well as other prominent black politicians, were not asked to assist in mobilizing the state's black electorate, a common ploy of black candidates seeking elected office.

Although Wilder carefully circumvented the utilization of tactics which might be construed as race-based, black voter turnout was, nonetheless, extraordinarily strong. As expected, black voters overwhelmingly endorsed Wilder (90 percent) and "in many black precincts, turnout was at presidential levels" (Sabato 1989, 32).

Unlike Bradley, who failed to mobilize the minority and leftist electorate effectively (Pettigrew and Alston 1988, 22–29), Wilder employed a two-pronged strategy to help ensure a large black voter turnout. The first prong entailed behind-the-scenes, grass-roots mobilization efforts (Jenkins 1989). Seven hundred and fifty thousand dollars were earmarked for a "get out the vote" drive. A list of 190,000 households representing a potential 340,000 voters produced by the Super Tuesday election was targeted by the Wilder camp. These households received voluminous campaign literature, as well as telephone and personal contact (Jenkins 1989, B-11).

The second prong of the mobilization strategy involved a reliance on the black church. Wilder used the black church as a surrogate to mobilize the black electorate in his behalf. During the last month of the election, he addressed the congregations of several black churches each Sunday. This strategy yielded low-visibility black mobilization, which was less threatening to the white electorate.

The third dimension of Wilder's deracialized political strategy involved the projection of a political image that would reassure white voters. Wilder consistently projected a statesmanlike image despite the pervasiveness of negative campaigning. His nonconfrontational style was further reflected in the manner in which he diffused a potentially explosive situation during a public appearance at the College of William and Mary. On this occasion, a group of strident young college Republicans accused Wilder of equivocating on the "right to work" issue. Instead of challenging the protesters, Wilder signed the placard of one of the picketers, a move that helped to fortify his image. Twice as many of the white voters felt that Coleman (32 percent) rather than Wilder (13 percent) was primarily responsible for the negative tone of the campaign (NYT-CBS News, 2).

An important outcome of the deracialized political strategy was the contribution toward minimizing racial polarization and conflict in the election. The absence of overt racial divisiveness, however, should not lead one to conclude that race has disappeared from the Virginia political landscape. Although most pre-election polls predicted that Wilder would win by a comfortable margin, he won by a mere 6854 votes. Moreover, Donald Beyers, a political novice, outpolled Wilder by a margin of 37,000 votes. Realities such as these underscore the fact that a deracialized campaign strategy presupposes racial bias on the part of the white electorate.

Wild Card Factor

The *Webster* v. *Reproductive Health Services* (1989) court decision constitutes the wild card factor in the election. The Supreme Court ruling,
which increased state powers to restrict abortion rights, energized the
pro-choice movement in the state. The saliency of the abortion issue
conforms with our description of the wild card component of the model—
the intrusion of an unanticipated factor which has a major impact on the
outcome of the election.

The Webster ruling spurred significant political activity which ultimately played to the advantage of Wilder. First, it was the catalyst that
mobilized several women's political organizations, including the Women's
Political Caucus (WPC), the National Organization for Women (NOW),
and the Pro-Choice Alliance. Virginia Armstrong, state chair of the Virginia Women's Political Caucus commented that "the *Webster* decision
clarified the importance of assuming an active role in the 1989 gubernatorial election" (Armstrong 1990). Members of these organizations
hosted fundraising events, sponsored political rallies, and staffed phone
banks and the polls in support of the Wilder candidacy.

Secondly, the pro-choice movement lent critical assistance in shaping
Wilder's response to the *Webster* ruling. According to Dr. Armstrong
(1990), the WPC was the "catalyst for moving the Wilder camp to adopt
a clear-cut statement on the choice issue." Initially Wilder vacillated on
the choice question. It was only after a series of meetings between the
leadership of the WPC and Wilder staffers that a firm pro-choice position
was adopted. The leadership of the Women's Political Caucus suggested
that the election could be won by addressing the abortion issue in liber-
tarian terms (Armstrong 1990). They were able to convince the Wilder
camp, on the basis of sheer numbers, of the potential political payoff of a
pro-choice stance. It was reported that there were 240,612 more female
registered voters than male, and that the majority of female voters favored
the individual's right to choose abortion.

Wilder acknowledged the instrumental role of the WPC in masterfully
managing the abortion issue in a letter to the state chair of the organization:

> I am especially grateful for your thoughtful efforts to assist us in producing a
> clear and unambiguous statement on a woman's right to choose. Our position
> on choice has set a standard for the nation. You were a vital part of the effort.
> (Wilder 1989b)

The presence of the gender gap in Wilder's electoral support illustrates the significance of the abortion issue. While the gender gap did not
materialize in the 1985 lieutenant governor's contest, in which Wilder
received identical support from females and males (54 percent from each),
it accounted for the margin of victory in this election. Exit poll data reflect

an 8 percent difference between female and male electoral support for Wilder. Of the female voters, 54 percent cast their ballots for Wilder compared to 46 percent of the male voters (*NYT*-CBS News 1989, 1).

Perhaps even more telling is the 13 percent Republican crossover vote. It is likely that this support was due to Wilder's pro-choice stance. Key's typology of the electorate helps to explain the dynamics of the abortion "wild card" in the election. The "switchers" in this election represented a small, but key segment of the electorate, which was sensitive to the candidates' positions on abortion.

The effective identification and framing of the wild card by Wilder was critical to his campaign success. Coleman's "freedom of choice" plan, which would allow students to enroll in schools regardless of their locations, was weighed heavily as a major weapon against Coleman (Johnson 1990, 3). However, the decision to attack Coleman's position on abortion proved felicitious.

CONCLUSION AND IMPLICATIONS

The purpose of this research has been to advance a theoretical model for examining black political success at the statewide level. Although this work applies the model to only a single case, the research nonetheless lays the groundwork for more systematic testing of a range of cases over time. The model is inherently limited in that it is designed to provide a blueprint for winning in nonblack majority political jurisdictions. Clearly, such a Machiavellian approach does not consider, nor does it seek to address, the ramifications of black political victories in majority white localities.

The phenomenon of deracialized politics, necessitated by the need to win in predominantly white districts, does in fact have grave agenda and leadership implications for the future of black politics. Specifically, a potential risk of expanding the electoral base of black office seekers—a key ingredient to black success in these districts—may be the abandonment of a political agenda that addresses the deprived status of black people. The critical question that remains unanswered is: On what basis do African-Americans forge coalitions with white moderates and conservatives? Additional research is needed on agenda setting, legislative initiatives, and the use of political capital by black office holders who were elected on the basis of a deracialized political strategy. Such research could enhance the ability to differentiate between tactical maneuvering (electoral strategy) and goal substitution (governance).

In conclusion, we should be reminded that Wilder's Herculean efforts did not translate into a wider margin of victory. As Elving (1989, 3210) has poignantly observed, "Wilder's win in Virginia, narrow enough to invite a recount, established that a black candidate can be elected governor—if he does everything right." Hence, the inevitable road to be traveled by black candidates in pursuit of higher political office, at this point in time, remains fraught with the continuing presence of the racial factor in American politics.

REFERENCES

This research was supported by the Institute for the Study of Minority Issues at Old Dominion University, Norfolk, VA. The authors acknowledge the invaluable research assistance of Phyllis Hardy.

Alkalimat, Abdul, and Doug Gills. 1984. "Chicago Black Power vs. Racism: Harold Washington Becomes Mayor." In *The New Black Vote.* Ed. Rod Bush, San Francisco, CA: Synthesis Publications, 55–179.

Armstrong, Virginia S. 1990. State Chair, Women's Political Caucus. Interview with the authors, February 26.

Axelrod, Robert. 1972. "Where the Votes Come From: An Analysis of Electoral Coalitions, 1952–1968." *The American Political Science Review* 66(1): 11–20.

Barker, Lucius J. 1987. "Ronald Reagan, Jesse Jackson, and the 1984 Presidential Election: The continuing American Dilemma of Race." In *The New Black Politics.* 2d ed. Eds. Michael B. Preston, Lenneal J. Henderson, and Paul L. Puryear, New York: Longman, 29–44.

Becker, John F., and Eugene E. Heaton, Jr. 1967. "The Election of Senator Edward W. Brooke." *Public Opinion Quarterly* 31(2): 346–358.

Black, Earl. 1976. *Southern Governors and Civil Rights.* Cambridge: Harvard University Press.

Bloice, Carl. 1982. "Why Bradley Lost." *People's World,* November 16.

Broh, Anthony C. 1973. *Toward a Theory of Issue Voting.* Beverly Hills, CA: Sage Publications.

Bullock III, Charles S. 1984. "Racial Crossover Voting and the Election of Black Officials." *Journal of Politics* 46(1): 238–251.

Carmines, Edward G., and James A. Stimson. 1989. *Issue Evolution: Race and the Transformation of American Politics.* Princeton, NJ: Princeton University Press.

Cavanagh, Thomas E. 1983. *Race and Political Strategy.* Washington, D.C.: Joint Center for Political Studies.

Citrin, Jack, Donald P. Green, and David O. Sears. 1990. "White Reactions to Black Candidates: When Does Race Matter?" *Public Opinion Quarterly* 54(1): 74–96.

Donovan, Beth. 1989. "The Wilder-Dinkins Formula Familiar to Blacks in House." *Congressional Quarterly Weekly Report,* November 11: 3099–3101.

Dye, Thomas R. 1988. *Politics in States and Communities.* 6th ed. Englewood Cliffs, NJ: Prentice-Hall.

Dye, Thomas R., and Harmon Zeigler. 1989. *American Politics in the Media Age.* Pacific Grove, CA: Brooks-Cole Publishing Co.

Edds, Margaret. 1987. *What Really Happened When Civil Rights Came to Southern Politics*. Bethesda, MD: Alder and Alder Publishers.

Elving, Ronald D. 1989. "Interpreting Elections: Keeping Perspective." *Congressional Quarterly Weekly Report,* November 18: 3210.

Goldstein, Michael. 1981. "The Political Careers of Fred Roberts and Tom Bradley: Political Style and Black Politics in Los Angeles." *The Western Journal of Black Studies* 5(1): 139–146.

Hamilton, Charles V. 1973. "Full Employment as a Viable Issue." In *When the Marching Stopped: An Analysis of Black Issues in the '70s.* New York: The National Urban League, 87–91.

————. 1977. "De-racialization: Examination of a Political Strategy." *First World* 1(2): 3–5.

Harwood, Richard. 1989. "Tilt! Tilt!" *Washington Post,* November 19, D6.

Henry, Charles P. 1987. "Racial Factors in the 1982 California Gubernatorial Campaign: Why Bradley Lost." In *The New Black Politics.* 2nd ed. Ed. Michael B. Preston, Lenneal J. Henderson, and Paul L. Puryear, New York: Longman, 76–94.

Jenkins, Kent. 1989. "Key Weapon: Getting Out the Vote—Mobilization Seen As Vital to Success. *The Washington Post,* November 6, B1, B2.

Johnson, Steven. 1990. "Wilder Says He Declined to Cast Vote." *The Daily Progress* (Charlottesville, VA), November 6, 1, 3.

Joint Center for Political Studies. 1989. "Black Elected Officials in the United States, January 1989." *Focus* 17(1): 3.

Jones, Charles E. 1987. "Wild about Wilder: The First Black Lieutenant Governor of Virginia." Paper presented at the annual meeting of the Western Political Science Association, Anaheim, California, March 26–28.

Key, Jr., V.O. 1966. *The Responsible Electorate.* Cambridge, MA: Harvard University Press.

LeBlanc, Hugh L. 1982. *American Political Parties.* New York: St. Martin's Press, Inc.

Lowen, James W. 1987. "Racial Bloc Voting in South Carolina." Paper presented at the annual meeting of the American Political Science Association, Chicago, IL, September 3–6.

Luebke, Paul, 1979/80. "The Social and Political Bases of a Black Candidates' Coalition: Race, Class, Ideology in the 1976 North Carolina Primary Election." *Politics and Society* 9(1): 239–261.

Mack, Kevin R. 1990. Tidewater Campaigns Coordinator, Clean Water Action. Interview with the authors, March 2.

Mason-Dixon Opinion Research Inc. 1989. *1989 Election Day Exit Poll Report.* Columbia, MD: Mason-Dixon Opinion Research.

McCormick, Joseph P. II. 1990. "The November Elections and the Politics of Deracialization." *New Directions: The Howard University Magazine* 17(1): 22–27.

Merrin, Mary Beth. 1979. "Independents, Issue Partisanship and the Decline of Party." *American Politics Quarterly* 7(1): 240–256.

New York Times-CBS News. 1989. *1989 Virginia Election Poll. New York Times*-CBS News, 1–3.

O'Hare, William. 1986. "Racial Compostion of Jurisdictions and the Election of Black Candidates." *Population Today* 14(6): 6.

Patterson, Thomas. 1980. *The Mass Media Election.* New York: Praeger.

Pettigrew, Thomas F., and Denise A. Alston. 1988. *Tom Bradley's Campaigns for Governor.* Washington, D.C.: Joint Center for Political Studies.

Piliawsky, Monte. 1989. "Racial Politics in the 1988 Presidential Election." *The Black Scholar* 20(1): 1–11.

Reed, Adolph L. 1986. *The Jesse Jackson Phenomenon: The Crisis of Purpose in Afro-American Politics.* New Haven, CT: Yale University Press.

Sabato, Larry. 1983. *Good-bye to Good-time Charlie.* Washington, D.C.: Congressional Quarterly Press.

———. 1987. *Virginia Votes 1983–1986.* Charlottesville, VA: University of Virginia Press.

———. 1989. "Virginia's National Election for Governor—1989." Unpublished paper. Charlottesville, VA: University of Virginia.

Virginia State Board of Elections. 1989a. "Official Election Results General Election—November 7, 1989." Richmond, VA: Commonwealth of Virginia.

———. 1989b. "Campaign Contributions and Expenditure Forms. January 1, 1989–December 31, 1989." Richmond, VA: Commonwealth of Virginia.

Wilder, L. Douglas. 1989a. Scheduling calendar, June 19—September 4.

———. 1989b. Letter from L. Douglas Wilder to Dr. Virginia S. Armstrong, state chair of Women's Political Caucus, November 21.

Wilhite, A. and J. Theilman. 1986. "Women, Blacks and PAC Discrimination." *Social Science Quarterly* 67(2): 283–98.

Williams, Linda. 1987. "Black Political Progress in the 1980s: The Electoral Arena." In *The New Black Politics.* 2nd ed. Ed. Michael B. Preston, Lenneal J. Henderson, and Paul L. Puryear, New York: Longman, 97–136.

NOTE

1. The office of the newspaper with the largest circulation in each of Virginia's 136 voting units was telephoned by our research assistant, Phyllis Hardy, to ascertain endorsement positions. Telephone calls were made during the period from January 20 through February 28, 1990.

Chapter
8

Andrew Young and the Georgia State Elections of 1990

Marilyn Davis
Alex Willingham

INTRODUCTION

This study reports on the 1990 campaign of Andrew Young for governor of Georgia and poses questions about the prospects and constraints facing minority race leadership aspiring to success in multiracial constituencies. Though American elections have become more racially diverse since passage of the national Voting Rights Act, statewide campaigns by blacks are rare. By the 1990 elections, merely 13 had been successful in just ten of the states; only five were then in office.[1]

In the 1989–1990 period several black politicians were serious candidates before statewide voting constituencies. L. Douglas Wilder was elected governor of Virginia; Roland W. Burris was elected state attorney general in Illinois; Richard Austin was reelected secretary of state in Michigan; Dwayne Brown was elected clerk of the superior court in Indiana; and J. C. Watts was elected to the corporation commission in Oklahoma. They joined Francisco Borges, the treasurer in Connecticut, elected previously, and Al Scott, the new Georgia commissioner of labor appointed to fill a term after the elections. Voters in California, Colorado, New Mexico, Massachusetts, and Wisconsin have elected black state officials though none were in office in 1990.[2]

In the 1990 elections Theo Mitchell, a state senator in South Carolina, ran unsuccessfully for governor. Alcee Hastings ran for governor in Florida. Kenneth Harris contested for lieutenant governor in Arkansas, Gene Crump ran for attorney general in Nebraska, Cliff Walker and Al Scott ran for their states' public service commissions in Alabama and

Georgia, respectively. Harvey Gantt ran for the U. S. Senate in North Carolina. In the short time since Wilder's dramatic victory in November 1989, there has been considerable activity at the state level.[3] These trends raise the possibility that black voting in America—which in the 1980s seemed to be settling into routine politics inside minority racial enclaves—may achieve parity by placing those who enjoy its support in higher levels of authority and power. Examination of this category of elections poses a special challenge as we assess the constraints on minority political empowerment in the 1990s.[4]

Young's race for governor is one of only four ever conducted for the highest state office where the candidate had a serious chance of winning (the others are the losing campaigns in 1982 and 1986 of Thomas Bradley in California and the Wilder election in Virginia). It was only the second in the southern states where the biracial character of the population makes the African-American group an integral and controversial element in the population.[5] With few exceptions these changes have been driven by candidates within the Democratic party raising the further question of partisan alignment as well as the way these efforts interact with race, region, and the quality of election discourse.[6] This study focuses on Young and the 1990 Georgia state elections as a way to join the debate about minority candidates in white majority constituencies and offers a frame of analysis for comparisons with other states. The focus on Young is appropriate. He is a pioneer of the civil rights movement of the 1950s and 1960s, and represents the most complete transition from the protest of that era to the politics of today. He was elected U. S. congressman for the Atlanta area in 1971, served as United Nations ambassador in the Carter Administration, and was elected for two terms as mayor of the city of Atlanta. When Young resigned from the United Nations in August 1979, it marked an extraordinary period in self-analysis within the black American leadership stratum that had begun with his endorsements and campaigning in the spring primaries of 1976.[7]

For partisans, especially Republicans, the politicization of Andrew Young symbolized the loss of innocence by the civil rights leadership, substantially expanding the grounds on which that leadership was to be criticized and dismissed. When Young left the United Nations, he rode a crest of popularity based on sympathy by those—especially in the African-American leadership and civil rights communities—who considered him ill-treated. The debate over black-Jewish relations took on a tone of great weight. Men and women of affairs solemnly debated the need for a recognized national leader and spokesperson patterned after Booker T. Washington who would fill a void deemed left by the untimely death of Martin Luther King, Jr. Dramatic gestures were made to construct consciously a program for leadership coherence. The forces unleashed during this period were to percolate through black political discourse until the 1984–1988 period when Jesse Jackson conducted two presidential primary campaigns that threatened to settle the question of a national black spokesperson, within constraints substantially less pretentious when measured in terms of concrete political power.

In focusing on Young and Georgia, we examine the campaign of an individual with a highly visible place in the struggle against racism, contesting for office in a state with a long history of discrimination in elections. We document the historical context in which black office holding in Georgia emerged. We introduce the 1990 cast of candidates, their backgrounds and positions on issues. We examine the role of money, strategy, style, polling, and racial appeals. We remain cautious about inferences to be drawn from this report to other elections in the state, region, or country. The 1990 Georgia state elections do demonstrate, however, that for a black candidate, many of the factors associated with electoral success—name recognition, media consultants, money, prior campaign experience, powerful connections, editorial support—are necessary but not sufficient to bring success.

THE HISTORICAL CONTEXT

Georgia is a typical Deep South state. Historically, its economy was based in part on slavery, and its politics evolved out of the attempted secession from the Union and subsequent defeat in the Civil War. Over time its population assumed a Protestant, biracial character and its social institutions were governed by the principles of white racial supremacy. With the overthrow of Reconstruction, the Democratic party returned to power, and except for a brief period of radical populist agitation in the 1890s, has been in control of state policy into the contemporary era. Blacks voted and held office during Reconstruction, but that period was volatile and marked by extensive violence. After Reconstruction the state was persistent in seeking ways to restrict popular participation, including severe restrictions on voting by its black citizens. Georgia enacted a series of constitutional and statutory measures that arranged election methods to the disadvantage of blacks.[8]

At mid-century, white rule in Georgia was propped up by two kinds of discriminatory practices in registration and voting: first, was a county-unit system that diluted the vote of urban areas where a few blacks did vote; and second, a campaign discourse (cultivated by the Talmadge Democrats) that turned state elections of the 1946–1966 period into a succession of referenda on white supremacy.[9]

A strong reform effort developed in response to these restrictions. Two tactics were used. The first entailed campaigns in an attempt to elect reformers or improve election practices. The second was courtroom litigation. The campaigns were of limited effect, although the litigation succeeded in bringing substantial reform. The changes involved invalidation of the White Primary[10] and the county-unit system;[11] suspension of its literacy test for voter registration;[12] redistricting in order to ensure equity among election constituencies;[13] the reversal of the attempt by the Georgia General Assembly to deny certification to a properly elected legislator because of political standards;[14] as well as several attempts to gerrymander the Atlanta area congressional district to ensure election of a white official.[15] In the 1990–1991 period, the state was defending in four voting rights lawsuits charging racial discrimination in the appointment of school boards, the use of the sole officer or one-person board for certain county commissions, the election of the judiciary in multimember districts, and the use of the majority vote/runoff requirement.[16]

Georgia is emerging from a painful process of accommodation to a postsegregationist world. Georgians who had no contact with segregation and who, conversely, are accustomed to seeing black faces in political campaigns and high national office, are emerging into adulthood. In 1990, babies born the year Georgia native and Nobel laureate Martin Luther King, Jr., was assassinated, had already been in the job market four years; their counterparts in college graduated in the class of 1990. The state had a 1980 population of 5.4 million, of which 27 percent were black. By 1990 there were 6.5 million Georgians, 27 percent black.

Georgia is no longer isolated from the larger national and international trends. During the 1980s the state was attracting 100,000 new residents a year, almost all due to in-migration by older Americans. In 1988, the Atlanta metropolitan area ranked thirteenth among the 131 American metropoles and exhibited the typical pattern where relatively affluent white suburbs ring an inner city populated by people of color and poverty. Jimmy Carter's election to the presidency gave the state special prominence. Foreign investment grew sufficiently to become an issue in state politics. Georgia ranked eighth among all states in the incidence of AIDS—a trend severely testing the traditional image of a sleepy state immune to outside influence or problems.[17]

THE EMERGENCE OF BLACK OFFICE HOLDING IN GEORGIA

Just as racial disfranchisement stands as a hallmark of Georgia's political history, we may measure current change according to improvements in the participation by blacks in the electoral process. In the decades since mid-century political change has been dramatic but uneven. The most basic measure is hostility to registration and voting by state officials. Such hostility was to decline slowly in Georgia. As blacks did participate during the 1940s and 1950s the emphasis was on voter registration and turnout in support of moderate white candidates. This sense of the place of the black vote was well established before the civil rights movement, and continues even as the most significant barriers—including the growing availability of black candidates—have been removed. Competition for that vote has been intense since removal of the county-unit system. Its defection was one factor in the defeat of then U.S. Senator Herman Talmadge in 1980, and its loyalty helped secure the victory of Wyche Fowler as a Democratic U.S. senator when the Democrats won back the old Talmadge seat in 1986. The basic idea that minority voting is a force merely in a contest among whites sets a crucial problem for black leadership.[18]

Office holding as a priority for blacks in Georgia was to arise slowly over the 1950s and 1960s. In 1954, Rufus Clements became the first black person to be elected to the Atlanta board of education in a controversial contest. No other black won office until 1962 when, because of a quirk in the state's constitution, reapportionment resulted in a situation where Leroy Johnson was elected to the Georgia Senate. The next success was Q. V. Williamson, who defeated Jimmy Vickers for an Atlanta aldermanic seat in 1965. Vickers, an incumbent, had been convicted of a felony before the election, and was denounced by then Mayor Ivan Allen, himself a major architect of the political accommodation.

By 1990, 28 blacks were elected to the 236-person state legislature.[19] All the Atlanta area jurisdictions—the state legislative delegation, city council, county commission, city board of education—had black majorities. The Georgia Association of Black Elected Officials (GABEO) and the Legislative Black Caucus command attention statewide. Calvin Smyre, a Columbus-area legislator, became a floor leader in the Joe Frank Harris administrations in office from 1983 to 1990. Max Cleland, the secretary of state, advocates affirmative voter registration. Martin Luther King, Jr.'s, son sits on the Fulton county commission; a son of Ralph Abernathy holds a seat in the general assembly.[20]

THE LIMITS OF POLITICAL CHANGE

There have been some other less positive trends that show the unevenness of the political change and show cause for caution about the success of efforts like that of Young.

1. The real improvement in political opportunities for blacks has taken place in the Atlanta area. Change outside the city has been slow and much less likely without time-consuming and costly litigation.[21] Only Augusta has a history mildly comparable to that of Atlanta due to the early successes of the Dent family and a history of minority voting under official tutelage. Yet, as we note below, the Augusta experience has been difficult to consolidate.

2. Few black Georgians compete for statewide office, and those who do rarely succeed. Before 1990, with one exception (to be discussed below), none had won a statewide office.[22] There had been campaigns by reasonably attractive candidates with some name recog-

nition, such as C. B. King, Maynard Jackson, and Hosea Williams. Jackson's 1968 race was against powerful incumbent U. S. Senator Herman Talmadge. King's race was in the crowded field that eventually elected Jimmy Carter governor in 1970. None of the other candidates really mounted a competitive campaign.

3. Most BEOs represent single-member districts with extraordinary black majorities. Even with the large number of legislators, blacks are underrepresented. In 1992 they comprised just 11 percent of the senate and a mere 12 percent of the lower house. If they were to double their numbers they would only approach their raw proportions in the larger population. The single-member district has been important in providing minimum representation, but persisting racial bloc voting by the white majority sets an artificial limit on those increases. The result is that black on white contests remain about as rare as ever and acquire a special saliency when they do occur.

4. Georgia continues to be a low voting state. In the 1988 presidential election between George Bush and Michael Dukakis, the state was forty-ninth in turnout among American states (and the District of Columbia). Less than 40 percent of persons of eligible age voted in that election.[23]

5. Counties with significant black populations continue to show underrepresentation. While redistricting guaranteed representation on multimember bodies, single-person offices continue to be monopolized by white males even in the 21 counties with black majority populations. This is striking in the case of the office of sheriff, long the symbol of repression in states like Georgia. In 1990 the one black sheriff in the state was Robert McMichael II, appointed to fill an unexpired term in Fulton County (Atlanta).[24]

6. Once elected black candidates face problems retaining office and governing. Edward McIntyre assembled a biracial constituency, won, and became a successful member of the Richmond County Commission showing prospects for higher office. He was later elected mayor of Augusta but had to leave office to serve a prison term when convicted in a kick-back scheme. Since that conviction, McIntyre has lost two comeback efforts including a run for mayor in 1990. In majority black Hancock County, John McGowan engineered a takeover of the county commission, but died under a cloud of charges about patronage, mismanagement, and negative relations with the all-white municipal government in the county seat.

   In the Atlanta area, federal sting operations and ethics investigations have resulted in the imprisonment of key officials with wide community leadership roles, including James Howard (city councilman), A. Reginald Eaves, Chuck Williams, John Evans (Fulton County officials), and Richard Lankford (Fulton County sheriff). There have been smears on others including the superintendent and assistant superintendent (both forced to resign) of the Atlanta schools and the president of the city council. There was a demoralizing scandal around the private life of Julian Bond, who like King and John Lewis, is an authentic symbol of the state's civil rights history. Bobby Hill of Savannah, another candidate in the 1990 elections, was disbarred.[25]

7. Resurgent terrorism and agitation by white hate groups may be involved in the mail bomb attacks, in the 1989–1990 period, on civil rights organizations and the federal courts. The political impact was specific: one victim was Robert Robinson, an NAACP lawyer and elected councilor in Savannah. Racial hate groups are contending for legitimacy. In one 1990 decision voiding a law prohibiting hooded marches, a state superior judge compared the Ku Klux Klan to a civil rights organization.[26]

8. Finally, change has occurred within the confines of one-party Democratic domination. Among the states of the old one-party South, Georgia is one of only two yet to elect a Republican governor; Mack Mattingly's 1986 defeat limited its only Republican U. S. senator to one term. In 1992 only 1 of its 10 U. S. House members was not a Democrat (Newt Gingrich). Some 245 of the 292-person state legislative seats were held by Democrats (see Table 8.1). Although there were over 200 Republican office holders including 11 sheriffs, they held a majority on just 11 of the 159 county commissions in the state.[27] The election machinery in these small counties is a significant delivery system in an otherwise large and complex state. The courthouse crowd of commissioners, county sheriffs, trial judges, probate judges, city councilors and voting officials remains largely Democratic, shifting easily from support for the Republicans in national politics, to loyalty to the Good Ole Boys around the statehouse, to tight partisan combat at the local level.

These factors show the uneven nature of the change in Georgia politics and pinpoint certain obstacles facing a black gubernatorial candidacy. It shows the disproportionate importance of Atlanta; limited multiracial

Table 8.1   PARTY AND RACE IN THE GEORGIA GENERAL ASSEMBLY

	Democrats		Republicans			Republicans (%)	NGOB* (%)
	White	Black	White	Black	Total		
Senate	30	6	10	0	46	0.22	0.35
House	187	22	27	0	236	0.11	0.21
Totals	217	28	37	0	282	0.13	0.23

*Non-Good Ole Boys (Republicans and blacks)

Source: *The Book of the States, 1988–1989* (Lexington, KY, Council of State Governments, 1988), p. 89; *Roster of Black Elected Officials* (Washington, D.C.: Joint Center for Political and Economic Studies, 1988).

campaigns at the state level; limited campaign experiences in majority white, biracial constituencies; generally low voter participation; limited success in the pivotal offices in majority black counties; and harassment and terrorism with the potential for reproducing the significance of race. The success of the Democratic party, which would normally be seen as a plus for a loyal national Democrat like Young, nevertheless remained problematic as the idea of a black nominee heading the party ticket invited fears of a Republican takeover (through the number of defecting Democrats motivated by race), thus providing a partisan cover for anxiety about the black candidate's reach for higher office and greater power. These were obstacles more formidable than those in the Virginia election. They confounded the Young candidacy in a way that only extraordinary success at the normal campaign techniques could overcome. The campaign was not able, as it turned out, to find those techniques.

THE CHARACTER OF THE 1990 ELECTORAL COMPETITION

The makeup of the 1990 Georgia election gives an idea of the character of electoral competition in the state today (see Table 8.2). Sixty-one persons filed to contest for twelve offices to be elected statewide. Two persons, incumbent Sam Nunn and one challenger, filed for the U. S. Senate seat. The other eleven were state offices, of which four—attorney general, school superintendent, secretary of state, and labor commissioner—were held by incumbents and uncontested. Of the three open seats on the state

Table 8.2   RACE, GENDER, AND PARTY IN THE 1990 GEORGIA STATE ELECTIONS: PROFILE OF QUALIFYING CANDIDATES*

	Number	(N=51) Percent
Democrats		
White Males	32	62
Black Males	5	10
White Females	1	2
Republicans		
White Males	10	20
Black Males	0	0
White Females	3	6

*Sixty-one persons contested for state office; 12 of these were nonpartisan candidacies for judges as required by Georgia law.

Source: Data provided by Georgia secretary of state.

supreme court, two were uncontested; of the three open on the appeals court, one was uncontested. The main foci of attention were the races for governor, lieutenant governor, insurance commissioner, public service commissioner, and an appeals court vacancy, all of which drew at least five candidates.

The candidates showed the new faces of Georgia politics, although some very traditional faces were also present. Lester Maddox and J. B. Stoner symbolized all the bigotry of an earlier and darker period in Georgia political development. Wealthy males were involved. Candidates like Lieutenant Governor Zell Miller, Roy Barnes, and Johnny Isakson were very much cut from the cautious mode of the Carter era—conservative overall but very much at home with the new biracial politics. They retain, for example, extensive links to black political officials and community groups, and convey an easy sense that white men can and should retain political power, but discharge it in a racially responsible way.

An array of Republican party candidates raised the challenge of two-party politics. Though a minority party, the GOP placed candidates in each of the contested positions. In all, 13 Republicans entered the partisan races, accounting for more than a fourth of the persons running there. Three Republicans entered the race for lieutenant governor.

In the 1990 election more blacks contested for political office than ever before. In addition to Young, there were: Bobby Hill, a Savannah lawyer and former state senator, running for lieutenant governor; Al Scott, a state senator, and Otis Smith of rural east Georgia, running for the public service commission; Robert Benham, an appeals court judge, running for the state supreme court; and Clarence Cooper seeking an appeals court seat.[28]

Women candidates were only a token part of these elections. Only four sought office; three were Republicans. The small number of women, and of women Democrats, is a sign that despite the exciting changes suggested by the presence of Young and the other minority candidates, traditional political patterns remain dominant. During the 1991 session of the Georgia General Assembly, the 29 female representatives who served in the house formed a caucus for the purpose of articulating issues of significance to women, such as child care and abortion rights.[29]

The dominant candidates for Georgia state office continued to be white male Democrats who held all of the uncontested seats and fielded 32, or 65 percent, of the candidates seeking the partisan seats. And while the candidates for judge did not declare official party membership, they, too, were overwhelmingly Democratic and all male.

THE GUBERNATORIAL CANDIDATES

Nine male candidates participated in Georgia's 1990 gubernatorial contest: five Democrats, and four Republicans. Democrat Zell Miller had served in the state's second highest executive position, Lieutenant Governor, for sixteen years. This position is elected in Georgia and coveted because its holder presides over the senate. Despite its controversial appeal in Georgia, Miller campaigned as the state lottery candidate. This took the form of pledging to place a lottery proposition on a ballot for a referendum vote. He promised to use the funds, if approved, for statewide education and other human service programs. Miller entered the race as a favorite. Roy Barnes, also a Democrat, was a former state senator. He spent a significant amount of campaign time attacking the state pension arrangements provided for elected officials and the private business dealings of Miller. His campaign also invoked the "traditional family values" discourse. He opposed the lottery and supported pro-life. Democrat Lauren "Bubba" McDonald, a former state representative, was the candidate running with the blessing of powerful state House Speaker Thomas J. Murphy—an archetypal Georgia Democrat whose support has been pivotal in recent governor elections. The Murphy connection received special attention in 1990 because of the rivalry between Murphy and Miller in legislative contests between the house and the senate. Young, himself, sought the Murphy favor, referring to him often and fondly. The McDonald/Murphy campaign counting on the legislative "machine" did not emphasize any particularly noteworthy issues and never caught fire. The final candidate was Democrat Lester Maddox, already well known, who said he ran to combat liberalism in Georgia!

The state's Grand Ole Party offered four candidates in the 1990 race for governor. Unlike the competitive Democratic primary, this lineup was dominated from the beginning by one man: Johnny Isakson, a former state representative. The Atlanta area businessman's campaign reflected the themes of the national party. He made the "no new tax" pledge. Isakson spent much of his campaign effort attacking the record and issue positions of Democratic gubernatorial nominee Zell Miller. Three other Republican candidates, who posed no threat to Isakson's nomination, garnered less than 30 percent of the vote in the small July 17 GOP primary which drew only 118,000 voters—a mere 10 percent of the primary voters. The other Republicans in the primary were a former superior court judge, Greeley Ellis, who ran on a law-and-order platform, and two others: Eli Veazey, a retired Army officer, and Robert Wood, a former school board member. Neither of them campaigned on any distinctive issues. These three candidates were also-rans in a minor party. They merely responded to prepared questions on selected issues presented to them by the news media.

The lineup in the governor's campaign was quite unremarkable and traditional overall. Compared to this lineup, Young was the "liberal" Democratic candidate of national and international notoriety. In February 1989, Young told *The New York Times* of his belief that "personality can prevail over ideology in elections, whether it can prevail over race, though, has yet to be proven." The statement exemplified one approach of the Young campaign strategy: be cautious about ideology and race before the Georgia electorate.

This generalized approach amounted to a "high road," or "presidential posture" similar to what had worked for Jimmy Carter in the 1976 national election. And while Ronald Reagan was much more specific about his ideology and programs, his radical notions were discounted by voters who related, instead, to his personalism and affability. Midway through the 1990 Georgia campaign, Young's style was, indeed, dubbed "Reaganesque."[30]

Insofar as issues were to be discussed, observers expected them to be: ethics in government, environmental protection, fiscal policy, abortion, death penalty, crime, and gun control—all typical elements of public controversy of the times.[31] When asked to rank issues themselves, the candidates listed such topics as crime and drugs, environment, education, taxes and spending, economic development, and abortion.[32] In an early effort to establish issue priorities, Young used focus groups, informal discussions with small groups, assembled in several communities around Georgia. It is not clear how these groups were formed. They met in suburban Atlanta, Savannah, and Macon and were all white in racial composition. Four issues emerged out of these focus groups as suggestions for priority issues for a campaign: international contacts in economic development outside Atlanta, abortion rights, quality education, and health care.[33]

Young's general theme was balanced economic growth through international partnerships. This reflected his generalized way of articulating his program. The contrast between this and the more orthodox approach of Miller was shown in a televised debate between them two days before the runoff election. When the question was put about how to pay for education in the state, Miller raised his lottery idea. Young compared his own plan with the virtues of a state lottery saying he was "going to get the money (for education) by doubling exports while you (Miller) are waiting on a lottery to be passed;" and by doubling "the chicken sales abroad, the carpet sales abroad," and "the peanut sales abroad before you (Miller) can get any money coming in from a lottery."[34]

Issues never dominated this election. Despite more than a decade of action in the very mire of partisan politics, the emphasis was on Young's personable qualities to the exclusion of any emphasis on hard decision making in office. Young was cast as a conciliator by the local press, and an international diplomat by the national press—always discussed as a personality. This was reinforced by the campaign dynamics of a state where the tendency to belittle the African-American candidate because of his minority race status argues for a response based on a genial, tolerant, and forgiving persona. In large part because of these characterizations, he could chance a campaign geared to his personality, to the "bigger picture" of things, conducted "above the fray." This came naturally to an individual who had so often assumed the duties of mediator. The challenge would be to ground such a posture in real politics. The campaign sought this grounding in two prior elections that seemed relevant.

One election was Wyche Fowler's successful 1986 Georgia campaign for the U.S. Senate. That victory reversed the trend where Atlanta area urbanites routinely lost to "populist" small-town politicians. Fowler had represented the majority black Fifth Congressional District (once held by Young). But Fowler defeated an incumbent, downstate Republican by carefully assembling a coalition of mainline Georgia Democrats. Two factors about the Fowler election seemed problematic for Young, however. First, though the 1986 Democratic primary was spirited (one opponent was Hamilton Jordan, the Carter White House aide), Fowler was able to garner the majority vote without a runoff. The second factor was the volatile voter turnout in the elections. In 1980 the Democratic senatorial nominee (Talmadge) lost when 1.5 million persons voted in the election. Six years later, Fowler won with turnout down to 1.2 million votes. The implication of the Fowler experience for Young was clear: hope for a primary with soft opponents enabling a party consensus and victory without a runoff; in the general election hope for a bare bones turnout with marginal increases in black voting to offset the Sunshine Democrats.

The second election experience was the Wilder campaign in Virginia. The comparison is not, of course, as direct (see Table 8.3). Indeed, any comparison raises a number of questions about differences in the political

Table 8.3 BLACK ELECTED OFFICIALS, GEORGIA, VIRGINIA (JANUARY 1990)

Type	Number	
	Georgia	Virginia
Federal Representative	1	0
State		
Governor	0	1
Senators	7	3
Representatives	23	7
County		
Commissioners	97	40
Others	4	3
Municipal		
Mayors	16	6
Others	235	78
Law, Law enforcement	23	11
Education/School Boards	89	xx*
Total	495	149

*Virginia school board members are appointed.

Note: Georgia has 1,286 local governments electing 6,556 officials; Virginia has 430 local governments electing 3,118 officials.

Source: "Focus" (Joint Center for Political and Economic Studies, Washington, D.C., Spring 1990); *1987 Census of Governments* Preliminary Report, (U.S. Department of Commerce, Bureau of the Census, December 1988).

cultures of the two states that we cannot explore here. The factor we do address was raised by Young just after the Wilder victory. It concerns the role of locally elected black officials in the broader campaigns. By calling attention to this, Young, while certainly wishful about his own chances, did finger what could be a crucial dynamic in the evolution of black politics. The raw figures looked favorable. Georgia's black Democrats now hold nearly 500 offices in local government, more than twice the number in Virginia when Wilder was elected. To what extent is the acquisition of higher office—in majority white biracial voting constituencies—a logical progression to be expected from the expansion of local elected officials? To what extent is this body of officials—all politicians themselves—a delivery system that can increase the impact of minority race voters? How do they compare to church mobilization or charismatic leadership—devices that received a lot of attention in the 1980 period?

Despite calling attention to the large number of BEOs, Young took care in the campaign to avoid a perception that defined his campaign organization along racial lines. In a well-publicized political address to the state legislative black caucus, Young actually "released" these officials from any obligation to support him in the election, saying that he would like to see blacks working in the other gubernatorial campaigns as well. His selections for key campaign positions were white men with intimate connections to Georgia politics. In this year of a record number of strong black candidates, there was no attempt to slate a state-level ticket systematically for special appeal to the black voter.[35]

Again, numerous questions, which cannot be answered here, are implied by these decisions. We do emphasize the way both these experiences served to sustain a sense of effective politics for a serious candidate. Young could then set off on a campaign for the most significant office in Georgia buoyed by his own self-confidence and by the results in recent campaigns on which he conceived his own.

POLLING AND THE ISSUE OF RACIAL APPEALS

The potential for racial appeals in the 1990 Georgia state elections was strong. The mere presence of six black candidates seeking statewide office was a noticeable item in a state long preoccupied with race in elections. Young's civil rights record was another factor. One Georgia farmer was blunt in his assessment of Young's appeal: "The association with Martin Luther King will make it so some whites would never consider voting for him."[36]

There were two white candidates closely identified with racial hate groups. Maddox had gained national and state notoriety (and the governorship of Georgia) in the 1960s as a symbol of defiance to the 1964 Civil Rights Act as a result of terrorist threats he made against blacks seeking service in a restaurant operated by him. The other volatile white candidate was Stoner (who ran for lieutenant governor). Stoner served time for a conviction in the bombing of the Bethel Baptist Church in Birmingham, Alabama. He remains an unreconstructed advocate of white racial supremacy, speaking often in state and national forums.

Finally the temptation for racial appeals is rooted in the very makeup of the electorate and the historic reluctance to vote as through ordinary civic duty. For the "normal" politician, the temptation to find a way to make a racial appeal is a natural by-product of the drive to win under these circumstances. Young's civil rights record was introduced by him to solicit support based on his role in the movement. The issue of race was discussed in heated debate by Miller and Isakson during the general election campaign. The two white candidates accused each other of being insensitive to racial justice as evidenced by Miller's opposition to the 1964 Civil Rights Act, and Isakson's opposition to making Martin Luther King, Jr.'s, birthday a state holiday. Race also showed up as these candidates promised minority appointments in their administrations.

Yet for all of the potential for racial appeals in this election, few were made by the candidates: the Maddox candidacy in 1990 did not represent a blatant appeal to racial fears and Stoner was viewed as a crackpot. Clearly the openly racial appeals of the Talmadge era have been abandoned. The more subtle appeals of an earlier Maddox era are more difficult to implement because of the shifting symbols and personalities in terms of which to discuss race. Also serious contenders now must be concerned about black voters who could be the basis of victory in competitive elections.[37] For these reasons, overt racial appeals of the kind once common in Georgia politics have declined.

There is a vigorous search to find other surrogates to thwart racial appeals. Thus, typical issues with some symbolic value—urban crime and drug use—were included in the public debates and forums.[38] In this campaign Maddox characterized Young as "a socialist, who has presided over Crime City, U.S.A." But Maddox was ignored and there was sharp rebuke on two other occasions when race was injected. One was an attempt to smear Young with crime statistics from the city of Atlanta; the other came when McDonald started to campaign on the theme that Young could not win in a general election against a white Republican.

But has race disappeared as a factor in Georgia state elections? We think not. Indeed, the tendency to discuss elections in racial terms is as strong in Georgia today as ever. What has changed is the locus of the discussion and the reformulation of the terms of its conveyance. Popular press coverage and election poll reporting in particular show that the central theme in the political discourse of the 1990 gubernatorial election was race.

In Andrew Young's race for governor, the earliest and most often repeated truism was that he had an inalienable bloc vote that would put him in a runoff primary no matter the content of the campaign, his record, or the worth of the opponents. On the eve of the first primary election the press reported that only 14 percent of the white voters supported Young compared to 70 percent of the black voters. Discussion of the campaign in these terms made race—already visible enough—the main vehicle for public consideration of these elections.

The major voter opinion polls in the election were conducted by *The Atlanta Journal-Constitution.* There were four between November 1989, and July 1990. On November 12, the weekend after Wilder's election in Virginia, it was reported that Young was "in solid position" for the governor's election. At that point he had higher support among likely voters, a more favorable approval rating and a field where he alone stood above the crowd in the minds of respondents.[39] Five months later, the newspaper survey results revealed increasing indecision among voters, eroded white support for Andrew Young, and a narrowing of the gap between Young and Miller in voter support.[40]

The November survey reported its results by race though the findings were not negative. It showed large white voter support for a Young candidacy—21 percent, with 40 percent supporting Miller. The overall undecided vote was 24 percent. Among all respondents in November, Young received 38 percent support, while Miller received 30 percent. The other two candidates in the contest, Barnes and McDonald, each received 4 percent of the respondents' support. Maddox was not included in the first survey.

The Atlanta Journal-Constitution made voter indecision and voter positions on selected issues major themes of its reporting on the second survey. The newspaper intended to show that the campaign was a fluid one, with no one candidate in a dominant position; that candidates needed to do more to make the campaign an issue-oriented one; and that a runoff was a distinct possibility. The second voter survey, of April 1990 revealed "a growing uncertainty among voters suggesting the campaign may not be a runaway two-man contest." Moreover, the paper reported that "doubt permeates the electorate."[41]

Two articles appeared with the larger poll results. One article attempted to relate the issue of crime to that of race. It stated that "black and white voters emphasized different levels of concern, particularly on the issues of crime and jobs. Forty-seven percent of black voters said the state was on the wrong track on crime compared with 56 percent of white voters." This statement implied that white voters are more concerned about problems of crime in society than are black voters.[42]

The second article dealt with the theme of the changing politics of race in Georgia since 1966 when Maddox had been elected governor. The author argued that Maddox's "slim showing" of 3.3 percent of likely Democratic voters in 1990 reflects a "big change in the politics of race," noting also that "49 percent of the likely voters recall him unfavorably" and that "55 percent of whites polled rated him unfavorably."[43]

Most significantly, the newspaper article argued that the Maddox gubernatorial tenure had not resulted from voter choice, but from a politi-

cal deal worked out in the Democratically controlled House of Representatives. When no candidate won a majority of the votes in the 1966 general
election, the Georgia House of Representatives selected Maddox to prevent the rise of Republicanism in the general election.[44]

To emphasize the race issue, an April 29 article stated that "even black
voters, who have seemed firmly committed to Young, showed increased
signs of indecision, with the poll showing about a quarter of blacks undecided." In another campaign article the prime discussion was the changing
race relations in the state over the past two decades. It was reported that
a majority of likely voters believed that race relations in Georgia were
good—whites, 67 percent and blacks, 44 percent. Even as the paper attempted to place the race question in a more positive context, it conceded
that "the issue of race remained a hurdle for the former civil rights leader,
Andrew Young." Miller's support of 60 percent among rural, older, and
more conservative whites revealed this trend according to the April poll.[45]

In June, a month before the July 17 primary, the newspapers reported
a third poll. In this poll, the number of blacks who believed that race
relations were good increased 14 percentage points; the white percentage
was unchanged. In reporting the results, the article noted that Zell Miller
had increased his support among the voters by 7 percentage points. The
newspaper revealed "across the board support for Miller in most voter
groups, except for African-Americans loyal to Mr. Young." It emphasized
that "white support for former Atlanta Mayor (Young) continues to leak
away." Black support for Young was stronger at 65 percent; however, he
was running third among white voters. According to these data, Young's
white support (except among whites with tolerant racial views) had continued to decrease since the November poll; he had gone from 21 percent
in November, to 16 percent five months later, and 12 percent one month
before the election. Moreover, the number of undecided voters, especially
in metropolitan Atlanta, declined. This important portion of the electorate—presumably attentive to appeals by candidates—was now more solidly in the Miller camp. The number of undecided white voters in the poll
had decreased to 19 percent.[46]

These reports characterized the racially polarized electorate and
raised questions about the effectiveness of Young's appeal to white voters.
For instance, the June poll article reported that "Mr. Young faces an
increasingly tough sell to white voters outside Atlanta, where he has
dropped to 8 percent of the vote, equal to Mr. (Lauren) McDonald." The
article noted that a Roy Barnes supporter said that he "can't vote" for an
African-American candidate. Moreover the voter survey showed that "at
least one-third of Georgia's white (voters) are outside Mr. Young's reach."
Young was termed a "long shot in becoming the next governor because
Miller was winning most of the support of whites who say they like Andy
Young."[47]

On June 26, *The Atlanta Journal-Constitution* addressed the question
of how Andrew Young could attract a significant portion of Georgia's

white voters while energizing African-American voters. Again, the newspaper reported the results of a poll. This time it was one in which Georgia voters were asked to compare the acceptability of Reverend Jesse Jackson with that of Young.[48]

To place the racial polarization on firmer ground, the newspaper implied that positions on certain public policy issues influenced white support for Young. For example, the June 16 poll article noted in closely placed, bold subtitles that "Young's white support slips" and that the issue of crime had an impact on voter support for a candidate. Here the paper subtly linked the Young candidacy with the crime issue.[49]

Of course, the newspaper cannot be held responsible for the racial views and voting preferences of the poll respondents. It is legitimate for the news media to establish the main trends among the electorate. But the reduction of election analysis to race—a reduction no doubt resulting from its saliency in the population—serves to keep the issue alive in the minds of voters and fails to provide alternate ways of looking at the political process. News analyses generally and opinion polls in particular serve this function. The challenge facing the candidates is to expand the discourse. The poll analyses reported here characterized the 1990 gubernatorial election through cumulative "scientifically conducted" polls during the election campaign period, and its strategic placing of issue-related articles with these reports. The effect was to substantiate a unique position on the character of the campaign.

In a July 14 opinion poll, Miller was expected to capture 36 percent of the Democratic vote, and Young, 30 percent. Nine percent of those voters polled were undecided about a candidate choice.[50] A comparison of candidate support among the newspaper poll respondents and candidate support among the voters on election day reveals interesting data. Miller garnered 5 percent more support in the election than he did in the July 15 poll. Young lost 1 percent support in the election. Roy Barnes, the third-place candidate, received 5 percent more support in the election than he did in the July 14 poll. The 9 percent undecided vote went to Miller and Barnes. Voter support for Young from this 9 percent of the undecided electorate may have given him a first-place position in the primary.

CAMPAIGN FINANCE AND CAMPAIGN STRATEGY

The 1990 elections were the most expensive in Georgia history. Campaign finance emerged as an issue in electoral mobilizing and in state election law reform. As of January 1, 1988, there were no campaign contribution limits in the state of Georgia. Omnibus ethics legislation passed the general assembly in the 1990 session. Among those supporting the reform were Miller, Barnes, and McDonald. The legislation limited individual cash and in-kind contributions (donations in the form of goods and services such as office space, transportation, and advertising) in statewide campaigns to $3,500 per election, or $10,500 for primary, runoff, and general elections. Then in April, Governor Joe Frank Harris signed Georgia's first-ever legislation to limit the role of money in elections. Harris later commented that "you cannot buy very much for $43,500." The legislative response to a growing concern throughout America about campaign spending had the effect of changing the rules in the middle of the game in this important election.[51]

When Young entered the 1990 campaign, his personal worth was less than that of any of the other candidates running. While none of the candidates was among the big rich, the net worth of each (see Table 8.4), shows that Young ranked last in the entire field. His main source of income was his salary as mayor. After leaving the mayor's office, Young took a position as a consultant with a legal firm, Law International. Three of the candidates, Republican Judge Greeley Ellis, Republican State Representative Johnny Isakson, and Democratic State Senator Roy Barnes, were millionaires. Andrew Young's campaign finance disclosure report showed a new worth of $394,300.

The state could not implement the ethics reform until it was precleared by the U.S. Attorney General. Clearance did not occur during these campaigns.[52] Large, unlimited contributions continued to the end of the primary campaign period. Secretary of State Max Cleland, among others, argued that it was unfair to impose a new campaign law during an election year. The law was also seen as being unfair to candidates who did not have significant personal wealth. Even after the general assembly passed the new law, Zell Miller accepted a $100,000 donation from the Medical Association of Georgia, and Roy Barnes raised $500,000 in bank loans secured by individuals. Young responded by refusing to abide by the law, saying it was not in effect until precleared—effectively giving him extra time to raise funds. Young did not believe that new limits on individ-

Table 8.4   GEORGIA GUBERNATORIAL CANDIDATES RANKED BY NET WORTH

	1989 Income	Assets	Liabilities	Net Worth
Roy E. Barnes	739,541	6,553,000	3,095,000	3,550,000
Greeley Ellis	145,065	2,650,000	221,854	2,430,000
Johnny Isakson	374,468	2,550,000	530,586	2,020,000
Lester Maddox	46,132	808,500	20,500	788,000
Lauren McDonald	87,399	939,000	160,000	779,000
Zell Miller	91,109	1,200,000	429,573	774,511
Andrew Young	120,700	553,700	159,400	394,300

Source: The Atlanta Journal-Constitution (May 5, 1990), compiled from financial disclosure statements filed with the Georgia secretary of state. Reprinted with permission from The Atlanta Journal and The Atlanta Constitution.

ual contributions were racially discriminatory in this case, however, as the last major gubernatorial candidate to enter the race, he argued that he was entitled to the extra fund-raising time. Other candidates had personal wealth, and two full years prior to the campaign in which to raise money.

Once the gubernatorial campaign began in earnest, financial contributions from wealthy interest groups drove the election. Young, while confident of the ability to raise the money needed, was nevertheless forced to raise funds from wealthy contributors who were often outside the state. Between January and June he collected $2.1 million. According to disclosure reports, a quarter of the $2 million came in contribution amounts of $30,000 or more.[53]

The leading candidates benefitted from hundreds of thousands of dollars in campaign contributions from bankers, doctors, plaintiff lawyers, nursing homes, labor unions, and realtors. Some prominent individual contributors received special attention in the local media two months before the primary election. Eight large campaign contributors were dubbed "sugar daddies" (those who enjoy influence in government in exchange for their contributions). An investment banker and an engineer/ realtor gave Zell Miller $100,000 for his campaign. Young benefitted from nearly $200,000 contributed from an international hotel magnate, a construction contractor, and an attorney.[54] Campaign contributions of this magnitude seem to establish "ties that bind" the victorious candidate to the contributors. These kinds of complex, financial bonds could have impeded the independence of a victorious Andrew Young as he, in the chief executive position, proposed and implemented policy in the state.

A news analysis of campaign contributions of at least $100 revealed that corporations and political action committees hedged more than 20 percent of the gifts they made; that is, they contributed to more than one campaign or remained neutral by giving token amounts of money or nothing at all to a candidate. This means that of the nearly $5 million contributed to gubernatorial campaigns, almost $1 million were spread among second candidates. Campaign contributions targeted for one candidate are more substantial than hedged ones. The hedging phenomenon had a negative impact on the candidacy of McDonald. During a meeting of the legislative subcommittee considering the ethics reform bill, McDonald was quoted as saying "if it's money that's going to elect you to public office, then I'm the farthest behind." McDonald ran fourth in a field of five candidates in the Democratic primary. Nearly one-third of McDonald's contributions from corporations and political action committees came from donors who also donated to another candidate.

Conversely, less than one-fifth of Young's contributions came from corporations and PACs that donated to at least two candidates. Some of his notable contributors were members of Georgia's organized labor movement. Other notable contributors to the Young campaign were out-of-state individuals in New York, California, Missouri, and Chicago, Illinois, as well as Hollywood entertainers. Members of former president

Jimmy Carter's cabinet and staff hosted fund-raisers for Young. Young was the only candidate with an extensive out-of-state fund-raising strategy, although Miller raised about $30,000 in Kentucky and received other contributions from New York investment bankers. According to Young's campaign manager Hobby Stripling, the campaign was financed primarily by money from inside the state of Georgia. Seventy percent of Young's campaign contributions came from within the state.

Money as a Campaign Asset

These candidates spent their money in the customary way: seeking to increase name recognition and get the attention of the electorate. Substantial spending went to television advertisements. The three major Democratic candidates for governor spent more than $3 million on television advertising in the critical month of June before the July primary. Miller spent the largest sum of money—almost $1.5 million—on television advertising, followed by Barnes, Young, McDonald, and Isakson, the major Republican candidate.

Most television money was spent in the Atlanta metro area. Atlanta television stations reach about 65 percent of voting-age Georgians.[55] Miller spent more than $1 million in Atlanta. His second target city was Macon, where he spent about $200,000. Barnes followed the same television spending pattern as did Miller. Young and Isakson both targeted Columbus as their second television area.

It is surprising that four of these five candidates spent the least amount of television money in Albany, Georgia. This city has "one of the most important television stations in Georgia politics" because it has "the only major network station that serves the southwest corner of the state, reaching about 6 percent of Georgia's voting-age adults."[56] The Albany station is considered "a key part of the strategy in a governor's campaign in which the two most dominating factors are money and television." Young was the exception. He did spend more television money in the Albany area, which is deep in Georgia's peanut country—the region that produced C. B. King and Jimmy Carter—and contains higher percentages of black voters.

The Young strategy was to hold television advertising for the final days of the primary campaign, which, his media consultants reasoned, was the right time to purchase television advertising. In this way, the electorate would have the Young name and message uppermost in their minds. The Young campaign organization released a commercial during the last week of the primary campaign directed at rural white voters who gave him 9 percent support in the polls.

Television advertising proved to be an effective way of reaching undecided voters. It was reported that Miller and Isakson spent the most money on television advertising during a six-week period from April to June and increased their support in the newspaper's opinion poll by seven points each. The argument advanced was that television advertising can help a candidate when it is used extensively and is not challenged by opponents on positions presented in the advertisements.

But the exact impact of advertising proved controversial. A poll reported just a few days before the election argued that television advertisements had failed to change voters' minds. In fact, it was reported that 41 percent of the voters who responded to the final pre-primary poll said the commercials simply reinforced their decisions to support a particular candidate. While 4 percent of the respondents said they were less likely to vote for a particular candidate as a result of the television spots, 34 percent of those polled said the commercials made no difference in their voting decisions.[57]

THE ELECTION RESULTS

The 1990 results were disappointing to the Young campaign: he finished second in both primaries.[58] The results are less negative when the returns of all black candidates are considered, however. Six black Georgians offered for statewide office: four ran as Democrats; two others were Democrats running for election to the nonpartisan state judiciary. An overview of the 1990 Georgia state elections appears in Tables 8.5 and 8.6.

In the 1990 elections the serious black candidates either won (in the case of Benham and Cooper) or achieved good results (Young and Scott). The more marginal black candidates did not do well. Turnout in the governor's election was high—drawing slightly more than 1 million votes—dramatically exceeding votes for the other offices. There was a drop-off of 10 percent between those voting in the governor's race and

Table 8.5   VOTES RECEIVED, BLACK STATEWIDE CANDIDATES FIRST PRIMARY, GEORGIA STATE ELECTIONS, JULY 17, 1990

Candidate/ Position	Total Candidates	Total Vote	Share	Rank	Percent
Andrew Young/Gov	5	1,052,315	303,159	2	28.81
Bobby Hill/LtGov	9	952,108	28,885	8	3.03
Otis Smith/PSC*	6	752,669	92,794	5	12.33
Al Scott/PSC*	3	821,914	191,763	2	23.33
Robert Benham/SC†	2	673,353	423,888	1	62.95
Clarence Cooper/AC‡	2	678,814	367,140	1	54.09

*State Public Service Commission

†State Supreme Court

‡State Court of Appeals

Source: State of Georgia, Report of Election Returns, 1990
General Primary and Primary Runoff, July 27, 1990, and August 20, 1990.

Table 8.6   1990 DEMOCRATIC PRIMARY ELECTION RESULTS

First Primary: Candidate	Votes	Votes (%)
Roy Barnes	219,136	20.82
Lester Maddox	31,403	2.98
Lauren McDonald	64,212	6.10
Zell Miller	434,405	41.28
Andrew Young	303,159	28.81
Runoff Primary:		
Zell Miller	591,166	61.84
Andrew Young	364,861	38.16

Source: Georgia secretary of state, Report of Election Returns, 1990.

those making a choice for lieutenant governor—the next highest office in vote totals. The "constituency" that determined the Democratic nominee for governor was different from the "constituency" selecting the lieutenant governor and nearly 400,000 more than that selecting the court positions won by Benham and Cooper.

The nature of the 1990 turnout was a complicating factor in Young's effort. The results made it difficult to replicate the Fowler election of 1986. Indeed, Young's first primary vote was comparable to Fowler's but actually came to a small percentage of the overall vote. Comparing these two elections highlights the treacherous role of dual nominating primaries. Fowler succeeded in getting a majority in the first primary.[59] Young, by contrast, was unable to place first in the primary, fueling accusations about his electability and leaving him at a disadvantage when turnout took the customary decline in the runoff. Electability took on singular urgency due to the special push by the Republican party. The specter of damage to the Democratic party's nominating an unelectable candidate was a theme of Young's opponents.

PERSONALITY, IDEOLOGY, RACE, AND PATRONAGE

While issues have been mentioned often, this campaign was not about issues when these are understood to be remote, general, and unrelated to interests. Not only did *race* remain a key term for discussing the campaign and of specifying its significance, but the campaign's own sense of strategy was cast in terms of Young's *personal appeal*. Finally, it was not about "issues" in the sense that, especially during the second primary between Young and Miller, there was a reemergence of the typical questions of *state patronage*.

For candidate Young, the focus on personal appeal was no problem given the persona of the conciliator he had long cultivated. The ideological problem was more thorny. The effort was to craft an ideological stance to respond to the Georgia electorate. There were two basic aspects of this effort. First was the effort to set a broad tone based on a universal good (i.e., economic development) of transcendent appeal. Much of the rhetoric that Young used when he claimed the state was getting "beyond race" came back to an effort to rotate the discussion to economic development issues. This was an appeal to business development interests, and it coincided with the concern about how development would occur given the globalization of the economy apparent in the late twentieth century. While this was a campaign tactic, it revived Young's belief in "public service capitalism," or "public purpose capitalism," first born in the civil rights movement and espoused next in the United Nations period of his career. Young polished the idea in a presentation to the Atlanta Hungry Club during this campaign. Closely associated with his life's work and philosophy, this continued a long-standing admiration for the will of American multinational corporations to do good.[60]

The second aspect of this ideological posture was designed to address more familiar values and issues to compensate for the limited appeal of social liberalism in Georgia. Young adopted a passive position on issues such as capital punishment, crime and law enforcement, drug policy, and the saliency of race. The economic growth issue and this neo-conservatism seemed to provide Young with a consistent stance, one that would set well with the expanding multinational corporations pressing for advantages in the southeast, as well as local boosters eager to have these companies do business in their often depressed communities. If civil rights allies would look the other way on the social conservatism, a new coalition would emerge in Georgia state elections!

But the difficulties facing Young were several. First, a good many Georgia voters lived in north Georgia and metropolitan Atlanta—the part of the state already enjoying growth, much of it linked to federal military spending. Second, recent governors had already adopted the international economic development theme, albeit on a low key. Young's own international connection is undeniable, but in election campaigns, politicians play to the state's long-standing nativism. Young made eloquent appeals to a new Georgia, but this did not reach the bread and butter issues of state politics. His call for more international business development was seen as a poor substitute—indeed a faraway dream—given his lukewarm attitude towards a state lottery. Miller, by contrast, warmly supported the lottery idea and made it a key part of his pitch to the black voters.

Finally, Young's outsider status was a liability in the area of state patronage. Support in these campaigns is often sheer reciprocity based in relationships of advantage actually worked out in the state policy process. During the 1990 Georgia elections, many donations went to candidates on the basis of their past positions on policy issues before state bodies. For instance, as presiding officer of the state senate, Miller supported a bill restricting the rights of parents to sue obstetricians for wrongful infant death due to birth defects. Although the bill died in the lower house, doctors showed their appreciation for Miller with financial support in the governor's race. As a kind of countermove, plaintiff attorneys, who customarily represent parents in such civil suits, donated nearly half a million dollars to the Barnes campaign. The nursing home industry gave more than $40,000 to the campaign of McDonald. As a chairman of the house appropriations committee, Barnes had supported substantial Medicaid reimbursements for nursing home patients.

The political action committees kept close tabs on known friends and enemies as they worked the political process. In such a game, the cards are stacked against the outsider. Even labor, a natural ally of Young, and a wedge in the drive for working-class white votes, was never fully behind the Young candidacy. At this level the campaign follows well-established tracks in American state politics, where a prime appeal is in the patronage enjoyed from control of state government machinery.

The neo-conservatism on social issues was difficult to sustain. Young's link with the "militant" civil rights movement—and with Martin Luther King, Jr., personally—was undeniable. His congressional voting record, while not a focus in this campaign, was so liberal that he consistently ranked in the ninety-fifth percentile on votes favored by the Americans for Democratic Action. His personal beliefs on abortion coincided with the "liberal" pro-choice position and he made this a public issue, believing it to be an asset in attracting voter support. Before the campaign was over he adopted the liberal side on two other "litmus tests" of recent liberalism: laws on gun control and flag burning. When the campaign was over, a white Georgia voter wrote to *The Atlanta Constitution* to clarify the record about the motivations for his vote against Young. He had voted against Young because of his stand on the issues and his political history; not his race. The repackaging on social issues had not worked.[61]

Presidential campaign postures are more difficult to apply in state elections where the reciprocity is so firm and Young's neo-conservatism simply seemed deceptive. To be successful, Young would have had to overwhelm the voting public by elevating the election discussion agenda to a plane on which these voters were not accustomed. But the very fire and determination required would have undercut the personalism deemed essential in persuading white Georgians to fill so powerful a state position with a black person. When assessing his campaign, Young seemed to acknowledge the "communications gap," saying that he had started too late to get his full message across. Wilder, commenting on the Young defeat, sounded a similar note, pointing out the difficulty of winning state elections without paying some dues through maneuvering within the structure of bargains established over time. It is difficult for any candidate; for a black candidate, it redirects our attention to the way discrimination in the politics of the past structures the limits of electoral opportunity in the present.

NOTES

1. Overall, some 18,000 officials of all kinds are elected in state governments in America. Our number includes only black persons elected to executive positions by statewide voting: about 285 such positions exist (although the number varies considerably among the states). Four states elect just one official by popular vote, Virginia elects three, Georgia elects eight. See 1987 *Census of Governments* (Washington, D.C.: Bureau of the Census, 1988); *The Book of the States, 1990–91 Edition* (Lexington, KY: Council of State Governments, 1990); volumes of *Black Elected Officials: A National Roster* (Washington, D.C.: Joint Center for Political and Economic Studies); "1990 Election Results for Black Candidates to the U.S. Congress and Statewide Seats," in *Focus* 18(10): 4, and data collected by the authors.

2. We know of no other compilation, similar to the *Roster*, of *attempts* to win office. Our most systematic information, then, is limited to those who have been victorious. We do not include those officials seeking or holding office during Reconstruction, nor persons seeking state office but elected from districts. Finally, we *exclude* from this tabulation persons seeking elected judgeships. Judicial elections are peculiar, however, and do not warrant inclusion here. This approach underpays the overall impact of blacks in state policy decision making but highlights electoral issues.

3. The results of our investigation so far suggest a larger universe of attempts that will weigh on any interpretation about black politics today. While we think it important to classify these campaigns with respect to some scale of import, such classification would require a refined local analysis not available at this point. We can report wide variation in these campaigns. Wilder, for example, has been a serious politician from the start. Hastings' 1990 race in Florida, on the other hand, was hardly credible coming, as it did, after he had been impeached from the federal judiciary. Yet in some elections where black candidates had limited support, mainly from voters of their own races, these candidates were actually pivotal in the outcome. King's long-shot campaign was the 1970 Georgia Democratic primary for governor (an attempt supported by Andrew Young). The example is not unimportant as the eventual winner was Jimmy Carter. Bell's campaign in the 1971 Louisiana governor's election made the difference in one of that state's most important elections. After losing, Bell returned to quiet community organizing work, but Edwin Edwards, the victor, became that state's first Catholic governor and its most dominant political personality in the last quarter of a century. Finally, there is a class of protest elections, mainly around the Mississippi Freedom Democratic Party (MFDP), where candidates campaigned without the standard expectation of victory. Protest elections, too, can evolve to have significant impact on the larger system as we see it, again, in Mississippi, in the several campaigns of Charles Evers. The importance of these election attempts will acquire added significance in the 1990 round of voting rights litigation due to the impact of such elections on determining the presence of racial bloc voting.

4. The status quo was twofold: the mayoral regimes elected in the central cities, and the local offices—primarily in the south and southwest—and the mayoral regimes elected in reapportioned election districts created under the federal Voting Rights Act. Abigail Thernstrom's *Whose Votes Count? Affirmative Action and Minority Voting Rights* (Cambridge: Harvard University Press, 1987)

is a useful discussion of the extension of racial constituencies in the voting rights area. However, her hysteria about affirmative action results in a pessimism wherein representation itself is cast as something innocent of empowerment. For a survey of the legal and policy concerns see Laughlin McDonald, "The Quiet Revolution in Minority Voting Rights," *Vanderbilt Law Review* 42 (5): 1249–1297 and Frank Parker, *Black Votes Count: Political Empowerment in Mississippi after 1965* (Chapel Hill: The University of North Carolina, 1990). For a discussion of voting rights and broader community empowerment see Margaret Edds, *Free at Last: What Happened When Civil Rights Came to Southern Politics* (Bethesda, MD: Adler and Adler, 1987), and Alex Willingham, "Voting Rights and Community Empowerment: Political Struggle in the Georgia Black Belt," in *Communities in Economic Crisis: Appalachia and the South,* eds. John Gaventa, Barbara Allen Smith, and Alex Willingham (Philadelphia: Temple University Press, 1990).

5. About half the African-Americans in the United States live in the 11 southern states of the old Confederacy. Other campaign attempts in the South are C. B. King (Georgia, 1970), Samuel Bell (Louisiana, 1971), and Charles Evers (Mississippi, 1971, 1983). Aaron Henry ran a protest campaign for Mississippi governor in 1963.

6. Adolph Reed, Jr., *The Jesse Jackson Phenomenon* (New Haven, CT: Yale University Press, 1986); Jeffrey Prager, "American Political Culture and the Meaning of Race," *Ethnic and Racial Studies* 10(1): 62–81; Barbara J. Fields, "Ideology and Race in American History," in *Region, Race, and Reconstruction: Essays in Honor of C. Vann Woodward,* eds. J. Morgan Kousser and James M. McPherson (New York: Oxford, 1982), 143–177. Our concern is reflected in events such as the 1988 Bush presidential campaign's use of the Willie Horton incident, and subsequent efforts in local elections to reorient campaign discussions to take advantage of racial bigotry. *Cf.* Dan Carter, "Two Faces of Southern Populism," *New York Times* (10 November 1990).

7. Reed, *The Jesse Jackson Phenomenon. Cf.* Andrew Young, "Why I Support Jimmy Carter," *Nation* (3 April 1976), 397–398; "Carter's Only Campaign Debt," *Time* (26 July 1976); Carl Gardner, *Andrew Young: A Biography* (New York: Drake, 1978) and James Haskins, *A Man with a Mission* (New York: Lothrop, 1979); Stuart Eizenstat and William Barutio, *Andrew Young: The Path to History* (Atlanta: Voter Education Project, 1973); H. E. Newsum and Olayiwola Abegrunin, *United States Foreign Policy Towards Southern Africa: Andrew Young and Beyond* (New York: St. Martin's Press, 1987); "Andrew Young Comments on Running for U.S. Senator from Georgia," *Los Angeles Times* (15 September 1979); Milton Coleman, "Andrew Young Seeks to Expand Role as a National Black Spokesman," *Washington Post* (23 August 1979).

8. Laughlin McDonald, "The Impact of the Voting Rights Act in Georgia," Proceedings, Conference on the Impact of the Voting Rights Act, Rice University, Houston, Texas (11 May 1990).

9. See chapters devoted to Georgia in various works, including V. O. Key, Jr., *Southern Politics in State and Nation* (New York: A. A. Knopf, 1949); Robert Sherril, *Gothic Politics in the Deep South: Stars of the New Confederacy* (New York: Grossman Publishers, 1968); Neal R. Pierce, *The Deep South States of America: People, Politics, and Power in the Seven Deep South States* (New York: W. W. Norton, 1974); Jack Bass and Walter DeVries, *The Transformation*

of Southern Politics: Social Change and Political Consequence Since 1945 (New York: Basic Books, 1976); Robert H. Swansbrough and David M. Brodsky, eds., *The South's New Politics: Realignment and Dealignment* (Columbia: The University of South Carolina Press, 1988); Alexander P. Lamis, *The Two-Party South* expanded ed., (New York: Oxford, 1988); James F. Lea, ed. *Contemporary Southern Politics* (Baton Rouge, LA: Louisiana State University Press, 1988).

10. *King* v. *Chapman* 62 F. Supp. 639 (1945).

11. *Gray* v. *Sanders* 372 U.S. 368 (18 March 1963).

12. Suspended by the Voting Rights Act, 1965, as amended.

13. *Wesberry* v. *Sanders* 376 U.S. 1 (1964).

14. *Julian Bond* v. *Sloppy Floyd* 385 U.S. 116 (1966).

15. *Busbee* v. *Smith* 549 F. Supp. 494 (1982).

16. *George Vereen* v. *Ben Hill County, Brooks* v. *State Board of Elections, NAACP* v. *Holder,* and *United States* v. *Georgia.*

17. The state growth estimates are from Max Cleland, Georgia's secretary of state, quoted in the *San Francisco Examiner* (1 January 1989). See "Metropolitan Statistical Areas," Table 36, in *Statistical Abstract of the United States* (Washington, D.C.: U.S. Department of Commerce, Bureau of the Census, 1990), 29–31 and "Spread of AIDS in Rural Areas Testing Georgia," *Atlanta Constitution* (18 April 1990).

18. The classic case is Atlanta and the classic study is Floyd Hunter, *Community Power: A Study of Decision Makers* (Chapel Hill: University of North Carolina Press, 1953). See discussion of the role of the black vote generally in Earl Black and Merle Black, *Politics and Society in the South* (Cambridge: Harvard University Press, 1987).

19. *Black Elected Officials: A National Roster.*

20. Affirmative registration is discussed in Frances Fox Piven and Richard Cloward, *Why Americans Don't Vote* (New York: Pantheon, 1988).

21. See the survey in McDonald, "The Impact of the Voting Rights Act in Georgia," and discussion in Willingham, "Voting Rights and Community Empowerment."

22. The 1984 campaign by Robert Benham for the state appeals court is the exception. The 1984 and 1988 presidential primary campaigns by Jesse Jackson, while not involving state office, did entail a black candidate vying before the Georgia state constituency.

23. "Non-Voter Study '88–'89" (Washington, D.C.: Committee for the Study of the American Electorate, 1988).

24. On the problem of mobilizing in one black majority county see discussion in Willingham, "Voting Rights and Community Empowerment."

25. Young was not involved in these scandals. His most prominent brush with an ethics problem occurred during his congressional years when he was involved with Michael Thevis, a convicted felon, referred to in the Atlanta newspapers as a dealer in pornography. See Howell Rained, "A Pornographer's Saga: Wealth, Disrepute, Jail and Now Escape," *New York Times* (15 May 1978) for a sketch of their relationship. In some instances (the Bond affair) Young played the role of minister/advisor. His public statements on the issue are sparse, but he considers attacks on minority officials to be part of the partisan game and calls for scrupulous conduct. See his comments in Yolanda W. Woodlee, "Expect Scrutiny, Blacks Told," *Detroit News* (22 May 1990). Formal charges

brought against these officials often resulted from "sting" operations and/or from practices typically engaged in by white officials. Such practices parallel charges brought at the national level and directed at other highly visible minority officials and some white officials whose base of support contains significant minority voters. All of the charges involved federal investigations under Republican administrations in the 1980–1990 period. An examination of this action as a racial conspiracy is Mary R. Sawyer, *The Dilemma of Black Politics: A Report on Harassment of Black Elected Officials* (National Association of Human Rights Workers, 1977) and *Harassment of Black Elected Officials: Ten Years Later* (Washington, D.C.: Voter Education and Registration Action, Inc., 1987).

26. Peter Applebome, "Bombings Echo Past, but Experts Hear Different Undertones," *New York Times* (26 December 1989).
27. A. L. May, "Campaign Could Wake up Voters, Shape Debate," *Atlanta Journal-Constitution* (1 January 1990), p. A-1.
28. The practice in Georgia is to appoint judges to vacant offices before the election as a form of official endorsement to potential candidates. Usually this is enough to slate a candidate and discourage opponents, but both Benham and Cooper drew opposition.
29. Jeanne Cummings, "Female Lawmakers Shut out of Leadership Posts," *Atlanta Journal-Constitution* (20 January 1991), p. C-1
30. Review coverage in A. L. May, "Candidates Dodging Gun Issue," *Atlanta Journal-Constitution* (5 August 1989), and Dick Williams, "Democrats' Race is Barnes, Miller Show," *Atlanta Constitution* (24 October 1989) for estimates of the issue by local journalists.
31. *Ibid.*
32. Deborah Scroggins, "Candidates Avoiding Abortion Issue, Coming Out Against Drugs, Pollution," *Atlanta Journal-Constitution* (1 January 1990), p. A-1.
33. A. L. May, "Breaking Ground: Young Getting Message Heard in South Georgia," *Atlanta Journal-Constitution* (11 February 1990), p. C-1.
34. A. L. May and Peter Mantius, "Candidates Let Charges Fly in Final T.V. Debate," *Atlanta Constitution* (August 1990), p. A-1.
35. See comments to Georgia Legislative Black Caucus reported in Alma E. Hill, "Young Makes Candidacy All but Official," *Atlanta Constitution* (16 March 1989). As noted, Benham and Cooper, the black candidates for judge, were slated following the usual practice in judicial elections.
36. Ronald Smothers, "Andrew Young Going Afield for Governor," *New York Times* (26 November 1989).
37. See discussion in Black and Black, *Politics and Society.*
38. In other elections during 1990, this effort was more successful and "quota" and "affirmative action" became effective code words. See Dan Carter, "Two Faces of Southern Populism."
39. A. L. May, "Poll Shows Young in Solid Position for Campaign," *Atlanta Journal-Constitution* (12 November 1990), p. A-1.
40. A. L. May, "Race Closer as Young, Miller Slip," *Atlanta Journal-Constitution* (29 April 1990), p. A-1.
41. *Ibid.*
42. Ron Taylor, "Crime Goes on an Ugly Mean Streak," *Atlanta Journal-Constitution* (4 April 1990), p. A-1.

43. David K. Secrest, "Maddox's Slim Showing Reflects Big Change in Politics of Race" (29 April 1990) p. A-14.
44. *Ibid.*
45. May, "Race Closer as Young, Miller Slip."
46. A. L. May, "Miller Gains Steam in Race Against Young," *Atlanta Journal-Constitution* (17 June 1990), p. A-1.
47. *Ibid.*
48. Campaign Digest. "How Respondents View Young, Jackson," *Atlanta Journal-Constitution* (26 June 1990), p. D-3.
49. May "Miller Gains Steam."
50. A. L. May, "Miller Has 6-Point Lead Over Young," *Atlanta Constitution* (14 July 1990), p. A-1.
51. Jeanne Cummings and A. L. May, "Young Suggests Rule: $1 Million Limit on Ads," *Atlanta Constitution* (18 April 1990), p. C-3.
52. The U.S. Department of Justice approved Georgia campaign finance laws in October 1990.
53. David Secrest and Peter Mantius, "Young War Chest Rivals Miller," *Atlanta Journal-Constitution* (9 June 1990), p. D-1.
54. Peter Mantius and David Secrest, "What Do the Sugar Daddies Get for Their Money?" *Atlanta Journal-Constitution* (27 May 1990), p. D-1.
55. Jeanne Cummings, "Candidates for Governor to Pour Money into Major Markets," *Atlanta Constitution* (23 May 1990), p. A-1.
56. *Ibid.*
57. Deborah Scroggins, "Few Ga. Voters Changed Minds," *Atlanta Constitution* (7 November 1990), p. A-6.
58. Because of the majority vote requirement, Young was eligible for a second runoff election where he came in second to Miller, who became the nominee. Miller was elected Georgia governor in the November general election.
59. Fowler got 50.3 percent of the vote, avoiding a runoff, with 315,000 votes.
60. The Hungry Club speech is cited in Alma E. Hill, "Andrew Young Says Georgia Is Ready for a Black Governor," *Atlanta Constitution* (23 October 1989). Elsewhere we examine the origins of "public service capitalism" in the civil rights movement and review its place in Young's United Nations days and urban mayor periods.
61. See the ranking of congressional votes in Michael Barone, Grant Ujifusa, and Douglas Matthews, *Almanac of American Politics, 1976* (New York: E. P. Dutton, 1977).

Chapter
9

Gantt Versus Helms

Deracialization Confronts Southern Traditionalism

Zaphon Wilson

INTRODUCTION

The 1989 elections sparked the notion of deracialization among analysts and observers as a way of characterizing a more mainstream, more deliberately racial crossover appeal by black candidates. As such, deracialization began as a process through which black candidates addressed political agendas that reflected a newfound set of political priorities that focused on nonracial concerns designed, in part, to disarm an alienated white electorate.

The 1990 United States Senate campaign in North Carolina was no different. This campaign more than any other in the state was the focus of newfound political priorities by black candidate Harvey Gantt. These new political priorities were formed into a political agenda based on non-racial issues and concerns that viewed modernizing the economy and diversifying the electorate as its capstones for greater levels of government commitment to reform.

Entering this historic United States Senate campaign as a decided underdog, Harvey Gantt attempted to build a coalition of blacks, women, labor, and liberals in the Democratic party in order to unseat incumbent Republican Senator Jesse Helms. The timing for an upset victory by Gantt seemed perfect. He had ridden a tide of popularity as Charlotte, North Carolina's, first black and arguably its best mayor. This tide of popularity also resulted in a new optimism by blacks in North Carolina who also vicariously enjoyed Douglas Wilder's gubernatorial victory in Virginia, as well as the successes of other black candidates in the South in 1990.

The purpose of this study is to examine Harvey Gantt's efforts to become the first black candidate to win a statewide election in North Carolina's history. A case study approach will be used in this examination of Gantt's ascendancy utilizing various newspaper accounts, campaign literature, and poll data to describe Gantt's overall strategy in running the campaign.

THE PERSISTENCE OF TRADITIONALISM IN NORTH CAROLINA POLITICS

As a conservative state, North Carolina has a tradition of favoring conservative candidates. Since Jesse Helms' initial victory for the United States Senate in 1972, Republican conservatism has grown in popularity at almost every level of government. Therefore, the Gantt versus Helms Senate contest presented a unique confrontation between two competing ideologies in the state.

These two competing frames of reference concern important political questions regarding just what roles government should or should not play in addressing the problems of the economy, industrialization, agriculture, and social-economic redistribution. In *Tar Heel Politics,* Paul Luebke places these competing ideologies into perspective by suggesting that traditionalist and modernizer ideals help to define the political reality in North Carolina.[1]

Modernizers, according to Luebke, favor growth in the state's economy as well as economic diversity. In this respect, modernizer politicians encourage renewed efforts in improving education at all levels in the state. Government, according to this ideal, must play a central role in education by increasing state expenditures to public schools as well as colleges and universities. Modernizer politicians also seek to accommodate blacks, women, and labor unions.[2] Consequently, better educational opportunities result in a more diversified labor force that can adapt to the changing demands of a modern, high technology market.[3] The end result, according to modernizers, would be a diversified economy that would enhance personal and corporate achievement.

Modernizer politicians argue that government must play an active role in achieving this ideal state because government has a responsibility to provide an adequate infrastructure through which economic growth can take place.[4]

Harvey Gantt fits into the modernizer category. As a trained architect, Gantt presided over one of the most rapid periods of growth in Charlotte, North Carolina—the state's Queen City. He was elected to the Charlotte City Council three times and served as mayor pro tem for one term. Gantt was later elected twice as mayor of the city which has a 75 percent white population.[5]

The traditionalist ideal on the other hand, differs markedly from modernizer interests. Traditionalists are skeptical of future economic change while modernists encourage change. The traditionalist view holds that economic change has the potential to lead to social disruption and economic competition.[6] Traditionalists see merit in maintaining the status quo and favor low-wage industries like textiles, agriculture, and manufacturing rather than service-oriented high technology industries.[7] High technology industries are not favored by this ideal because it (they) would bring large numbers of outsiders into the state thereby disrupting the harmony of the community. Another reason why traditionalists do not favor high technology industries is because such industries would compete with the existing low-wage industries in the state.[8]

The traditionalist ideal also differs from modernizer ideals in regard to the role of religion. Modernizers represent every religious denomination including Catholicism, Judaism, Episcopalianism, and Hinduism. Traditionalists on the other hand, base their faith on fundamentalist Protestantism. This basis for religious conviction provides traditionalists with a framework based on deference. Traditionalists feel that social deference is important in all walks of life. Therefore, wives defer to husbands, poor people defer to wealthier ones, and political deference is always displayed to respected public officials.[9] In this regard, traditionalists were forced to accept integration, which contributed to their feeling that blacks and women have gained unfair advantage as a result of affirmative action and equal opportunity laws.[10] Therefore, traditionalists feel that blacks should go only as far as whites will tolerate and blacks should never challenge white patriarchal authority.

By the same token, traditionalists are opposed to government intervention because it results in higher taxes (which traditionalists oppose) and waste.

Jesse Helms falls squarely on the side of the traditionalist ideology and may also be its strongest defender in North Carolina politics. This is not surprising because Helms was reared in a modest family in Monroe, North Carolina, a Charlotte bedroom community. Jesse Helms did not run for any public office before 1972. Prior to that period Helms served in his father-in-law's radio station as an editorialist for WRAL in Raleigh, North Carolina. This media format provided Helms with a loyal audience throughout eastern North Carolina. From this soapbox, Helms editorialized against communist expansion, the civil rights movement, hippies, and anti-Vietnam activists.[11]

Helms championed the causes of a rural electorate fixed to agriculture, religion, and economic conservatism. As a result of this following, Helms was encouraged to run for the United States Senate in 1972.[12]

These two competing ideals, modernization and traditionalism, stand in stark contrast to each other and provide a useful framework for understanding North Carolina politics.

THE HARVEY GANTT BURDEN

Harvey Gantt was well aware of his uphill battle in this election. However, after winning the Democratic party nomination to face Helms in the general election, there appeared to be quite a bit of momentum across the state for Gantt. This momentum was in part sustained by the fact that Gantt represented a serious challenge and could become the first black person to win a statewide election in North Carolina's history.[13]

In order to overcome the burdens of race and a liberal philosophy of government, Gantt felt that a coalition of blacks, women, labor, and progressives could overcome problems of race. Therefore, Gantt portrayed himself as a "New Deal–New South" Senate candidate. The "New Deal" aspect reflected Gantt's faith in government. As a "New Deal" Democrat, Gantt tied himself ideologically to Franklin D. Roosevelt and embraced the New Deal policies of Roosevelt's era as a fitting role for government.[14] The "New South" reflected Gantt's notions of the social progress that the region had experienced since the civil rights movement and the Voting Rights Act of 1965. The "New South" is a South of equal opportunity, economic expansion, and development. In this context, race was an issue that had been resolved and was not an important part of the overall problem.

Nonetheless, Gantt had to disarm the electorate of any misconceptions they might have held against him because of his race in particular, but also about his liberalism in general.

Therefore, Gantt felt that he had to present a nonthreatening image to the white electorate while also reinforcing democratic ideals to the black electorate. This dilemma was Gantt's main concern toward deracializing his campaign. In this vein, Gantt shied away from racial problems by casting them in the rhetoric of progressive change for the state.

Gantt's burden of race was particularly important in a state where so few black candidates win elections at any level of government, much less statewide. For example, in 1968, only nine blacks served as mayor or council members in the state. The data in Table 9.1 illustrate the small numbers of black officials in the state.

As Table 9.1 illustrates, black elected officials have greater success in local elections. In the categories of mayor/city council members, black official representation increased from 1968 and each period thereafter culminating with 279 in 1989. However, between 1983 and 1989, substantial decreases occurred in the election of county commissioners. By 1989, this number of county commissioners increased to 42. There are a total of 300 county commissioners in the state who represent 100 counties. Most commissioners are elected at-large with only 8 commissioners in the state being elected by district.[15]

Between 1983 and 1985, school board membership for blacks decreased by 50 percent, but by 1989, this number increased by 16 for a total

Table 9.1   BLACK ELECTED OFFICIALS IN NORTH CAROLINA

Office	1968	1971	1974	1983	1985	1989
Mayor/City Council	9	63	112	151	162	279
County Commission	0	3	13	35	31	42
School Board	1	12	29	123	66	82
Sheriffs	0	0	2	4	2	4
Legislators	0	2	3	12	13	15
Judges/Trial Appellate	0	2	0	15	9	21
Council of State*	0	0	0	0	0	0
Congress	0	0	0	0	0	0

*Council of State refers to offices that require a statewide election such as: Governor, Lt. Governor, Secretary of Agriculture, Insurance Commissioner, Secretary of State, Attorney General, Secretary of Labor, Superintendent of Public Instruction, State Auditor. Other members are appointed by the Governor.

Source: U.S. Civil Rights Commission, *The Voting Rights Act: Ten Years After;* North Carolina Association of County Commissioners; North Carolina Local Government Advocacy Commission; North Carolina School Board Association; Voter Education Project, Atlanta, GA; Joint Center for Political Studies, Washington, D.C. 1985 and 1989 figures compiled from *Focus,* a Joint Center publication.

of 82 black school board members in the state. This increase in the number of black school board members must be weighed against the fact that the state has 950 elected board members who serve 140 school districts in the state's 100 county districts and 40 city districts.[16]

Out of the state's 100 sheriffs, 4 are black and were elected in counties with large black populations, including Wake, New Hanover, Northampton, and Warren Counties. Beside mayor/city council members, school board members, and county commission members, the most dramatic increase in black elected officials was in the category of judges/trial appellate. This category went from 9 in 1985 to 21 in 1989. From this total, one judge, Henry E. Frye, serves as an associate justice for the state supreme court. The other judgeships include ten superior court judges, two court of appeals judges, and eight district court judges.[17]

Between 1983 and 1989, the number of black legislators increased slightly with three blacks being elected to the general assembly. This new addition brought the total to 15 blacks and in January 1991, Dan Blue of Wake County became the state's first black speaker of the house.

By contrast no black served on the council of state which requires either a statewide election or appointment by the governor. This trend is also evident in the United States Congress, even though H. M. "Micky" Michaux ran in 1982 from the Second Congressional District, forced a second primary runoff with Tim Valentine, and narrowly missed the nomination from the Democratic party. Following Michaux's lead in 1984 came Kenneth Spaulding in the Second Congressional District; however, he was defeated in the Democratic primary by incumbent Tim Valentine.

Explanations for the failure of black candidates to win abound. However in the mid- to late 1980s when black representation reflected dramatic declines, the primary explanation could only be political reactionism within the electorate. Black voters tended to vote for black candidates while white voters supported white candidates with very little racial crossover voting.

Black candidates, therefore, continued to struggle with image problems. They were either too liberal or lacked government experience. Harvey Gantt was accused of both. Linda Williams points out that

> [b]lack political candidates still suffer from negative stereotypes and white bloc voting. Not only do whites perceive blacks as less capable of achieving goals, less likely to possess important personal attributes, and less qualified . . . but a majority of whites also agree that most whites vote on the basis of race rather than qualifications.[18]

BUILDING THE GANTT COALITION

Facing the reality that Williams aptly describes, the Gantt campaign engaged in a twofold approach to the election. One aspect of the campaign utilized a county tour approach that required extensive travel throughout the state.

Gantt, in an old-fashioned way, campaigned tirelessly throughout every rural town, major city, and county of the state preaching his view of a revitalized economy brought forth by a revitalized government.[19] During these stops, Gantt attempted to build upon his coalition by arguing for programs designed to enhance the quality of life for women, the young, and the very old. In order to solidify the basis of this coalition, Gantt covered topics on education, abortion rights, and higher levels of government funding for child care in the state. These services could be funded by redirecting the so-called peace dividend to domestic funding, while also establishing higher taxes for the wealthy.[20]

The second aspect of Gantt's approach was a systematic attack on Jesse Helms' Senate record. Through a comprehensive series of television commercials, Gantt was able to reach the people of the state with ads that depicted Helms as a defender of large business interests, often at the expense of the poor. These ads also attacked Helms' lack of support for education.

These challenges to the Helms record coupled with the county tour approach personalized the campaign and appeared to benefit Gantt's efforts toward coalition building. Surveys taken during the early stages of the campaign showed the contest as a dead heat between the candidates. As early as June 1990, Gantt was leading in the campaign by 4 percentage points in the polls at 44 percent to Helms' 40 percent.[21] The telling story in the early stages of the campaign was the extremely high number of undecided voters. Sixteen percent of those surveyed in June 1990 were undecided in their support for either candidate. Obviously, the undecided voter played an instrumental role in the outcome of the race.

By September 1990, just three months later, the polls showed a clear shift in the electorate toward Jesse Helms. Helms picked up 7 percentage points during this period that resulted in narrowing the gap 45 percent to Gantt's 46 percent.[22] By the same token, 9 percent of those surveyed in September were undecided.[23]

A breakdown of the poll data shows that Gantt had a 5 percentage-point edge over Helms among female voters with 48 percent compared to Helms' 43 percent support from this group, with 9 percent being undecided.

Gantt spokeswoman Susan Jetton argued that the support of women was vital for the Gantt campaign. Jetton argued:

> We want women to know we need their help . . . not only because it's important to us, but (because) we believe it's important to them. Absolutely, there's no question but that Mr. Helms' record is one of voting against women, whether it be on the subject of choice or education or child care or working women.[24]

Issues of pro-choice and women's rights appear to have been clouded by the dictates of Protestant fundamentalism in the state. As a Protestant stronghold, many North Carolinians appear to be guided by the Biblical dictates on the position of women vis-à-vis men. Therefore women by this definition play a subordinate role to men in every aspect of life. This is particularly important because of the large numbers of women who are employed in low-wage industrial jobs in the state.

Men also tended to favor Helms over Gantt. Fifty percent of the men surveyed favored Helms compared to 41 percent favoring Gantt.[25] By October 1990, only 35 percent of white males favored Gantt compared to 65 percent favoring Helms.[26]

Although Gantt attempted to engage white males by reassuring them that his approach to business development would benefit them, white males could not be persuaded. Older white males just did not favor Gantt and felt that he was just too liberal on other issues for their taste.[27]

Regional breakdowns of the polling data also reveal interesting results. In eastern North Carolina, for example, Helms' support was seen as a predictable outcome. After all, this region is comprised primarily of farms and has always been a Helms stronghold. Ironically, Gantt led in the polls in this region by 12 percentage points over Helms at 52 percent compared to 40 percent for Helms.[28] This surprising lead is best explained by the fact that Helms did not campaign at all in the region. Therefore voters responded with a negative reaction to Helms for not taking the region seriously. Nevertheless, this early lead fueled the Gantt campaign in the region and resulted in an extra effort by Gantt to maintain this edge in eastern North Carolina.

Conversely, the Piedmont Region which includes Charlotte, Greensboro, and Winston-Salem was viewed as a Gantt stronghold. It was felt that the Piedmont area, with its diversified economy and regional universities as well as its sizable black population, would provide substantial support for Gantt. However, Gantt led in the Piedmont area by only 1 percentage point over Helms with a 46 percent advantage to Helms' 45 percent.[29] The closeness in the campaign in this region is best explained by the growth of the suburban communities in the region. The suburbs were largely white and conservative, resulting in a ground swell of support for Helms.

The Mountain Region of the state was overwhelmingly in favor of Helms 61 percent to Gantt's 29 percent. One explanation for this lop-sided distribution is the relatively small number of blacks living in the region.[30] This region nevertheless has always been conservative and Re-publican. Moreover, this region lags behind both of the other regions of the state economically, and its economy is based on furniture and textile manufacturing industries, with strong fundamental Protestantism as its moral base.

Racial breakdown of the polling data also illustrates the degree to which race still plays a dominant role in North Carolina politics. Borrow-ing from Linda Williams, the issue of race has been replaced in the South by issues of conservatism which directly affect political agendas. Blacks in this respect favor more liberal government policy while whites favor more conservative alternatives. As a result of this split in the ideological perspec-tives of the electorate, black candidates can expect little support from white voters.[31] In North Carolina this was indeed the case. Gantt received a favorable rating from 90 percent of black voters while Helms received 10 percent support ratings from blacks.[32] White voters tended to favor Helms by a 56 percent margin.[33]

These data are significant because Gantt needed at least 30 to 41 percent of the white votes and at least 90 percent of the black votes in order to win the election.

In the early stages of the campaign Gantt was in a dead heat in the election only if the undecided voter element were excluded. The size of the undecided vote coupled with the serious television attacks on Gantt by Helms led to a close race. The coalition of women, blacks, and progres-sives did not gel in the early stages of the campaign and even began to dissolve as the election grew near.

MEDIA COVERAGE OF THE CAMPAIGN

The mass media were clearly divided between Jesse Helms and Harvey Gantt. Eastern newspapers tended to favor Helms while Western newspa-pers from metropolitan areas favored Gantt. Each of the candidates, how-ever, relied heavily upon media coverage in their campaigns. And, both camps developed extensive media advertisements on radio, television, and area newspapers. As the campaign drew to an end, media coverage became the most important instrument for both candidates.

Table 9.2   GANTT-HELMS: RACING FOR DOLLARS

Total Raised	Gantt $4 million	Helms $11.2 million
Raised from July through September	3.2 million	3.4 million
Raised from PACs	466,561	588,235
Cash on Hand	788,768	100,147
Debts	-0-	192,414

Source: The Charlotte Observer, October 17, 1990.

Ironically, Gantt had more than enough financial backing to challenge Helms in the final weeks of the campaign. The data in Table 9.2, taken from *The Charlotte Observer*, highlight this point.

Although Helms had $7.2 million more than Gantt in campaign funds, both candidates raised about the same amount of money from July through September. Both candidates also received similar contributions from political action committees. The bulk of Gantt's contributions came from individual donations across the nation. These contributors included celebrities with a majority of Gantt's contributions coming from labor unions and human rights groups.[34]

Almost one-half of Gantt's money was spent on television advertisements ($1.4 million). He also spent more than $100,000 on telephone fund-raising and $72,500 on political polling.[35] Television provided the most useful vehicle for each candidate and proved to be the deciding factor in the campaign.

The central theme running throughout Gantt's commercials was the failure of Jesse Helms to represent the needs of North Carolina's poor people in the United States Senate.

The following excerpt from the Gantt-Helms television campaign illustrates this point.

Gantt Challenges Helms' Congressional Voting Record
Democratic challenger Harvey Gantt says Sen. Jesse Helms, R-N.C, often votes against legislation that could help North Carolina in areas where it ranks poorly:

PROBLEM: North Carolina's rate of 11.5 deaths per 1,000 births is 4th highest in the country.
VOTE: Increase by $31 million the Women, Infants and Children food program for poor women and their children by cutting other programs in agriculture bill by 0.7%. July 1988. Passed 87–4. Helms: No.
HELMS SAYS the program already was getting a $125 million increase.

PROBLEM: N.C. high school students taking the SAT this year had an average score of 841 out of 1,600—49th in the country.
VOTE: Allocate $7.5 billion to elementary and secondary schools to help

disadvantaged children and to states for block grants. December 1987. Passed 97–1. Helms: No.
HELMS SAYS education is a state and local responsibility.

PROBLEM: From 1979 to 1990, 30,000 N.C. farms were abandoned, more than in any other state.
VOTE: Revise and extend program for price supports, exports, soil conservation, farm credit, agriculture research and food assistance for poor people. July 1990. Passed 70–21. Helms: No.
HELMS SAYS the best farm bill would be a balanced budget, which would lower interest rates for farmers.

PROBLEM: The 1980 census found that North Carolina had more dwellings without public sewers or septic tanks—99,400—than every state but one. About 70 N.C. towns and cities have no more sewage treatment capacity.
VOTE: Authorize $18 billion to state and local governments to build sewage treatment plants. January 1987. Passed 93–6. Helms: No.
HELMS SAYS he supported then-President Ronald Reagan's $12 billion version of the bill, which failed.

PROBLEM: North Carolina has four metro areas that exceed national standards for ozone and mountain areas threatened by acid rain.
VOTE: Clean Air Act includes new limits on tail pipe emissions of cars and light trucks, as well as acid-rain controls requiring scrubbers and coal-burning utility plants. April 1990. Passed 89–11. Helms: No.
HELMS SAYS the act is too expensive for industry and will result in the loss of thousands of jobs.[36]

As the preceding excerpt clearly demonstrates, North Carolina has one of the nation's highest infant mortality rates, one of the nation's lowest Standard Achievement Test averages, and one of the nation's poorest records on environmental quality. In each category, however, Helms argued against expanding programs in order to hold down taxes and suggested that concerns raised by Gantt throughout the campaign were best addressed at the state and local government levels.

Helms countered Gantt's attacks on him by depicting Gantt as a big government liberal with "extremely different values," and called upon the electorate to return to good old-fashioned conservative North Carolina values.[37] Obviously, the traditional values Helms called for were designed to incite the white electorate to maintain the state's status quo of conservative interests. Helms' response to Gantt revolved around Gantt's lack of experience and his lack of a voting record.

Helms on Television

The ad opens by saying that Gantt has been distorting Helms' record on education. It then says:

> Look at the facts. The official Congressional Record shows Senator Helms sponsored competency tests for teachers to raise standards and quality; increase school lunch funds by cutting foreign aid; $900 million to make our schools drug free.

And on February 20, Senator Helms voted for the dropout-prevention program—the one Gantt implies Helms didn't support.

Harvey Gantt's record on education: None.[38]

Competency testing for teachers was one of Helms' amendments that was tabled in February 1990. Moreover, Helms voted ten times in the 1980s to decrease funding for school lunch programs.[39]

Gantt's commercials continued to link Helms with big oil interests and accused Helms of being out of touch with the real issues facing the state.

Gantt on Television

What's more important? Protecting the big oil companies? Or fighting price gouging at the pump?

Harvey Gantt supports a law that would prosecute any oil company that tries to make a fast buck in a national crisis—up to five years in jail and a half-million dollars fine.

But Jesse Helms has refused to even criticize the oil companies. No surprise: They're bankrolling his campaign. They've given him almost $100,000 in campaign contributions.

We've had enough of Jesse Helms' priorities.

Harvey Gantt for Senate. Because protecting North Carolina, not oil companies, is what really matters.[40]

Linking Helms to big business interests was underscored with presenting a broad spectrum of North Carolinians for Gantt. Gantt always used middle-class people who were mostly white and female in his commercials. These individuals spoke on behalf of Gantt, supporting his views on pro-choice and the environment. Gantt never directly addressed the issue of race or affirmative action in his campaign, except to deny his support for them. Rather than using issues of affirmative action, Gantt relied on strategic issues developed throughout the campaign on education, pro-choice, and economic development in order to solidify a common framework of interests for his coalition.

These interests and the groups that supported them provided Jesse Helms with cannon fodder to attack the Gantt campaign as a campaign run by communists, homosexuals, lesbians, and organized labor. Helms argued in one interview that:

[h]e (Gantt) is being run by the NARAL (National Abortion Rights Action League) and homosexuals, the labor unions, people like that . . . I know that his campaign is being run by others . . . He is going around saying anything these advisors are telling him to say. He is far worse than Jim Hunt ever was. The liberals—people for the American Way, and the American Civil Liberties Union—they always misrepresent the conservative and his position. And that is exactly what Mr. Gantt is doing. Or Mr. Gantt's campaign.[41]

Jesse Helms' obvious defensiveness in the campaign rested on the fact that he could not link Gantt to the Democratic machinery of Ron Brown, Jesse Jackson, and the Democratic party elite. Gantt made a conscious effort not to invite black liberals into his campaign, especially Jesse Jackson.

In essence, the Gantt campaign developed a series of television commercials that depicted him in nonracial and nonthreatening terms. This strategy resulted in favorability ratings for Gantt by likely voters in the areas of education (51 percent) and law and order issues (43 percent), even though Gantt was opposed to the death penalty.[42]

These results were encouraging to the Gantt camp and provided a lift going into the final week of the campaign.

With just one week remaining in the election the Jesse Helms camp aired its most effective commercial in the campaign. The commercial showed a white male dressed in work clothing seated behind a desk. This unidentified individual was in the process of opening a letter of employment rejection. The letter was smeared with red, black, and green ink across the bottom. In a provocative commentary, a voice booms out over the television saying that the white male applicant was the most qualified applicant, but due to the company's affirmative action policy a minority candidate was offered the job. The applicant is then heard saying that he really needed this job. At this point the commentator says that Harvey Gantt supports Ted Kennedy's quota bill.[43]

This commercial more than any other addressed the issue of racism in the campaign. Helms played on the fears of white working-class voters in an area that they fear the most, economic competition from black workers. Moreover, President George Bush had just vetoed the 1990 Civil Rights Bill by arguing that it promoted quotas.

The Gantt campaign was caught off guard and could not adequately respond to this commercial. In short order, Gantt was back to square one. Race had proven to be the most effective weapon for Helms in a campaign that played on concerns for traditional society grounded in the preservation of old South values and racist sentiments.

THE ELECTION RESULTS

The 1990 Senate campaign between Harvey Gantt and Jesse Helms was a classic confrontation of classical conservatism against liberalism. This off-year election was met with enthusiasm in the state and across the nation. It resulted in the largest number of voters in the state's history going to the polls in an off-year election. A total of 2,054,909 North Carolinians voted. From this total Jesse Helms received 1,080,208 votes (53 percent) to Harvey Gantt's 974,701 votes (47 percent).[44]

Jesse Helms received 478,671 votes (55 percent) in rural areas compared to Gantt's 392,336 votes (45 percent). A remarkable turnout of 59.9 percent of rural voters voted in this election.[45]

Gantt faired a little better in large urban areas than Helms. In these areas, Gantt received 334,341 votes (56 percent) compared to Helms'

266,215 votes (44 percent). Urban areas also experienced a larger than average turnout with 62.6 percent of large urban dwellers voting.[46] Again the substantial numbers of suburban voters tended to vote for Helms.

In the category of "Other Urban Areas" in the state, Helms outpolled Gantt 335,322 votes (57 percent) to Gantt's 248,024 votes (43 percent).[47] Sixty-two percent of "Other Urban Area" voters voted in the election.

The final statewide tally showed that Helms' margin of victory was 105,507 votes with an overall voter turnout in the state of 61.4 percent.[48]

Gantt's efforts toward building a coalition of young voters, women, and progressives was lost in the backlash of more conservative voters going out to vote. Gantt needed at least 40 percent of the white vote to win; however, Gantt received only 35 percent of that vote. White voters were just not disposed to vote for Gantt. The data in Table 9.3 highlight voter turnout by race.

Table 9.3 clearly illustrates the degree to which racial bloc voting took place. Even though Gantt received 35 percent of the white vote, Helms received 65 percent of that group's vote. Women were split equally between the two candidates, which suggests the degree to which issues of ideology and gender are split in the state. This group was pivotal to Gantt's success but showed no overwhelming support for him. Men also favored Helms over Gantt by a 16 percent margin. Gantt's political success could have been ensured had more women shifted to Gantt.

The 7 percent of black voters who favored Helms in the election are indeed an anomaly. There are those who voted for Helms simply because they felt Gantt had no chance of winning. And then, there are those who did not agree with Gantt's pro-choice position. Still yet, there are blacks throughout the state who agree with the conservative position Republicans hold regarding policy. Nevertheless, this subgroup of black voters for Helms represents a numerically small percentage of the vote. Conversely, the overall percentage of the black vote has been recorded at 22 percent of the total votes cast.[49]

The second element of Gantt's coalition included the young and older voter. This group split between Gantt and Helms with the younger voters going for Gantt while the older voters carried Helms. Table 9.4 illustrates the age distribution in the election.

As Table 9.4 shows, Gantt won only in the 18- to 29-year-old category.

Table 9.3   VOTER TURNOUT BY RACE: GANTT-HELMS SENATE CAMPAIGN

	Black Voter	White Voter	Male	Female
Harvey Gantt	93%	35%	42%	50%
Jesse Helms	7%	65%	58%	50%
Totals	100%	100%	100%	100%

Source: Compiled from The Charlotte Observer, November 8, 1990.

Table 9.4   AGE DISTRIBUTION IN GANTT-HELMS
            SENATE RACE

Age	Gantt	Helms	Total
18–29	54%	46%	100%
30–44	42%	58%	100%
45–59	42%	58%	100%
60+	41%	59%	100%

Source: Compiled from *The Charlotte Observer,* November 8,
1990.

This could bode well for the future of the state's politics in terms of progressive reform, but a full 46 percent of this age group favored Jesse Helms. By the same token, the 30- to 44-year-old category went decidedly with Helms, while the 45- to 59-year-old group also favored Helms over Gantt by 16 percentage points. The 60-plus category also favored Helms over Gantt by a 17-point edge. This suggests that Gantt did make some inroads into each category but not nearly enough to maintain a winning coalition.

Income and education categories also reveal an interesting set of outcomes in the election. As shown in Table 9.5, lower income groups favored Gantt while individuals with less than a high-school education favored Helms. The more prosperous voters also favored Helms, but college graduates, another important element in Gantt's coalition, favored Helms.

These results are perhaps the most interesting of the election returns. An interesting dynamic occurs in this table because people with lower levels of education overwhelmingly favored Jesse Helms 61 percent to Gantt's 39 percent. Conversely, people with lower incomes favored Gantt

Table 9.5   INCOME/EDUCATION RESULTS: GANTT-HELMS
            SENATE RACE

Income	Gantt	Helms	Total
Less than $15,000	60%	40%	100%
$15,000–$30,C00	48%	52%	100%
Over $30,000	42%	58%	100%
Education			
High School or less	39%	61%	100%
College Grad.	48%	52%	100%
Post Grad.	63%	37%	100%

Source: Compiled from *The Charlotte Observer,* November 8, 1990.

60 percent to Helms' 40 percent. Explanations for this dynamic surely revolve around issues of race and the manifestations of racism. Blacks represent a disproportionately high percentage of the state's poor people, but blacks also have comparable high school graduation rates with their white counterparts. As such, the white population enjoys a higher standard of living as reflected in average hourly wages and are fearful of losing ground economically to blacks.

Poor whites and blacks would appear to have more in common through the development of a poor people's coalition rather than interests focused on middle-class concerns. However, Gantt was never able to link the interests of the poor people of both races to his coalition. Jesse Helms on the other hand was clearly able to pit the interests of working-class blue-collar whites against the interests of blacks through interjecting race into the campaign. This linkage is also seen in the number of college graduates who favored Helms. Racial cleavage is evident in the higher educated groups in North Carolina who fear that their job security is somehow threatened by the expansion of educational opportunities for blacks, which is further fueled by their resentment of affirmative action programs.

On purely economic levels, job competition in North Carolina is much more prevalent in the low-wage industries. Consequently, Helms' effort to play on job security in the campaign rallied poorer white workers and reassured more prosperous whites that their status would not be threatened by federal government interference.

Jesse Helms was able to gain the support of the undecided voter in every region of the state as a result of the so-called Wilder factor.

The Wilder factor is best described as the reluctance of white voters to tell pollsters that they favored the white candidate over the black candidate. The size of the undecided voter group helps to establish this point. Rather than telling pollsters they supported Helms, white voters responded that they were undecided on a candidate.

Post-election polls reveal that Helms received 52.6 percent of the vote in the Eastern Region and 57 percent in the Mountain Region.[50] In the end, 17 of 20 small urban counties voted for Helms, who carried 71 of the state's 100 counties. Gantt, on the other hand, carried 29 counties including 3 small urban counties.[51] The cities carried by Gantt included Charlotte (his home city), Durham, Winston-Salem, Greensboro, and Raleigh.

Unlike Wilder in Virginia, Gantt was not able to win a narrow victory that a modernist crossover appeal could provide. His efforts fell short in the end due to a strong effort by Jesse Helms, an old pro at race baiting.

Gantt's approach toward the campaign provided for a strong appeal to nonracial issues designed to provide white crossover voting. Although Gantt did make some inroads into the white community he could not convince enough white voters with his appeal toward modernization. Consequently, suburban and rural areas overwhelmingly favored Helms and provided him with a substantial margin of victory.

CONCLUSION

The Harvey Gantt–Jesse Helms Senate campaign provides a classic study in ideological politics in the state. There are two competing frames of reference, modernism and traditionalism, which provide the framework of state politics. This political dichotomy establishes the issues to be discussed in politics, economics and social order. It also establishes racial relationships and issues of power.

This senate campaign also resulted in other important outcomes for the political future of the state. As an indirect result of Harvey Gantt's efforts, Dan Blue became the first black in the state's history to serve as speaker of the house in the North Carolina General Assembly. This was due to significantly larger numbers of Democrats voted into the general assembly on Gantt's political coattails.

Gantt's political future is not in doubt. He may still yet run for Congress, if the general assembly under Blue's leadership can carve a majority black or Democratic district in or around Charlotte. Or, Gantt may opt to follow Wilder's lead by running for one of the offices of state which includes lieutenant governor or maybe even governor.

Be that as it may, Harvey Gantt must realize by now that race and poverty are important political issues but difficult ones on which to build coalitions. These two realities are not separate and establish unique sets of interests that define politics in North Carolina. These interests also confine the state's politics to modernist or traditionalist ideals.

Modernists favor greater levels of economic development and diversification through high technology industries. Modernists argue that the future of the state rests on concerns for economic expansion rather than low-wage industry. In this respect, minorities would benefit economically and politically. Modernist politicians therefore rely on an agenda that addresses the environment, minorities, and greater levels of government involvement.

Traditionalists do not favor the type of economic expansionism advocated by modernists. They argue that more government involvement leads to higher taxes, more waste, and unnecessarily challenges the state's status quo. In this respect, the political interests of the poor are tied to the political interests of the wealthy.

As a traditional politician Jesse Helms was more than able to maintain his view of Republican conservatism in the state. The data throughout this chapter shows that Helms was able to solidify his position in the campaign by arguing for a revival of Old South values, grounded in religion, family, and limited government involvement.

Harvey Gantt could not overcome the deep convictions of traditionalism in the state's electorate. His efforts to build a multiracial coalition and his efforts to deracialize the campaign through nonracial issues of environmental protection, better educational opportunities, and economic development were not enough to change the perspective of the state's voters.

With these differing political interests based on economics, race, and religion, how can biracial political coalitions work?

Political coalitions are difficult to achieve and even more difficult to maintain under the best of circumstances. But beyond that, political coalitions must be based on perceived mutual interests and not popular issues. To this end, Gantt's efforts, however noble, could not redefine the state's political interests, nor its socio-cultural context.

NOTES

1. Paul Luebke, *Tar Heel Politics: Myths and Realities,* (Chapel Hill: University of North Carolina Press, 1990).
2. *Ibid.,* 20–22.
3. *Ibid.,* 18–20.
4. *Ibid.,* 19.
5. Harvey Gantt, Committee to Elect Harvey Gantt U.S. Senate, campaign literature, 700 East Stoulwall Street, Charlotte, NC 28202.
6. Luebke, *Tar Heel Politics.*
7. *Ibid.*
8. *Ibid.*
9. *Ibid.*
10. *Ibid.*
11. Taken from Jesse Helms' campaign literature *Conservative Digest* (January/ February 1990), 7–17.
12. Luebke, *Tar Heel Politics.*
13. Harvey Gantt was the second black person to run for a statewide office in North Carolina. The first was Howard Lee, who ran unsuccessfully for lieutenant governor in 1972.
14. Paul Collins, "Gantt Visits Surry, Wilkes, and Alleghany," *Winston-Salem Journal* (August 14, 1990), 1B.
15. *Black Elected Officials: A National Roster* (Washington, D.C.: Joint Center for Political Studies Press, 1989) 323.
16. *Ibid.,* 323.
17. *Ibid.,* 323; 336–337.
18. Linda F. Williams, "White/Black Perceptions of the Electability of Black Political Candidates," *National Political Science Review* (2), 62.
19. See, for example, Jim Morrill, "Senate Candidates Campaigns: A Study in Contrasts," *Charlotte Observer* (August 19, 1990), 1A, and Elizabeth Leland, "Campaign Teams Help Call Shots," *Charlotte Observer* (October 7, 1990), 1A.
20. Jim Morrill, "Gantt Is Betting on Peace Dividend to Help Pay for Spending Proposals," *Charlotte Observer* (September 9, 1990), 1A.
21. Jim Morrill, "Voters Split Over Gantt-Helms Race," *Charlotte Observer* (September 22, 1990), 1A.
22. *Ibid.*
23. *Ibid.*
24. Elizabeth Leland, "Female Voters," *Charlotte Observer* (September 17, 1990), 1A.
25. Morrill, "Voters Split Over Gantt-Helms Race."

26. *Ibid.*
27. *Ibid.*
28. *Ibid.*
29. *Ibid.*
30. *Ibid.*
31. See, for example, Linda T. Williams, "Blacks and the 1984 Elections in the South: Racial Polarization and Regional Congruence," in *Blacks In Southern Politics,* ed. Lawrence W. Moreland (New York: Praeger, 1986), 77–98.
32. John Drescher, "Undecided Voters Big Factor in Gantt-Helms Race," *Charlotte Observer* (September 23, 1990), 1A, and Jim Morrill, "Voters Split Over Gantt-Helms Race."
33. John Drescher, "Undecided Voters Big Factor in Gantt-Helms Race."
34. See, for example, Jim Morrill and John Drescher, "Gantt Raises Money at Helms' Pace" *Charlotte Observer* (October 17, 1990), 1A, and Ted Melnik and Jim Morrill, "Both Camps Bank on Helms' Image: National Stature a Money Magnet," *Charlotte Observer* (October 21, 1990), 1A.
35. Morrill and Drescher, "Gantt Raises Money."
36. This extensive quote was taken by John Drescher, "Senator No? With Reason, Helms Says," *Charlotte Observer* (October 10, 1990), 1B.
37. Helms even went so far as to call for a religious revival of conservatism. See, for example, Ken Ottenbourg, "Helms Urges Religious Revival: He Blames Fiscal and Educational Problems on Democrats," *Winston-Salem Journal* (September 8, 1990), 18B.
38. Ken Ottenbourg and Chris Geis, "Latest Ad May Have a Devastating Effect on Race," *Winston-Salem Journal* (September 19, 1990), 1.
39. *Ibid.*
40. *Ibid.*
41. John Mark and Jim Morrill, "Others Run Gantt's Race, Says Helms," *Charlotte Observer* (October 7, 1990), 4B. Helms also made this charge in Elizabeth Leland, "Campaign Teams Help Call Shots," *Charlotte Observer* (October 7, 1990), 1A.
42. See Morrill, "Voters Split."
43. This controversial commercial aired continously the week before the election on all of North Carolina's major network stations: ABC, CBS, and NBC.
44. These statistics were taken from a series of articles from *Charlotte Observer* including "Gantt Expected Gains Tail" (November 8, 1990), 1A, and "Pollsters Seek to Square Predictions" (November 8, 1990), 1A.
45. *Ibid.*
46. *Ibid.*
47. *Ibid.*
48. *Ibid.*
49. *Ibid.*
50. *Ibid.*
51. *Ibid.*

Chapter
10

The Election of Gary Franks and the Ascendancy of the New Black Conservatives

Georgia A. Persons

*I*s it or is it not black politics? That is the compelling question raised by the November 1990 election of Gary Franks to the U.S. House from the Connecticut Fifth District. Franks' election was an anomalous event for several reasons. First, he became the first black Republican elected to the U.S. House in several decades; since the departure of Oscar DePriest of Chicago in 1935. Franks' election also follows by more than a decade the departure of Edward Brooke, the black Senator from Massachusetts who served from 1966 to 1979. Franks thus became the only Republican among the 26-member Congressional Black Caucus. Second, Franks won the election from an overwhelmingly white district with only a 4 percent black population. While Franks is not the first to be elected from a majority white district (Wheat of Missouri, Dellums of California are others), he is the first to represent a congressional district with such a very small black population. One can hardly argue that Franks' election was the result of a biracial coalition.

Third, Franks ran as a conservative Republican, espousing issue positions consistent with the Reagan-Bush philosophies on many issues of salience to the larger black community, including many civil rights issues. During his campaign Franks supported a reduction in welfare benefits, a constitutional amendment to prohibit burning the American flag, the death penalty for drug traffickers, and a cut in the capital-gains tax rate. He opposed the Civil Rights Act of 1990, family-leave legislation, and raising the federal income tax (*New York Times* 11/25/90, p. 1).

Campaigns by black candidates involving deracialized political strategies as examined in earlier chapters of this book clearly provoke questions about the directions of black politics, particularly in terms of its future issue content. However, the election of Gary Franks, given the issue positions he espoused and given the demographic makeup of his district, starkly joins the issue in a somewhat more profound way: Just what defines black politics?

Some observers, and some analysts, have dismissed the Franks election as simply not black politics. However, while one might understand this dismissal as an initial reaction, it is nonetheless a mistake, for to dismiss the significance of the Franks election is to close one's eyes to a host of practical questions this election raises about the future of black politics. Also, to dismiss this development would be bad social science, as we would abdicate our responsibility to seek to explain the significance of what Franks' election represents as a political and philosophical phenomenon: the emergence of a new conservative voice in black politics as part of a broader political movement. This chapter argues that, properly understood, the meaning of the Franks election may be far more important than any change signalled by most other deracialized campaigns of 1990.

This chapter seeks to illuminate the significance of the Franks election by explaining the origins and central thrust of the new black conservative movement. To do so, it is necessary to review briefly the shaping of what has been in recent years, the traditional mobilization of bias in black politics in terms of interest articulation and partisan identification. The discussion then shifts to the 1980 Reagan election as the critical defining event in the construction and promotion of a black conservative movement. The final portion of the discussion focuses on the entry of the new black conservatives into the electoral arena, of which the Franks candidacy was the second wave.

THE SHAPING OF THE TRADITIONAL POSTURE OF THE NEW BLACK POLITICS

Whether the individual efforts of Du Bois, Booker Washington, Garvey, or Adam Clayton Powell, or the collective efforts of the civil rights movement and the early days of black electoral politics, black politics has been defined by an expressed commitment to the uplift of the race, socially, economically, and politically. To be sure, there have been differences over the most appropriate or most effective methods by which to pursue this commitment. Such differences have been exemplified by the conflicts between Washington and Du Bois, and more recently, between black nationalists and blacks who hold the liberal integrationist perspective. However in the modern era, with the demise of black politics as individual followings and the rise of more collectivist efforts, there have emerged at least periods of generalized consensus on the appropriate strategies to be utilized in pursuit of black liberation. Walters refers to these periods of generalized consensus as involving somewhat conscious shifts in strategy: the first occurring between 1955 and 1957 in the movement for civil rights, the second in 1966–67 with the black liberation movement, and the third in the early 1970s with the movement for black electoral politics (Walters 1980).

The strategic shift from the short-lived black liberation or black power movement to the emphasis on pursuit of electoral politics involved a particularly difficult struggle. In the aftermath of the civil rights movement and with the mobilization and nationalization of the black electorate spurred by passage of the Voting Rights Act, there was a perceived necessity of arriving at a consensus for optimizing the impact of the expanded resources and growing power of the black community. Efforts to structure such a consensus were undertaken in a series of national conferences which continued long-standing historical efforts to arrive at ideological unity and strategic consensus regarding black political efforts.[1] In recent years, these conferences were held in Newark in 1967, Atlanta in 1970, Gary in 1972, and Little Rock in 1974. Each of them involved often rancorous debate and struggle between groups adhering to variants of black nationalist ideology who were "radical" and sometimes fringe activists associated with organizations such as the Black United Front, Congress of Racial Equality, and the American Communist Party, pitted against veterans of the more liberal integrationist organizations such as the National Urban League, the NAACP, and newly elected black officials. The struggle between these two major factions pivoted around the fundamental questions of whether blacks should pursue efforts to transform or dismantle the U.S. capitalist system and eschew any cooperative or dependent involvement with the white-dominated and inevitably oppressive U.S. social and economic structure; or alternatively, blacks should seek to reform the system to eliminate social and economic injustice and work to become integrated with full parity into the social, economic, and political life of the nation as promised by the American democratic creed. The first option, advocated by black nationalists, was viewed by its opponents as separatist in intent and unlikely in outcome, while the second option was viewed by its opponents as a grand delusion which would at best result in blacks presiding over the mechanisms of their own oppression.[2]

The integrationists won out of course, in no small part due to the fact that their positions were more palatable to the white majority (and less threatening to the maintenance of the U.S. economic and social system) and were seen as more promising to the majority of black Americans. With a peaceful coexistence having been reached between leaders of civil rights organizations and the newly emergent black elected officials, there emerged a generalized consensus in regard to a set of issues which became known as the black agenda. The defining essence of the black agenda was the goal of manifold justice for blacks with specific objectives of achieving parity with the white majority in a number of areas including education, employment, housing, voting rights, and political representation, health care, and income. It was a broadly defined, social reform agenda and was taken as defining the objectives of all black political efforts.

At the core of this consensual framework developed some specific policy positions, sometimes proffered by black political leaders, and sometimes resulting from legislative and other compromises reached in efforts to translate broad social goals into operational policies with specific impacts. Perhaps most important of all in terms of the broader calculus of two party politics, the black agenda became a bargaining tool in efforts to exact promises from major white political candidates in exchange for black voter support. In turn, support of the black agenda became the overarching standard by which the masses of black Americans evaluated white candidates for major political office. While one does not hear much about "black unity" these days, there has been nonetheless an implicit and generally understood unity of objectives and agreement on acceptable issue positions. There exists an institutionalized mechanism, the loosely organized Black Leadership Roundtable, for forging, reinforcing, and advocating consensual positions. The Roundtable serves to link a mobilized black electorate with liberal white groups who frequently jointly advocate preferred positions on major policy issues. The partisan linkage has been to the Democratic party, a linkage forged by the national Democrats championing the civil rights movement.

While this partisan bonding has been beneficial to the black community, it has not been without criticism from diverse perspectives. Within the black community and among the black leadership corps, there has been a growing complaint that blacks have not been rewarded in proportion to their support of the Democratic party. This complaint has led to diverse propositions, including proposals to deliver strategically the black vote in a more pivotal manner between the two major parties. There have also been the reemergence of calls for formation of an independent black political party to facilitate the creation of a viable third-party system. Indeed, the 1984 Jesse Jackson campaign was designed in part to structure a more policy supportive environment for the black agenda within the Democratic party. For the Democratic party, the conflicts which grew out of issue positions deriving from the push of the black agenda led to charges that the party was losing its white voter base (Weissberg 1986). In the aftermath of the Carter loss in 1980, this concern led to efforts to redefine the party's platforms and image in a manner designed to gain distance from racially charged issues. One result of this was the undercutting of the clout of the institutionalized black leadership. Then came Reagan.

THE "REAGAN REVOLUTION" AND THE NEW BLACK CONSERVATIVES

The election of Ronald Reagan in 1980 marked a turning point in many respects. First, his landslide victory over Carter served to suggest a repudiation of the Democratic philosophy and programs by the masses of voters. The entire Democratic coalition was placed on the defensive. The defeat of many veteran Democratic officials and the Republican win of the U.S. Senate in the 1982 mid-term elections only served to heighten a general sense of a conservative political tidal wave to be resisted at the peril and folly of the would-be brave. The mood was not conducive to pursuit of liberal or progressive political efforts. Second, the Reagan administration made a concerted effort to discredit the civil rights leadership corps and attempted to annoint and establish an alternative black leadership which would be supportive of conservative Republican principles and policies.

Initial efforts to achieve the establishment of an alternative black leadership emanated from "The Black Alternatives Conference" held at the Fairmont Hotel in San Francisco on December 12 and 13, 1980, a month after the first Reagan win. The conference, with a theme of "rethinking the black agenda" was formally convened by black economist Thomas Sowell, a senior fellow at the Hoover Institute of Stanford University, with the support of conservative Republican institutions including the Heritage Foundation and the Institute for Contemporary Studies. The latter played official host. The conference report, published as "The Fairmont Papers," called for new ideas on racial and ethnic issues (Institute for Contemporary Studies 1981).

The major black participants included Chuck Stone, a journalist and former aide to Adam Clayton Powell, who likened the ideas of the Black Alternatives Conference to those he had heard at three black power conferences in 1966, 1967, and 1968. Stone was referring to ideas such as black self-reliance and black self-determination. Noted political scientist Charles V. Hamilton attended and was recorded as speaking on the need for increasing black voter participation. Other black participants included Martin Kilson, a Harvard political science professor; Walter E. Williams, a professor of economics at George Mason University; Percy Sutton, former Manhattan Borough president and former counsel to Malcom X and the Black Panthers; television journalist Tony Brown; Bernard Anderson of the Rockefeller Foundation; and Clarence Pendleton and Clarence Thomas, who were soon to become major players in the Reagan Administration's efforts to redirect major civil rights policy implementation. Major white participants were Edwin Meese, then legal counsel to the President, and Nobel laureate economist Milton Friedman (Institute for Contemporary Studies 1981).

The objectives of the conference were clear: to establish a cadre of blacks of some prominence who would speak to a new thrust in domestic policies in regard to black Americans, with the hope and anticipation that they would emerge as alternative leaders to the civil rights leadership group. A review of the conference report suggests that the conference was a decidedly disjointed one in terms of ideas and foci. Speakers raised a highly mixed set of issues which ideologically might be variously characterized as very conservative, Democratic liberalist, black nationalist, and a few perspectives defying any ready label. The central, underlying theme was that the civil rights era had come to an end and that the established black leadership did not represent black Americans. For some participants the problem was that the civil rights leadership were not independent leaders, while for some other participants the problem was that the established black leadership had run out of useful ideas. Otherwise the positions pressed were as diverse as the backgrounds of the participants.

As reported by Washington journalist Fred Barnes, the Reagan White House developed a strategy which they committed to written memorandum, for identifying and bestowing publicity upon blacks who could in turn be annointed as credible, alternative black leaders. In the early days of his administration, Reagan steadfastly refused to meet with the established black leadership. The Reagan administration also effectively shunned the more moderate black Republican cadre as well. Instead, his staff recruited an alternative group of blacks for a set of highly publicized meetings. Initially, a group of about 20 blacks including conservative activists, businesspeople, policy analysts, and academicians met with White House staff and formed the Council for a Black Economic Agenda, selecting as its head one Robert Woodson, who ran the National Center for Neighborhood Enterprise as an adjunct to the American Enterprise Institute. This group later developed and announced its agenda focused around spurring entrepreneurial activities in inner cities. Later, upon the request of this newly formed group, a meeting with Reagan was held at the White House (Barnes 1985). Thus the ritualistic and symbolic foundations were laid for an alternative black agenda and an alternative black leadership.

Moreover, a small cadre of very articulate black intellectuals emerged to lend their voices to a cacophony of conservative voices seeking to lend intellectual support for what was to become known as the Reagan revolution in regard to domestic policy generally, including the traditional black agenda. This group consisted of economists Glenn Loury, Walter Williams, and Thomas Sowell. In part, the utterances of this group centered around black self-help and black economic development, themes historically central to black political thought. However, the other dimension of (new) black conservative thought, that governmental intervention in the lives of blacks has been more detrimental than helpful to the interests and well-being of blacks, especially the black poor, was the tenet which signalled their distinction from other black advocates. In place of governmental intervention, this group of conservatives favored instead a laissez-faire capitalism with a presumed rectifying hand of the free market (Sowell

1975, 1981; Williams 1982). To these positions, Glenn Loury added his assertions that many of the problems of black America were moral in nature, with the remedies having to emanate from within the black community (Loury 1984a, 1984b, 1985).

The final role in the burgeoning black conservative movement was played by a group of black appointees within the Reagan administration who had the task of manipulating the critical components of the administrative public policy apparatus to attempt to bring the transformation full circle. These included Clarence Thomas as chairman of the Equal Employment Opportunity Commission (EEOC), and Clarence Pendleton as chairman of the U.S. Commission on Civil Rights. Both of these individuals spearheaded policy initiatives in direct opposition to what had been the previous thrusts of their respective agencies. The EEOC and the Civil Rights Commission were both turned against the very purposes for which they were originally established (Bawden and Palmer 1984).

What we see then is a newly emergent black conservative movement engendered and largely sustained by conservative white Republicans. If, as many critics have long contended, the traditional civil rights leadership has always been an appendage of the liberal Democratic white establishment, the conservative black Republicans may legitimately be characterized as an appendage of the recently ascended, white Republican establishment. If one group was "hustling" the plight of the downtrodden black masses to legitimate and maintain their claim to leadership, then the other group seemed quite ready to "hustle" their proclamations of the poor as being harmed by government intervention and/or as morally deficient. This "hustle" was run as their claim to legitimacy as alternative, allegedly independent, black leaders. Perhaps the most independent black activist cadre has been the black nationalist camp, which has not recently had significant voice in black politics. Interestingly, while the liberal integrationists of the civil rights establishment have generally held the far right position on the continuum of black political thought, they now find themselves in the middle. The new black conservatives are on the right.

The complexity of the philosophical predispositions of black conservatives is belied by the interestingly awkward position within which they find themselves politically. As one observer put it, they are whipping boys for black liberals and game pieces for whites on the right. Judging from the repeated utterances of several in attendance at the Black Alternatives Conference, they see themselves as a group of freethinkers who dare, and feel compelled, to challenge the conventional wisdom regarding the causes of and solutions to the black predicament in America. They see themselves as being "excommunicated" and castigated by the civil rights establishment for daring to think for themselves. They hold that they do not oppose government programs for the poor because they feel that government gives too much help to the poor; but rather they feel that the government creates too much harm to the poor, that too many programs pay people to stay disadvantaged. Perhaps most importantly, they feel that they know the path to black economic liberation. However, a seemingly major part of their mission is a consistent exhibition of a considerable angst toward the established black leadership. Thus, given that they are frequently associated with positions that are laden with racist sentiments, their attacks on the established black leadership contributes to their relative political alienation within the black community and largely precludes their having credible voice in the political debate.

One must not assume that the presence of the black conservatives in the Republican party has been a comfortable one for either group. Indeed the contrary is true. The recent relationship between blacks and the Republican party has been fraught with conflict and contradictions. It should be noted that not all black Republicans are a part of this latest conservative cadre. Some blacks trace their roots in the Republican party to the party's identification with the emancipation of black slaves, and generations of family identification as Republicans. Indeed, at least one contradiction regarding the black presence has been inherent in the notion that some black Republicans hold in regard to how the party should define itself in relationship to its historical role in the liberation of blacks. This has converged with the contradiction between the efforts of the party to create greater visibility of black Republicans in ways that are beneficial to the party and the refusal of the party to afford blacks access to and membership in the policy-making bodies of the national Republican party. Although the party was aggressively cultivating a new black leadership group, it did not feel obliged to alter the role and status of blacks within the party organization.

At the 1988 Republican National Convention, during perhaps the height of the black Republican ascendancy, the issues of the contradictory status of blacks in the party were raised. An interracial, New York–based group called Freedom Republicans, with a reported membership of 1000 issued a report that attacked the party's rules for delegate selection and determination of membership on the Republican National Committee (RNC). The Freedom Republicans argued that delegate selection rules favored small states and disadvantaged larger, more populous states which had larger minority populations, with the result that blacks and other minorities were grossly underrepresented. The Freedom Republicans argued for reforms which would have made the party's governing body more directly reflect the demographics of the nation (*New York Times* 6/26/88, p. E26). In 1988 there was only one black voting member, from the Virgin Islands, on the RNC, and only 3.2 percent of Republican delegates were black. In that same year, 16 percent of the Democratic National Committee membership was black, and black delegates comprised 23 percent of the delegate total. The rule changes proposed by the Freedom Republicans were soundly defeated on a voice vote as such proposals had been repeatedly defeated in RNC meetings of previous years (*Washington Post* 8/12/88, p. A9). The Democrats had confronted the issue of its delegate selection processes and the makeup of the DNC, starting in

1968 in response to the challenge by the Mississippi Freedom Democratic Party. Through a series of reform commissions, the Democrats instituted rules to have the party's convention and national committee reflect the demographic makeup of the party's mass voter base (Crotty and Jackson 1985).

The reasoning of the RNC in regard to its refusal to make accommodations to blacks was that the RNC simply refused to recognize the demands of any special interest or group, rather dealing with members as individuals. An eloquent response to that reasoning was presented by one Lugenia Gordon, who was 67 years old in 1988 and who then served as president of the Freedom Republicans and leader of the reform movement. Ms. Gordon was quoted as saying, "If this party is so color blind, how come they can see well enough to make this committee lily white?" (*Washington Post* 8/12/88, p. A9). Ms. Gordon threatened to sue the RNC, challenging the party's right to receive millions in funds from the Federal Election Commission. At that same 1988 convention, George Bush announced formation of the "Coalition of Black Americans for Bush." That coalition was headed by then Howard University President James E. Cheek who, apparently as part of some grand strategy, secured the appointment of RNC Executive Director Lee Atwater to the Howard University Board of Trustees. Atwater's appointment led to a major student protest which resulted in Atwater's resignation, and ultimately the dismissal of Cheek as president of the university.

THE NEW BLACK CONSERVATIVES IN THE ELECTORAL ARENA

Also in 1988, despite the contradictions and conflicts surrounding blacks in the Republican party, some half-dozen blacks sought high-level political office under the Republican label. Aside from their general conservatism, they all shared the goal of persuading more blacks to vote Republican, and they all received support of the national Republican party. The candidates included Maurice Dawkins, who challenged Charles Robb for the U.S. Senate from Virginia; former Reagan State Department appointee Alan Keyes, who ran against Paul Sarbanes for the U.S. Senate from Maryland; Jerry Curry, a retired army major-general, who challenged Representative Owen Pickett for the U.S. House from Richmond, Virginia; former Reagan HUD appointee James Cummings, who ran for the U.S. House from Indianapolis; Michael Webb, who ran against Peter Rodino for the Newark U.S. House seat; and Ronald Crutcher, who ran for the U.S. House from Akron, Ohio. None of these six was successful, but a new political strategy was fully underway.

Thus, what analysts observed as major changes "taking place" in a host of elections in 1990 were actually manifestations of change which had

already occurred. As discussed in Chapter 2, the trend toward the diminution of race (as conventionally defined) had already occurred among black
mayoral candidates prior to the 1990 elections. What was evident from the
aforementioned 1988 campaigns involving black Republicans was that
most of them did not seek to use race as a political resource in the traditional manner. What is also notable from the 1988 campaigns is that many
of the black candidates were pushing an ideological alternative, in some
instances, using race as a kind of *lagniappe,* in contests against liberal
white Democrats. Robb, Sarbanes, and Rodino, for example, were well-
known white liberals. The fact that these black Republican candidacies did
not receive greater attention from scholars or the media is no doubt
attributable to a fixation on the Jesse Jackson presidential candidacy of that
time as *the* contest of any significance involving a black candidate. Thus,
analysts were late in identifying an emergent trend toward deracialized
black politics.

The 1990 elections thus entailed deracialization in two variants. One
was a shift among liberal black Democrats as a genre from a traditional
and expected insurgent-style politics, which summoned up interests and
issues divided racially around a social reform agenda, to race neutral,
mainstream issues. Black candidates of this variant (discussed in Chapters
6–9) retained the core liberal Democratic philosophy. The other variant
of deracialization involved campaigns in which black candidates did not
pursue mainstream interests structured to facilitate the building of a new
common ground between black and white voters. Rather, they advanced
issues which were framed within an ideological context which decisively
set these candidates apart from what had been mainstream black politicians and traditionally defined black politics. Second, they advanced issue
positions which have traditionally formed the basis for divergent interest
identification between blacks and whites, and which indeed have been
frequently used as thinly veiled, anti-black signals. Third, they advanced
issues which primarily required and encouraged black voter support
based on the symbolic appeal of a common racial identification. There was
a secondary appeal to those blacks who identify with themes of black
self-sufficiency and self-determination as the path to black liberation despite the cloaking of these themes in conservative political garb.

Thus given the message of the new black conservatives, they had even
less of a need for a sizeable black voter base than the group of new
converts to deracialized politics. While the deracialized liberal Democratic candidacies of 1990 evidenced a transformation of the new black
politics as defined by the legacy of the civil rights movement, the deracialized black conservative candidacies had their roots in a more contemporary, anti-civil rights ethos, largely borne of the "Reagan Revolution."

Franks' candidacy was not the only one among black conservatives
seeking national office in 1990. J. Kenneth Blackwell was persuaded by
Bush-appointed Housing and Urban Development (HUD) Secretary Jack
Kemp to leave a top-level HUD post to run for the U.S. House from the

Cleveland, Ohio, First District. That district was then changing hands from Democratic Representative Thomas Luken (no relationship to Representative Donald Luken of Ohio, who was charged with sexual misconduct) to his son, Cincinnati Mayor Charles J. Luken. Thus the Republicans calculated that the Democrats might be vulnerable in a district which gave Bush 63 percent of the vote in 1988. Blackwell had briefly served as mayor of Cincinnati in 1979–80, and had served on the city council. The Ohio First had a black population of 16 percent. Blackwell ran on a platform of opposition to the 1990 Civil Rights Act, opposition to abortion, and opposition to federal subsidies for art exhibits like the controversial works of Robert Mapplethorpe. Blackwell's campaign benefitted from the support of such Republican notables as Jack Kemp, Dan Quayle, Oliver North, and Barbara Bush. His detractors charged that Blackwell had become a Republican one month after Reagan's 1980 win (*New York Times* 10/24/90, p. 14; *Washington Post* 9/27/90, p. 11; *Wall Street Journal* 10/4/90, p. 20).

Also in 1990, Al Brown ran unsuccessfully for the U.S. House from the Louisville, Kentucky, Third District, a district with a black population of 18 percent. Brown, a local businessman, ran with the full support of the RNC, which judged Brown clearly to be the superior candidate in comparison to his white Republican opponent. Brown assumed an anti-governmental assistance position, asserting, "I don't believe in handouts. . . . People must take advantage of opportunities" (*Christian Science Monitor* 5/29/90, p. 6). Brown campaigned in support of affordable housing and job opportunities, and opposed more sanctions against South Africa, arguing that "America needed to sweep around its own door first."

The Franks Victory

In comparison to the candidacies of Blackwell and Brown, the circumstances surrounding the Franks candidacy were rather propitious. Franks' biography was perfect for the "boot straps" legend. His father had been a mill worker who never achieved more than a grade-school education. However, all six of the elder Franks' children had been college educated, three with doctorates. Gary Franks received a bachelor's degree from Yale in 1975, and owned a successful real estate firm. He was a popular three-term alderman from Waterbury, a largely working-class town in the Connecticut Fifth. Franks had run unsuccessfully for state comptroller in 1986, but had received more votes than any other Republican on the ticket. He had supported Ronald Reagan in 1980, and had later supported Reagan's bid for a line-item veto. In regard to governmental intervention in the lives of the poor, Franks held that, "The key to the American way is making people self-sufficient. The worst myth out there is that you can do this through tax and spend, tax and spend, tax and spend. . . . Welfare dependency leads to a spiral of governmental dependency" (*New York Times,* 8/9/90, p. B1). Given the context of the district in which he ran, and given Franks' issue positions (cited at the beginning of this chapter), Franks' political credentials were impressive indeed.

Patterns of voting behavior in the Connecticut Fifth provide a testimony to recent shifts in the political fortunes of the Democratic and Republican parties and the ascendancy of the latter. During the Kennedy and Johnson years and into the early 1970s the district was solidly Democratic. Since the early 1980s the district has been solidly Republican. Preceeding Franks, Representative John Rowland won the district in 1984 at age 27 to become the youngest member of Congress. Rowland's win over his Democratic opponents had been in the range of 61 to 74 percent of the vote. In 1988, the Connecticut Fifth gave George Bush a higher percentage of support than any other Connecticut district. In 1990 the district had a low unemployment rate due in part to a significant presence of defense related activities, and polls showed a high level of satisfaction with the policies of the Republican administration (*Almanac of American Politics* 1990). Thus for a conservative Republican, this was an ideal district.

Franks' opponent, liberal Democrat Toby Moffett, entered the race with several disadvantages. First, Moffett was attempting to make a political comeback. He had served in the U.S. House, 1974–1982, but had left for an unsuccessful run for the U.S. Senate (and had lost the Fifth District in that race). He had unsuccessfully sought the Democratic nomination for governor of Connecticut in 1986. Moffett also fell victim to the label of opportunistic carpetbagger. Moffett had been a very short-term resident of the Connecticut Fifth District when he mounted his campaign. He had lived for the previous three years in the Third District. When he had earlier served in the Congress, he had represented the Sixth District. Moreover, Moffett had asserted: "I am running against the Reagan era" (*New York Times* 8/9/90, p. B1). Franks, on the other hand, was running in support of the Reagan-Bush era policies.

However, Franks' victory over Moffett was a slim one of only 5 percentage points. Franks had won the Republican nomination in a fiercely fought, five-candidate, seven-hour, nine-ballot, party convention. Many of his fellow Republican operatives were fearful that Franks' race would be a barrier to his election. Indeed, Franks reports that on the campaign trail, most whites tended to dismiss him as just another liberal black Democrat seeking office. Franks stated: "Then, as they were walking away, I'd say, 'wait, I'm a Republican!' And they'd turn around and say, 'Oh in that case, we'll give you some thought.' People just assumed because I was black I was a Democrat" (*New York Times* 1/25/90, p. 1). Despite his issue positions and despite being characterized by Moffett as another Jesse Helms, "who forgot where he came from," Franks carried seven of the eight mostly black districts in heavily Democratic Waterbury. Political scientist Terry Alan Baney of Teikyo Post University in Waterbury attributed Franks' margin of victory to the unexpected loyalty of affluent white Republicans (*New York Times* 11/15/90, p. 1). National Republican party officials hailed his victory as evidence that the Republican party was the party of opportunity, and predicted that Franks would be eagerly sought for speaking engagements and would be a major draw at party fund-raisers. Franks held: "My message will be different from what many people have heard from a black congressman" (*New York Times* 11/25/90, p. 1).

CONCLUSIONS

The election of Gary Franks simultaneously represents an expansion, albeit small, of the established black leadership as well as its fracturing along partisan and ideological lines, which will undoubtedly be significant over time. While there is a significant role to be played by black conservative intellectuals and political appointees in the Republican ascendancy, election to office bestows a different kind of legitimacy on an individual. That Franks was hailed as the highest ranking black Republican in the country attests to the yet smallness of this group of elected black conservatives. Of course the deficiency in Franks' claim to legitimacy as a black leader is a profound one: the constituency which elected him is overwhelmingly white. His claim to legitimacy then must be based solely on his racial identity as a black man. Thus, his political message as such may be significantly viewed as that of a representative of white interests, and/or as the positions of an individual who happens to be an elected official who is black. What we see here are some aspects of the contradictions between the predicament of blacks in American society, a predicament which has been defined by race and racial oppression, and the manipulation of black identity as a symbolic resource in efforts to achieve political gains (whether by black conservatives or liberal integrationists).

In regard to the ascendancy of the new black conservatives, the interests of the Republican party in fielding these candidates and in attracting more blacks to the party must be understood in both its partisan and ideological contexts. Presently the pattern of black support for Democratic presidential candidates in the 85 percentile range constitutes a very telling commentary of rejection by African-Americans of the Republican philosophy. This constitutes something of an image problem for the Republican party as it suggests that Republicans have little legitimacy with blacks on a full range of issues. One objective of the Republican strategy in regard to blacks is to attract 20–25 percent of the black vote to make the Republican party the majority party in congressional as well as presidential elections. Since the Republican party is not interested in changing its philosophy, its objective in regard to recruiting an alternative black leadership is to attempt to (1) change the political message and its messengers in regard to some issues and thereby alter public perceptions generally and black perceptions specifically of the nature and causes of the black predicament; (2) delegitimate one set of demands being made on the political system by African-Americans and legitimate an alternative set of demands; and (3) thereby legitimate a different set of policy responses to a significant range of domestic policy issues.

Is it, or is it not, black politics? What we call black politics in the 1990s is almost exclusively an electorally oriented phenomenon. It is thus a set of activities directed toward winning elective office in which the character of those activities is increasingly defined merely by the racial identity of the contestant. As such, black politics is frequently a set of tactics directed toward the immediate goal of winning a particular political office—political scoring. Except coincidentally, black politics is increasingly cut off from any larger philosophical grounding and, indeed, it is increasingly cut off from the social movement which gave it birth. What black politics collectively provokes as an analogy is the biblical story, found in Genesis 11:1–9 (King James version) of the building of the Tower of Babel, the essence of which is captured in verse 7: "Go to, Let us go down, and there confound their language, that they may not understand one another's speech."

NOTES

1. An excellent and detailed examination of these conferences is part of a yet unpublished two-volume study of black politics being prepared by Robert C. Smith, Department of Political Science, San Francisco State University, San Francisco, California. Of particular interest is a chapter, available for limited distribution: "The Failure to Learn the Lessons of History: An Anatomy of the National Black Political Convention, 1972–1980."
2. For explication of black nationalist political thought, see John Bracey, Jr., August Meier, and Elliott Rudwick, eds., *Black Nationalism in America* (Indianapolis: Bobbs-Merrill, 1970), and Milton Morris, *The Politics of Black America* (New York: Harper & Row, 1975), especially Chapter 6.

REFERENCES

Almanac of American Politics. 1990. Washington, D.C.: Borone and Company.

Barnes, Fred. 1985. "Invent-a-Negro, Inc." *The New Republic* (April 15), 9–10.

Bawden, D. Lee and John L. Palmer. 1984. "Social Policy: Challenging the Welfare State." In *The Reagan Record: An Assessment of America's Changing Domestic Priorities.* Eds. John L. Palmer and Isabel V. Sawhill. Cambridge: Ballinger Publishing Co.

Crotty, William and John S. Jackson III. 1985. *Presidential Primaries and Nominations.* Washington, D.C.: Congressional Quarterly Press.

Institute for Contemporary Studies. 1981. *The Fairmont Papers: Black Alternatives Conference,* San Francisco, California.

Loury, Glenn. 1984a. "Redirecting Priorities to Help the Black Underclass." *Point of View* (Summer 1984).

———. 1984b. "A New American Dilemma." *The New Republic* (December 31), 14–18.

———. 1985. "The Moral Quandary of the Black Community." *The Public Interest* (Summer 1985), 9–22.

Sowell, Thomas. 1975. *Race and Economics.* New York: McKay Co.

———. 1981. *Markets and Minorities.* New York: Basic Books.

Walters, Ronald. 1980. "The Challenge of Black Leadership: An Analysis of the Problem of Strategy Shift." *Urban League Review* 5(1), 77–88.

Weisberg, Robert. 1986. "The Democratic Party and the Conflict Over Racial Policy." In *Do Elections Matter?* Eds. Benjamin Ginsberg and Alan Stone. Armonk, NY: M. E. Sharpe.

Williams, Walter. 1982. *The State Against Blacks.* New York: New Press.

Part
Three

ENDURING DILEMMAS OR INEVITABLE TRANSITION?

Chapter
11

Ideology as the Enduring Dilemma of Black Politics

Robert C. Smith

Several of the papers in this volume use the concept of deracialization to suggest that black politics may be undergoing a fundamental transformation in ideology, strategy, or both. In a short essay that appeared in a symposium devoted to the 1989 elections, this author argued that this was not the case but that instead the patterns observed in the 1989 elections were a continuation of the post–civil rights era pattern of pragmatic, "mainstream" black politics.[1] The differences between the elections of 1989 and those of the late 1960s and 1970s then are more symbolic than substantive. The election of the first black governor in the nation's history is obviously of great symbolic significance; a significance heightened by the fact that Wilder was elected from the South. Wilder's election as Virginia's governor led many observers to tout him as a new conservative, mainstream alternative to the liberalism of Jesse Jackson and other establishment civil rights and black elected leaders. Wilder thus becomes the standard bearer of a new black politics as the torch is passed from civil rights era black leadership to a new generation of moderate and less race-conscious leaders. This oversimplifies the situation, which is not unusual in a society where even scholarship tends to be driven increasingly by media myopia and historical obtuseness. When analyzed in proper historical and comparative context the differences between, for example, a Jesse Jackson and a Douglas Wilder are, as one observer writes, "neither large nor new. These men are like two threads of the same cloth when examined within the larger context of the black community and American political minorities generally."[2] The point is that in order to understand the contemporary discussion and debate about deracialization, it is useful to locate it within the broad spectrum of traditional political thought as it has evolved in black America. Therefore, the purpose of this chapter—adapted from a larger in-progress project on post–civil rights era black politics—is to lay out a detailed historical and comparative framework for analysis of contemporary black ideologies. The analysis is organized in terms of the three major traditions in black political thought—nationalism, liberal integration, and radicalism.

Going back to the formation of African-American thought, there has always been enormous ideological diversity, ferment, and debate, especially when compared to the relatively narrow range of political thought and opinion that has characterized the country as a whole since its founding.[3] As Marguerite Barnett has written ". . . in comparison with other groups in American society, black communities produce inordinately large numbers of talented individuals and organized groups concerned with fundamental systemic change."[4] Thus, radicalism of some sort or another is an abiding feature of black thought in the United States. Yet there is also an important element or strain of conservatism in black thought, although historically it tends not to be articulate or coherent.[5] However, the most basic cleavage in African-American thinking has been between nationalism and assimilation or integrationism (although these latter categories are not really "-isms" since they are amorphous and lack a clear, coherent tradition. Indeed, much integrationist thought has been worked out in reference to the nationalist tradition). Within each of these broad tendencies—nationalism and integrationism—there may be identified various permutations in thought that bridge the classical left-right ideological spectrum in Western thought. Finally, within black thought there is a socialist and, in the twentieth century, an explicit Marxist-Leninist pattern of political thinking. Thus, in dealing with black ideology one is dealing with a rich variety of politics, and this very richness constitutes a major dilemma in the effort of African-American leadership to develop and sustain movements of solidarity to deal with the subordinate status of the group.[6] This essay analyzes historically and comparatively the problem of ideology in black politics and seeks to explain its significance and implications for the contemporary discussion of deracialization.

IDEOLOGY

One of the problems in framing analysis of the ideological implications of deracialization is the conceptually flawed way in which the term *ideology* is generally used. Within Western social thought and especially its derivative, the American science of politics, the term *ideology* has been used in a bewildering variety of ways. As one review of the literature concludes, the "ambiguity in the concept is reflected from author to author in a wide variety of definitions, explicit and implicit and lack of agreement regarding even the basic properties of the concept."[7] Ideology is probably best understood to require the following elements: a more or less logically coherent system of symbols that (1) includes some conception, more or less sophisticated, of historical causation and (2) links cognitive and evaluative perceptions of one's conditions and its prospects for change with (3) a program of collective action for the maintenance, alteration, or transformation of the status quo.[8] In this usage ideology tends to be largely an elite phenomenon, developed and articulated by specialists in symbols and politics who conceive of their tasks as providing education and leadership to less ideologically inclined mass followers.

NATIONALISM

Given this concept of ideology, we can turn to analysis of ideology in black America beginning with nationalism. Perhaps, as Professor Rodney Carlise has suggested, because of the fragmentary and discontinuous production of scholarship on black nationalism, there is an impression that the ideology and its advocates are *sui generis*, unique to a specific time, place, or person.[9] This impression may result also from the cyclical character of the saliency of nationalist ideas in African-American politics. Whatever the explanation, there is a tendency for observers, especially in the press but the academy as well, to view recurring nationalist expressions, whether by Marcus Garvey, Malcolm X, Stokely Carmichael, or Louis Farrakhan as phenomena that somehow require wholly new explanations.[10] Yet as Carlise and others posit, black nationalism in the United States constitutes an integral tradition of thought that is 200 years old; a tradition that has as much continuity and vitality as the liberal or radical traditions among white Americans. Over the years nationalist thinkers have developed a set of ideas, doctrines, and strategies that have considerable continuity and repeatedly appear in the tradition.[11] It is ignorance of this tradition that results in the predictable talk about some ominous new force in black society whenever a new cycle of nationalism produces a Garvey, Malcolm X, or Farrakhan, when in fact the basic elements in the thought of these men are almost as old as slave society in the United States.

Stuckey, in his admirable work on black nationalism, has shown that as a sentiment and later as a doctrine nationalism has its origins in the slave culture and has emerged more as a result of African traditions of cultural autonomy and hegemony than any borrowing or adaptation from European theories or models.[12] Because of the North's relative freedom, nationalism as a developed doctrine emerged there. However, its roots are in the southern slave culture where the relative isolation from Europeans and the large and frequent infusion of Africans from the continent reinforced African consciousness and group solidarity (until as late as the nineteenth century the slaves referred to themselves as Africans and probably did not consider themselves American until after the Civil War).

What, then, are the core or fundamental elements of this tradition or system of thought? First, in terms of historical causation there is an acute consciousness of oppression at the hands of Europeans as the source of the African predicament in the Americas. Second, there is an awareness and appreciation of the persistence of group traits that distinguish Africans from others, traits that survived the slave experience and that provide a cultural basis for group autonomy and struggle. Third, there is a Pan-African consciousness that posits bonds and obligations among Africans everywhere.[13] Fourth, in terms of intervention strategy, there is the belief that the subordinate status of the race can only be altered as a result of group self-reliance and unity. Related to this last factor is the constant refrain in the nationalist tradition, often exaggerated, that blacks have failed to do for self, and all too frequently accommodate rather than resist oppression.

In its formative years these basic elements of the tradition were worked out by a variety of thinkers in various media but received their clearest and earliest articulation as doctrine in the works of Edward Wilmot Blyden and Martin Delaney, intellectuals of the first rank.[14] Delaney, frequently referred to as the "Father of Black Nationalism," is probably the most uncompromising of nationalism's founding fathers. He rejected the possibility of integration with whites, suggesting they were either culturally or genetically "devils" and that their whole history as a people was characterized by one impulse "to [crush] the colored race wherever found."[15] Delaney also emphasized the cultural retrograde character of European civilization compared to African civilization's special spiritual and aesthetic values of soul. As a result of these attitudes regarding the enduring traits of the race, he was the first of the founding fathers to insist on the indispensability of a separate nation as the basis of African liberation in the United States.

This goal of a separate homeland—probably always viewed as utopian by most nationalists—has colored most interpretations of the tradition as many scholars (especially in the twentieth century), on the basis of often facile dismissal of this objective, have rendered the entire tradition as "fantasy" or "romanticism."[16] Yet this notion of a separate homeland had some influence on the formation of African states as well as black towns in Kansas and Oklahoma.[17] But perhaps the most telling criticism of the critics of land-based nationalism is in terms of its alternative—integration on the basis of justice and equality within the American system. As Stuckey writes:

> When nationalists advocated the total removal of their people from America—and few indeed have been those who have thought this strategy either realistic or desirable—it should not be said that even they, considering centuries of merciless oppression of Afro-Americans, were less realistic than believers in the American dream. Moreover, the record seems to suggest rather the opposite; that those people of color (and their white allies) who believed in the absorptive powers of America were vastly more deluded than those blacks who decided to depend mainly on their own people, their own energies in a hostile land.[18]

More importantly, this particular variety of the ideology is only that—one variety of many—and a minority one at that among both the intelligentsia and the masses. Indeed, one of the analytic problems of nationalism is that within the core elements of the tradition identified above there are a bewildering variety of nationalist tendencies and programs. As Bracey, Meier, and Rudwick write, black nationalism has been defined to describe "[a] body of social thought, attitudes and actions ranging from the simplest expression of ethnocentrism and racial solidarity to comprehensive and sophisticated ideologies of Pan-Negroism or Pan-Africanism. Between these extremes lie many varieties of nationalism."[19] Historically and today these varieties may include (1) religious (Christian and non-Christian including Islam and sundry sects), (2) cultural, (3) economic (bourgeois and socialist), (4) political (reform and revolutionary), (5) territorial separatism, and (6) Pan-Africanism.[20] Within the black community in the twentieth century each of these varieties of nationalism has attracted some measure of elite and mass support, especially in the big cities of the North. The saliency and intensity of nationalist thinking as a whole or any particular variety has of course varied over time, although it appears that when nationalism is prominent in any given period each of the varieties and subvarieties finds some adherents among both the intelligentsia and some element of the masses, although the latter is hard to document.[21]

In their cyclical theory of nationalism, Bracey, Meier, and Rudwick suggest that there have been four relatively distinct periods when nationalist thought was salient in African-American society and politics, each coinciding with especially disappointing or difficult times for the race in its relationship with the larger society. The first was between 1790 and 1820, occurring as a result of disappointment with the failure of the new nation to include blacks within its liberal, democratic covenant. The second was in the period of the 1840s, coinciding with the failure of the abolitionist movement to make major advances in the struggle against slavery, and resurfacing for a third time in the 1880s in the aftermath of Reconstruction as black civil rights gains were sharply reversed. The final cycle occurs in the late 1960s through the early 1970s as a result of disappointment with the pace of the civil rights revolution, especially in the big-city ghettos of the North.[22]

In each of these cycles essential elements of the tradition—acute consciousness of the nature of white oppression, doubts as to the essential humanity of whites, race consciousness, solidarity, and insistence on the necessity of self-reliance and collective action—became prominent in the full variety of nationalist ideologies, from religious particularism to territorial separatism, from cultural revitalization movements to organizations of revolutionary change. In several of these cycles mass organizations emerged, national in scope, including Garvey's Universal Negro Improvement Association, Muhammad's Nation of Islam, and the Black Panther party. Although these organizations declined after relatively brief periods—largely as a result of the twin problems of internal personality conflict, leadership, and ideological factionalism, and the external, near-constant campaigns of government surveillance, infiltration, harassment, and repression—their contributions in terms of heroes, myths, and ethos are important elements in the tradition's vitality.[23]

In brief, this is one of the ideological tendencies that shapes political discourse in black America. Before turning to analysis of the integrationist ideology and the radical tradition in black politics, one might do well to note that given the identification of cycles of nationalist ascendancy with periods of disappointment and disillusionment, it is probable that we will see a fifth cycle of heightened nationalist expressions. This is so because of the widespread dissatisfaction with the pace of change in the post–civil rights era struggle, the perception of a turning back of the clock on civil rights and race advancement policies in this period of conservative ascendancy in the federal government, periodic reports of racial harassment and violence, and the enduring reality (vividly chronicled in the daily media) of one-third of the race mired in the misery and degradation of the so-called underclass.[24] This point is also touched on in the conclusion where there is a discussion of its relationship to the deracialization strategy.

INTEGRATION

In his influential work on the nature and character of the discourse that shapes the maintenance or transformation of a social order, Mannheim draws a distinction between "ideologies" and "utopias" that is useful in making sense of ideological conflict in black America. For Mannheim, ideology is a peculiar kind of social thought that is used to stabilize a social order, while utopia is thought employed in system transformation. This distinction is helpful in understanding the "ideology" of the black establishment—integration—and its tensions with the "utopias" of nationalism and radicalism. The essential analytic distinction here is between the thinking of established groups that seek the maintenance and stability of a social system and the thinking of certain oppressed groups interested so passionately in social transformation that they focus only on those things that would lead to that transformation.[25] Historically, the dominant or establishment leadership group in black America, while interested in change in the racial character of the social system, has otherwise been bound to it, and it has generally sought reforms, usually incremental, that would preserve the system absent its racial characteristics. This is so in part because the black leadership establishment has always been an appendage or, in Matthew Holden's term, clients of elements of the larger, external white establishment. And from the time of Frederick Douglass to the present, the dominant liberal integrationist black leadership establishment has been heavily influenced in its thinking by the system stability and maintenance concerns of its white patrons. As Bunche, writing from the perspective of the radical tradition, argued in his critique of liberal integrationist politics, white men exercised too much influence on black leaders and this leadership in its quest for respectability and access to the authorities showed too much concern for the opinions of whites and too little for the plight of the black masses.[26]

Thus, while the liberal integrationist black establishment is not a ruling group in America and has always been committed, more or less, to transformation of the racist element of the social structure, it is the dominant or ruling group inside black America and it has extensive linkages (ideological, financial, and personal) to the white establishment. As a result the character of the struggle against racism has been bound to the interests of system stability, perhaps, as Mannheim suggests, in an unconscious way that obscures the real conditions of the masses of blacks. Thus, ideological conflict in black America, as it did during the 1970s, often takes the form of rhetorical charges by nationalists and radicals of "sell-out" and appeasement, while establishment blacks charge their opponents with being "unrealistic" and "utopian." This likely is a structural feature of the struggle because along with the status quo, interest-bound character of the establishment, Mannheim writes, "utopian thinking is incapable of correctly diagnosing an existing condition of society. They are not at all concerned with what really exists; their thought is never a diagnosis of the situation; it can be used only as direction for action."[27] The black establishment, past and present, has certainly been frequently timid in the struggle, relying on moral suasion and gradualism rather than militant protest. It is also true, as Morris contends, that nationalist thinking tends to be linked to unrealistic goals with little coherent programmatic content and frequently burdened with "empty posturing" and a "disparate assortment of ill fitting 'socialist' or 'marxist' ideological fragments which further confuse rather than clarify goals."[28]

The ideology of liberal integration, unlike its radical and nationalist counterparts, lacks a tradition of a *self-conscious* set of ideas, doctrines, and myths that have been passed down from generation to generation. Rather, integrationist thinking, like its patron ideology in the larger society, tends to be ad hoc, characterized by philosophical pragmatism. There is no founding father like Martin Delaney or classical doctrinal statements such as Blyden's *Christianity, Islam and the Negro Race*. Rather, the ideology has been developed on the run, without systematic attention to problems of historical causation or internal consistency or coherence. Again Du Bois (who except for the eclecticism of his thinking, which in his long life ranged over the entire spectrum of black thought including liberal integration, several varieties of nationalism, and radicalism, might be considered the intellectual founder or father of integration) is useful here in understanding the absence of integrationist doctrine in his constant refrain: "We face a condition not a theory." Therefore any philosophy, ideology, or program of action that gave promise of altering the condition of the race should be embraced. This of course is an exacting formula for ideological incoherence, contradictions and political opportunism, of the best and worst sorts.

Trying to discern the fundamental elements of the integrationist belief system is therefore difficult, but the following seem to be enduring: (1) the historical basis or cause of the subordinate status of blacks is racism, the doctrine and practice of white supremacy; (2) contrary to some nationalist thinking, white racism is not invariant (in terms of culture or genetics) but can be altered; (3) change in the racial order requires race/group solidarity, but just as important, it requires interracial cooperation or coalition; (4) except for racism the American social system is fundamentally sound; (5) there is an inescapable interdependence between black and white Americans and there can be no liberation for the race outside of the United States; and (6) programs for racial reform, given the fundamental soundness of the system, must employ conventional processes of political activity that are consonant with system stability. Down the line, from Douglass to Washington, to Du Bois, to Randolph, to Martin Luther King, to Jesse Jackson, to Douglas Wilder, these have been core cognitive and evaluative elements of integrationism.[29]

Within this broad ideology there are of course permutations or varieties, ranging from conservatives such as Booker Washington or Thomas Sowell to the consensus liberalism of Douglass, the early Du Bois, or a modern-day Jesse Jackson, to the democratic socialism of a Randolph, the middle Du Bois, or a Congressman Ronald Dellums. The democratic socialist strain of integration, never very prominent in the overall thrust of the ideology (in part because black socialists have no powerful patrons in the external white establishment), is close to, but ideologically distinct from, the radical tradition in black thought.

RADICALISM

More so than integration but less than nationalism, black radical thought in the United States does not exhibit the character of a well-developed tradition. Black radicalism in the United States is indeed often tied in critical ways to integration and especially nationalism. For example, Cedric Robinson in the most detailed effort to trace out the fundamental elements of a black radical tradition has difficulty in disentangling its Marxist elements from nationalist personalities and doctrines.[30] Similarly, Cruse argues that both black nationalist and Marxist thinking in the United States have been distorted in their development as a result of the influence of the Soviet-dominated CPUSA and the paternalism of radicalism's principal white patrons—Jewish Americans—given their confusion about their own ethnic nationalist tradition and their ambivalence about their status in American society and culture.[31]

Like integration, then, radicalism is not identifiable by distinct historical founders or advocates or a coherent body of doctrines and ideas that evolved over time to shape generations of thinking and practice. Du Bois is viewed by some as a candidate for the mantle of radicalism's founding father. But Du Bois is also credited with the intellectual parentage of the civil rights establishment ideology of integration and was a major contributor to the elaboration of one variety of nationalist ideology, Pan-Africanism. Thus, unless one can trace continuity in Du Bois' thought from his early NAACP days to his post–World War II embrace of communism, then it is difficult to see how his ideological eclecticism can be made to fit easily any but all of the various patterns of black thought.[32] Other important figures—Richard Wright and Paul Robeson, for example—are too ephemeral in their thinking and behavior to make much of a doctrinal contribution to the tradition, except in Wright's case to show the utter intellectual bankruptcy and perfidy of the various CPUSA involvements in black radicalism's evolution.[33]

The basic elements of the tradition as it has been worked out—especially in the 1970s—adopt and attempt to apply, often in a rigid and mechanical way, classical Marxist doctrine to the condition of African-Americans, yielding the following core elements: (1) inherent capitalist economic exploitation is the basic historical agent in the subordination of Africans, with racism as an important but subordinate epiphenomenon of this process; (2) racial solidarity or unity, while important in the African-American freedom struggle, must be ultimately subordinate to the unity of the whole working class in the struggle against the bourgeoisie, including the black petite bourgeoisie and capital's functionaries in the black leadership establishment; and (3) the goal of black liberation in the Americas can only be achieved as a result of a socialist revolution that removes the structural basis for racial subordination.[34]

The foregoing are of course a summary of black radicalism's fundamental principles; each of which is often frequently debated in terms of nuance and subtlety as well as emphasis by persons operating within the tradition. Indeed, such discussions sometimes occasioned as rancorous an exchange in the 1960s and 1970s as did the debates between black Marxists, nationalists, and integrationists. Then there is the problem of trying to blend elements of the traditions of nationalism and Marxism in a single analytic and political project. This tenuous exercise was the source of bitter dispute in the late 1960s as the Black Panther party sought to define itself doctrinally and in practice as a revolutionary nationalist Marxist-Leninist organization to the consternation of both cultural nationalists and orthodox Marxists.[35] This ideological confusion was compounded with disastrous results for black solidarity when Amiri Baraka, perhaps the leading cultural nationalist of the period, changed his ideology to Marxism-Leninism in the midst of his tenure as a leading official of the National Black Political Convention, leading to bitter recriminations between cultural and revolutionary nationalists and the liberal integrationist leadership establishment, and the eventual collapse of the convention process.[36]

CONCLUSION

The purpose of this essay has been to sketch the basic elements of the three major ideological tendencies that have developed over time in black politics in order to provide a historical and comparative framework for analysis of the contemporary debate about deracialization as a new direction in black politics. When viewed within this framework, the new deracialized politics manifested in the elections of 1989 and 1990 is clearly a variant of the historic commitment of the black leadership establishment to the ideology of liberal integration. This ideological spectrum has always included a fairly broad range of perspectives, from left to right and in terms of emphasis on racism, racial reform and race consciousness, and solidarity. Deracialization, to the extent that it represents a new departure in black politics, is a strategic change that places less emphasis on racism, racial reform, and race solidarity than did the electoral politics that emerged in the immediate aftermath of the civil rights and black power movements of the 1960s. This development is not unusual or unexpected. As social movements become institutionalized the tendency over time is for them to become routinized as a result of what Weber called their interaction with the enduring institutions and material interests of the society.[37] Thus, deracialization constitutes a heightened level, an advanced stage of the institutionalization of the African-American freedom movement, a stage in which blacks may now compete for offices beyond the confines of the black community. While this creates a new strategic environment, the ideological content of this new black politics is more a matter of form than substance.

The election of a Douglas Wilder in Virginia or a David Dinkins in New York City takes place against a background of a growing sense of disappointment and despair in the African-American community. The optimism generated by the election of the nation's first black governor is tempered by the reality of one-third of the race living under unspeakable conditions of poverty, misery, and degradation. As the twenty-first century dawns, it is becoming increasingly clear to blacks that the status of the race—its society, family, culture, and community—is in a state of decline and that the strategies employed by its leadership in the post–civil rights era have not been effective in arresting this decline. There is also a sense that the larger society does not care; that the ongoing Reagan revolution continues to turn back the clock on the quest for racial justice. Historically, conditions such as these have been fertile ground for the rise of nationalist and radical challenges to the liberal integrationist establishment. This may be the most important dilemma posed by the new politics of deracialization. It is not likely to be able to arrest and reverse the decline of the black community and in its strategic calculus which deemphasizes issues of race and racism, it suggests that even black leadership itself may be turning away from the problem. It is possible, therefore, that by pursuing a strategy of deracialization, the liberal integrationist establishment will, paradoxically, stimulate a renewed emphasis on race among blacks and encourage growth of the more radical and nationalist ideologies that are enduring elements of the African-American experience.

NOTES

1. Robert C. Smith, "Recent Elections and Black Politics: The Maturation or Death of Black Politics," *Political Science and Politics* 22 (June 1990): 160–162.
2. Richard Shingles, "Wilder and Jackson: Threads of One Cloth," *Focus* 18 (May 1990): 160–162.
3. On the relatively narrow confines of American thought as encapsulated in the liberal consensus or tradition the best treatment is still Louis Hartz's *The Liberal Tradition in America* (New York: Harcourt, Brace, 1955).
4. Marguerite R. Barnett, "A Theoretical Perspective of American Racial Public Policy," in *Public Policy for the Black Community,* eds. Barnett and James Hefner (New York: Alfred Publishing, 1976), 23. I should also note that black thought has been disproportionately the product of political activists rather than detached, unengaged observers. Thus, it also tends, like much of American thought, to be directed toward change or problem solving in orientation. Indeed, while it is possible to discern a "tradition" in black ideology, there is also an ad hoc quality to it as it evolves to meet the changing realities of race oppression. This characteristic is nowhere better seen than in the changing ideology or changing emphases in the ideology of W. E. B. Du Bois, the prototype black activist-intellectual. This quality of black thought led Gunnar Myrdal to conclude radically and erroneously that it lacked internal coherence, that there was no tradition, but rather black thought should be ". . . in the main considered as secondary reactions to more primary pressures from the side of the dominant white majority." See *An American Dilemma* (New York: Harper & Row, 1944), lxxv. This view shows Myrdal's unfamiliarity with the historical development of black ideology and his misunderstanding of the realities of black thinking he observed in the 1930s and 1940s. Yet this view of black political thought and behavior as mere reactions to whites shaped a generation of scholarship on black leadership and ideology, especially among political scientists. For a critique of Myrdal and social science research on black leadership thinking see Robert C. Smith, *Black Leadership: A Survey of Theory and Research* (Washington, D.C.: Howard University, Institute for Urban Affairs, 1982), 20–34, 67–80, 92–96.
5. See Hanes Walton, Jr., "Blacks and Conservative Political Movements," *Quarterly Review of Higher Education Among Negroes* 37(1969): 177–83, and Alex Willingham, "The Place of the New Black Conservatives in Black Social Thought: Groundwork for the Full Critique." Paper presented at the Annual Meeting of the Association for the Study of Afro-American Life and History, Philadelphia, 1981.
6. Historically, black leadership efforts to create and sustain all inclusive institutions of black solidarity and political action—the 1830s National Negro Congress, the 1930s National Negro Congress, and the 1970s National Black Political Convention—have failed as a result largely of ideological conflict. On the

1830s convention see Howard Bell, "National Negro Conventions of the Middle 1840s: Moral Suasion vs. Political Action," *Journal of Negro History* 22 (1957): 247–60; on the 1930s Congress see Lawrence Wittner, "The National Negro Congress: A Reassessment," *American Quarterly* 22(1969): 883–901. On the 1970s convention see Robert C. Smith, "On the Failure to Learn the Lessons of History: An Anatomy of the National Black Political Convention, 1972–80." Paper presented at the Annual Meeting of the National Conference of Black Political Scientists, Atlanta, 1990.

7. Willard Mullins, "On the Concept of Ideology in Political Science," *American Political Science Review* 66(1972): 458.

8. *Ibid.* Dealing specifically with the problem of black ideology, or what he calls "value judgments," Mack Jones identifies three essential elements: (1) a description of an empirical situation (factual base), (2) prediction of future developments, and (3) an intervention strategy, the operations which must occur or be performed if future developments are to occur in the desired way. See "Scientific Method, Value Judgments and the Black Predicament in the U.S.," *Review of Black Political Economy* 7(1976): 4–18.

9. Rodney Carlisle, "Black Nationalism: An Integral Tradition," *Black World* 22 (1973): 4–10.

10. Most recently this may be seen in the media's coverage of the controversial remarks of the Nation of Islam's Minister Farrakhan during the 1984 presidential campaign. Taken out of the context of the nationalist tradition, Farrakhan's rhetoric appears much more tasteless than it really is as did the rhetoric of Malcolm X when he first received national press attention.

11. Carlisle, "Black Nationalism." On nationalism as a tradition see also E. Essien-Udom, *Black Nationalism: A Search for Identity in America* (Chicago: University of Chicago Press, 1962), Chapter 2; John Bracey, Jr., August Meier, and Elliott Rudwick, *Black Nationalism in America* (Indianapolis: Bobbs-Merrill, 1970); and Harold Cruse, *The Crisis of the Negro Intellectual* (New York: William Morrow, 1967); 4–6. The most sophisticated evidence and argument for nationalism as an integral tradition in African-American thought is the work of Sterling Stuckey. See *The Ideological Origins of Black Nationalism* (Boston: Beacon, 1972) and *Slave Culture: Foundations of Nationalist Thought* (New York: Oxford, 1987).

12. Stuckey, *Slave Culture.* Stuckey's *The Ideological Origins of Black Nationalism* gives us an excellent collection of the earliest nationalist sentiments and doctrines including Robert Young's 1829 "Ethiopian Manifesto," Henry Garnett's famous address to the slaves, and Martin Delaney's "The Political Destiny of the Colored Race." When read in conjunction with the Bracey, Meier, and Rudwick collection it is fairly easy to see the continuity and coherence of the thought.

13. Stuckey shows that one of the positive effects of slave culture in the development of nationalism was its detribalizing effects which forced Africans from various tribes and nations to think of themselves as a single people. Thus, ironically, African nationalism has its origins in the Americas.

14. On Blyden see Hollis Lynch, *Edward Wilmot Blyden: Pan Negro Patriot, 1832–1912* (New York: Oxford, 1967), and on Delaney see Victor Ullman, *Martin R. Delaney: The Beginnings of Black Nationalism* (Boston: Beacon, 1971).

15. Delaney, "The Political Destiny of the Colored Race" in Stuckey, *The Ideological Origins,* 198. Delaney's "devil" theory of whites is a notion that appears

frequently throughout the tradition but it was given its most profound elaboration in Elijah Muhammad's *Message to the Black Man* (Chicago: Nation of Islam, 1965).

16. Theodore Draper dismisses this aspect of the tradition as a "fantasy" in *The Rediscovery of Black Nationalism* (New York: Viking, 1969), and Matthew Holden, Jr., in his uncompromising critique uses the term *romanticism* to dismiss virtually all varieties of black nationalism with the possible exception of the cultural expression. See *The Politics of the Black "Nation"* (New York: Chandler, 1973), 68–130.

17. Carlisle, "Black Nationalism."

18. Stuckey, *The Ideological Origins of Black Nationalism*, 29. For example, Holden in his critique of nationalist programs in the 1960s argues that integration is the only rational goal for blacks in the United States. Pursuant to that goal he proposes a series of five-year strategic plans in such fields as education, and politics, that by 1976 would have set in motion a process where race would not predict the distribution of "material benefits or psychic esteem in any significant degree." See *The Politics of the Black "Nation,"* 131–42. A generation later his thinking seems almost as farfetched as the goal of a separate nation as race more and more predicts life chances in the United States in nearly every important area—education, health, mortality, the economy, office holding, and mental health. For detailed documentation of this race disparity see Gerald Jaynes and Robin Williams, *A Common Destiny: Blacks and American Society* (Washington: National Academy Press, 1989).

19. Bracey, Meier, and Rudwick, *Black Nationalism*, xxvi.

20. *Ibid.* There is much overlap between the varieties of types of nationalism. For example, each variety usually includes a cultural component of some sort and each variety usually emphasizes some form of economic self-sufficiency as part of its thought and program of action.

21. The available survey data provide hardly any insights on mass opinion in this regard.

22. Bracey, Meier, and Rudwick, *Black Nationalism*, xxx–liii. See also Milton Morris, *The Politics of Black America* (New York: Harper & Row, 1975), Chapter 6.

23. On Garvey see Tony Martin, *Race First* (Westport: Greenwood, 1976), and Theodore Vincent, *Black Power and the Garvey Movement* (San Francisco: Ramparts, 1972); on the Nation of Islam see Essien-Udom, *Black Nationalism*, and C. Eric Lincoln, *The Black Muslims in America* (Boston: Beacon, 1961); and on the Panthers see Gene Marine, *Black Panthers* (New York: New American Library, 1969), and Chris Booker, "The Rise and Decline of the Black Panther Party," unpublished manuscript, 1983.

24. Past cycles of nationalist saliency have often been presaged or accompanied by a names controversy. What should Africans in America call themselves, African, Colored, Oppressed Americans, Black, etc. These name controversies have usually occasioned conflict and tension between the integrationist establishment and ascendant black nationalism. Thus, it is interesting that the most recent instance of this change in preferred designation—to African-Americans—has been adopted by virtually all elements of the black intelligentsia, almost without debate. This *may* mean that the fifth cycle of nationalist prominence may occasion less intergroup conflict than earlier ones, which would be an important historical advance in the African-American freedom struggle.

25. Karl Mannheim, *Ideology and Utopia* (New York: Harcourt Brace, 1963), 40.

26. Ralph Bunche, "The Programs of Organizations Devoted to the Improvement of the Status of the Negro," *Journal of Negro Education* 8(1939): 542–43. On this point see also Lerone Bennett, "The Black Establishment," in *The Negro Mood and Other Essays* (New York: Ballantine, 1965).

27. Mannheim, *Ideology and Utopia,* 40.

28. Morris, *The Politics of Black America,* 111–112. Nationalist thinking tends to be especially weak or utopian when it comes to what Jones calls the "intervention strategy"—the "how to get from here to there" with respect to programs of action. One searches nationalist thinking in vain for sensible programs of cultural, economic or political change that would lead to revolutionary transformation of the racial order.

29. Holden's *The Politics of the Black "Nation"* and its companion volume, *The White Man's Burden* (New York: Chandler, 1973), are probably the most systematic elaborations of the integrationist ideology available.

30. Cedric Robinson, *Black Marxism: The Making of the Black Radical Tradition* (London: Zed Press, 1983).

31. See Cruse, *The Crisis of the Negro Intellectual,* 147–70. Also on the Jewish intelligentsia and the development of black integrationist thinking see David Lewis "Parallels and Divergences: Assimilationist Strategies of Afro-American and Jewish Elites from 1910 to the early 1930s," *Journal of American History* 71(1984): 543–64.

32. Gerald Horne, *Black & Red: W. E. B. Du Bois and the Afro-American Response to the Cold War* (Albany: SUNY Press, 1986).

33. See Wright's essay in Richard Crossman's *The God That Failed* (New York: Harper & Row, 1949).

34. There is of course a long, often acrimonious history of debate within the black radical tradition and within the American left on these elements fundamental to black radicalism, a debate that resurfaced in the late 1960s and early 1970s. On the foundations of the debate see Wilson Record, *Race and Radicalism* (Ithaca: Cornell, 1964), and Henry Williams, *Black Response to the American Left* (Princeton: Princeton University Press, 1973). On this debate in the late 1960s and 1970s see I. A. Baraka "Why I Changed My Ideology: Black Nationalism and Socialist Revolution," *Black World* 24(1975): 30–42, Tony Thomas, "Black Nationalism and Confused Marxists," *Black Scholar* 4(1972): 47–52, and Earl Ofar, "Marxist-Leninism: The Key to Black Liberation," *Black Scholar* 4(1972): 35–46, and more generally Manning Marble, "Black Nationalism in the 1970s: Through the Prism of Race and Class," *Socialist Review* 10(1980): 57–107.

35. On the Black Panthers see Booker, "The Rise and Decline of the Black Panther Party." On the conflict between the Panthers and their cultural nationalist critics represented for a while by Baraka and throughout by his colleague Ron Karenga see Karenga's "Kawida and Its Critics: A Socio-Historical Analysis," *Journal of Black Studies* 8(1977): 125–48.

36. See Smith, "On the Failure to Learn the Lessons of History," 91–101.

37. Max Weber, "The Sociology of Charismatic Authority." In *From Max Weber: Essays in Sociology,* eds. H. H. Gerth and C. Wright Mills (New York: Oxford, 1958), 54–55.

Chapter
12

Towards a Reconstituted Black Politics?

Georgia A. Persons

What we have seen in the analyses of Chapters 1 through 11 are manifestations of a significant change in the relationship between black political leaders and the mass-level black population. This continues an historical series of changes. The analyses also yield insights into visions of black liberation, black political leadership, and illuminate as well the emergence of strategy in relationship to changing visions and varied contexts. In the first portion of this concluding chapter we reflect on how the foregoing analyses have informed our understanding of the changing relationship between black political leaders and black voters. The second section entails an analysis of broader changes within black politics with which the deracialization movement converges. This final section addresses the future of insurgent-style black politics as well as the probable future of black politics generally.

BLACK POLITICAL LEADERS AND THE BLACK VOTER: A CHANGING RELATIONSHIP

Over time there have occurred major shifts in the relationship between black political leaders and the mass-level black population. Black political leaders of the Du Bois genre and time were not leaders with significant mobilized followings, for the circumstances and conditions of the black race did not permit active mobilization of the masses. Rather, black leaders of that era were individuals who seized severely circumscribed forums to engage in articulation of grand visions for the uplift of the race. For leaders of the Du Bois genre, their visions of racial uplift both incorporated a definition of the problem confronted by the race, a conceptualization of strategies necessary for liberation, and a prescription of the appropriate role for black political leadership. This was an era of post-slavery, pre-electoral black politics when political visions held significant currency. Although there was little consensus among them, black political leaders of that era were great visionaries.

One might identify a second era of black leadership dominated by individuals in high-level positions in black civic and religious organizations. This group functioned at the national level, but their presence and clout were supplemented by select black entrepreneurs and civic and religious leaders at the local level. This latter group functioned with especially high visibility in those locales which did not yet elect any blacks to office. These unelected, reputational leaders generally served as liaisons between the black and white communities with status frequently determined by the nature of their connection to the white community.

The contemporary era of black electoral politics is not the first manifestation of black electoral activity. The earliest stage of black electoral politics, not counting the brief experiences of the Reconstruction era, was primarily an era of individualized followings due, in large part, to the fact that mass mobilization of the black community had not yet occurred. Early black elected officials such as Oscar de Priest, Arthur Mitchell, William Dawson of Chicago, and Adam Clayton Powell of New York City, were exceptional men in exceptional circumstances due to the fact that they were able to get elected to Congress (between 1928 and 1944) during a period when black voting was very limited and occurred under severely restricted circumstances. These black representatives were thus much revered by their black followers, and due to their stature and status as black leaders, commanded a degree of respect from white elites as well.

This was not yet the "independent black politics" as would be practiced many decades later, rather early black elected officials were frequently tied into the white-dominated political machines of their day and were thereby able to deliver benefits to many of their supporters. Their relationship to their followers was a kind of patron-client relationship in which these black leaders functioned as brokers in a network of relationships: delivering a limited black vote in support of select white candidates at the local and state level; delivering particularistic benefits such as jobs and access to social service benefits to many of their black constituents; and attempting to utilize their access to the political process to advance the collective status of blacks nationwide (Gosnell 1935, 1937; Moon 1948; Wilson 1960). While the objective conditions of black Americans might have dictated a grand vision for liberation, the exigencies of early-stage black electoral politics appear to have precluded all but the most inchoate vision. It is this general lack of an effective vision to sustain strategic directions which in large part is at the heart of the seeming perpetual lament echoed by Cruse (1967, 1987), Reed (1986), and others.

The rise of large-scale black electoral politics, essentially as developed in the post–Voting Rights Act years characterized by mass-level mobilization, merged political leadership and political representation via attainment of elective office. This development greatly expanded the ranks of the black leadership and, at the same time, led to the existence of two distinct groups of black leaders: those who could, or chose to, lay claim to leadership of the race by virtue of leadership in diverse organizational settings and/or community based activities, and those individuals who were able to obtain elective office. Many of the latter group had previously been members of the former group but many were relatively new to politics. The emergence of the latter group was to have a profound effect on black politics. Within the electoral arena, political leadership as the articulation of a grand vision was slowly eclipsed, while strategy as deliberate actions calculated to obtain electoral victory became paramount. This was not an insignificant shift in the determinants and manifestations of black leadership.

Although electoral politics emerged out of a general consensus on a collective strategy for black liberation, and as a strategic shift it presupposed a vision for transformation of the black community, in hindsight, the vision of transformation was, relatively speaking, quickly lost. Electoral politics is by definition a game of strategy. Candidates for elective office must effectively mobilize voters, articulate issues in a way which garners the support of large segments of voters, and assemble winning coalitions of diverse groups. Strategy dictates success. While black elected officials may well hold broad visions of how they can best serve the needs of the black community, such visions are generally not systematically contemplated, not well developed, and rarely articulated as such. Rather, the political visions of black politicians seeking elective office must be gleaned from their campaign strategies, if they are discernible at all. Black voters then must increasingly rely on the shorthand of issue positions and the "color coding" of black candidates as proxies for visions of political leadership.

Although the new black politics was originally conceived as a means of operationalizing a vision of racial uplift and transformation, the analysis in Chapter 3 suggests that black electoral politics has, over time, actually contributed to an erosion of the general consensus about racial uplift. The early black mayors who ran against white candidates and white power structures were almost involuntarily political insurgents who were able to mobilize black voters by issue positions and a call for black political empowerment which conveyed a message of social reform. Thus the strategies of individual black insurgents fit the pattern associated with the collective vision of social and political transformation which presumably underlay the electoral politics strategy. These black politicians defined their relationship to the black voters as one of political deliverers and political clients/supporters. Thus insurgency functioned as both strategy and style for most first black mayors. However, strategies and styles began to change at different electoral junctures in the institutionalization of black mayoralities. As mayoral contests evolved to pit one black politician against another, the collectivist tenor of the electoral strategy began to dissipate with a shift toward individual black politicians crafting situation-specific strategies directed toward the individual goal of winning elective office.

As early as the reelection stage in a first black mayoralty, when the mayoralty had been proven to be an obtainable goal for black aspirants, black challengers to the incumbent began to undermine the potential of insurgency. At this stage black challengers crafted their strategies to exploit the dual tendencies of strident resistance on the part of some white voters and the acceptance of the inevitability of black mayoral leadership among other white voters with, in both cases, a preference for the most moderate black leadership obtainable.

We have seen that at the succession stage of black mayoralties a more definitive effort at political differentiation among black competitors emerges as black contestants split the black vote and, in instances where whites constitute a pivotal swing vote, woo the white vote by resorting to strategies involving stereotypical stigmas. Such tactics were an early form of racial reconciliation in which some black politicians offered themselves to white voters as alternatives to the objectionable styles and policies of insurgent reformers. On the other hand, in cases of involuntary succession, a majority of black voters appear to have become disenchanted with the social and economic decline and political paralysis which accompanied long-term insurgency and moved to elect candidates with a more accommodationist style and identifiable managerial skills. These developments suggest that the decline of insurgency as a style and strategy in black politics was inevitable. Indeed, the institutionalization of black mayoralities had led to a more conservative posture among black politicians and the erosion of consensus about broader strategic goals. While the coin of race continues to be used as a political resource by black politicians, it is increasingly exploited by black candidates, white elites, and white voters in what are effectively mutually agreed upon efforts to control the outcome of electoral contests and the symbolic and substantive rewards of the political game.

The Richmond case offers interesting insights into other dimensions of insurgency and its limitations. Black leaders in Richmond used insurgency as a means of mobilizing the black electorate, and over time, changing demographics facilitated the obtaining of a degree of independent black political power. Upon election as the first black mayor, Henry Marsh moved to reassure the white business community that his administration would champion economic development, but joined with blacks on the city council in an effort to direct aggressively the path of economic development and to leverage its impact in support of the priority goal of alleviating poverty. In the abstract this appears to have been a reasonable strategy for governance, designed to test one way in which to operationalize effectively the goal of social and economic transformation of the black community implicit in black political empowerment. However, the black leadership in Richmond did not have the political power to take control of downtown development. Moreover, the goal of alleviating poverty was effectively forsaken by the black leadership in their pursuit of minority business set-asides, a program which largely benefited the black middle class. The obvious question is whether this rather limited goal was the only strategic maneuver which the Richmond white power structure would countenance. In the end, the insurgents' strategy of calculated cooperation proved to be very difficult to execute and a very limited one in its outcome.

We also see with particular luminosity in the Richmond case how insurgent-style politics as pursued by one group of black politicians led to conditions which were exploited as opportunity structures by other black politicians. In effect, Roy West offered himself to the white power structure as a moderate alternative to black insurgents. By joining with white councilmen to secure his election as mayor, West placed himself in a position clearly dependent on white support, thus ensuring that his politics would not be at significant variance from the wishes of his white supporters. On the other hand, given the demographics of the city which favored the black majority, a strategic "defection" by a black politician represented the best outcome whites could hope for. As in several of the cities examined in Chapter 3, in Richmond the politics of insurgency was undermined by black politicians crafting individualized strategies to obtain white support to secure electoral victory. With the election of Roy West, Richmond's politics returned to status with a new accommodation having been worked out at the level of black and white elites. The Richmond case and other similar cases suggest that with the demise of insurgency, the relationship of black political leaders to mass-level black supporters became largely one of descriptive representation, with at best, an aspiration of substantive representation.

There are lessons to be learned from the Cleveland case, not the least of which is "what's old is new again." As the first black mayor of a major city, emerging in the turbulent period of the waning days of the civil rights movement and during the days of urban riots, Carl Stokes had attempted what we might characterize as a populist version of a deracialized campaign. This was not a style unique to Stokes. Indeed most black mayors of the insurgent period and beyond have adopted similar stances. Stokes appealed for racial solidarity, vowed to be mayor of all the people, emphasized issues which trandscended race, vowed to improve the economic climate of the city, sought to redirect major municipal institutions to be more responsive to the needs of the black community, and avoided contact with black activists who were known to incite the angst of white voters. At the same time Stokes sought to mobilize the black community for long-term, effective exercise of power. This was an ambitious agenda indeed and one set within the context of the times. This was a period of great hope for urban America, when responsive leadership was assumed to be the fulcrum for transforming many urban ills, including healing the breach between blacks and whites. Stokes' populist deracialization differed from the contemporary version in that he and other black insurgent mayors of that era took strong positions on issues such as improving and increasing the available stock of low-income housing, creating jobs, eliminating police brutality, increasing minority representation in the municipal work force, and more equitably distributing and delivering municipal public services. These were the issues of the urban policy agenda locally and nationally, and advocacy of these issues was the natural political stance to assume. Advocacy of these issues also incorporated an agenda for the uplift of the black community. Contemporary deracialization too takes its cue from the national political mood in regard to issues of social transformation. Thus deracialization as a political strategy and style is void of any identifiable issue stances which might be characterized as a black agenda.

The second lesson to be learned from the Cleveland case is also a major reminder that in many cases black insurgency was frequently manifested primarily at the rhetorical level, while a major bonding took place between insurgents and the white business community. This was apparently a major part of the role played by George Forbes who was a long-time insurgent politician in the Cleveland arena. Indications of Forbes' ties with the white business community were evident by the impressive array of endorsements he received during his mayoral campaign against Mike White. Whereas Forbes had apparently engaged in a reconciliation with white elites, he was still perceived as an insurgent by rank and file white voters, and apparently by the majority of black voters as well. He lost the support of the former group, garnered the support of the latter, and lost the election to Mike White, who campaigned on a theme which can be characterized as racial reconciliation.

We saw in the analysis presented in Chapter 4, that deracialization was actually proposed as an agenda-setting strategy designed to avoid articulation of black interests in presidential campaigns in a way which would create opportunities for countermobilization of white voters by the Republican party. Under a deracialized agenda-setting strategy, priority issues of the black agenda such as employment, comprehensive health care, education reform, and crime prevention would be advanced in such a way as to appeal across racial lines and thus garner broad-based support as opposed to risking the polarizing effects of race-specific policy appeals. Thus deracialization was initially proposed as a strategy geared toward the realization of collective ends. While we might characterize deracialization in agenda setting as a strategy for overcoming the limits of race to transform the collective status of blacks, we might characterize deracialization as electoral strategy designed to overcome the limits of race so as to transform the opportunities for individual black politicians. In effect, the deracialized electoral strategy entails an interesting idea about political marketing wherein the product, a black candidate, is understood to have a built-in base of consumers; that is, black voters, with a strong preference for the product, and the presumption is made that there is a potentially much larger consumer base which can be tapped with strategic product design, packaging, and promotion.

Since racial concerns have been a perpetual by-product of American politics whether or not a black was present in the campaign as a candidate, then blacks pursuing deracialized political strategies have to work a unique political magic. They have to render their own skin color and racial identity irrelevant (for example, Wilder's assertion that he never ran as a black man), and at the same time avoid those issues which have a clear racial valence. Failing that, they must reverse the charge of the racial valence (as is done by a black championing the cutting of welfare rolls), and articulate issues which most readily transcend race (such as fiscal restraint, or abortion). In short, blacks pursuing deracialized electoral strategies must avoid championing any issues which could be interpreted as specifically benefiting blacks except in the most tangential manner. Thus many black politicians pursuing deracialized strategies do not risk making even the traditional calls for racial harmony. Rather, they act as if, or indeed explicitly assert, that all questions of race are irrelevant.

However, one can argue that the most critical tests of the deracialized electoral strategy have not worked, as in the Georgia and North Carolina cases covered in Chapters 8 and 9. Indeed, analytically, one of the most interesting factors in the Wilder case was how close he came to losing. Wilder won by less than a one-percentage-point majority. For a deracialized electoral strategy, Wilder was the perfect candidate. He had served a two-decade-long political apprenticeship; he had declared as far back as his contest for lieutenant governor that he had never run as a black man. He was not strongly identified with the civil rights movement. His campaign theme of "the new mainstream" was easily interpreted as racially acquiescent, nonthreatening, and nonoffensive. His complementary theme of "law and order" was reminiscent of the similar Nixonian theme and likewise suggested a recognition of white concerns and positions on crime, and suggested as well a protective posture in response to these concerns. His other issue positions bespoke a generally conservative political posture, except for his position on the abortion issue, a position which adroitly capitalized on the widespread support among white women in particular for legalized abortions. Wilder had critical party support and media support. That Wilder almost lost despite his record and stellar profile as a candidate is rather telling of the idealism and limitations of the deracialized strategy.

In applying the model of deracialized electoral strategy developed by Jones and Clemmons, in Chapter 7, to the Andrew Young candidacy, presented in Chapter 8, we readily see the limitations of this strategy in overcoming race. Young had not served an apprenticeship in state-level politics, but he had well-established political credentials as a former U.S. Congressman, ambassador, and as mayor of the major city in his state.

Young did all of the right things in terms of deracializing the issue content of his campaign. He never mentioned his civil rights history and even asserted that racism in the state had declined from the level of cancer to the equivalent of an acne-type nuisance. However, Young's presence in the campaign—his racial identity—remained an issue. His fellow Democratic partisans were openly fearful that his nomination for governor would result in a victory for Republicans. The influential Atlanta media supported his candidacy and generally played racial ombudsman, but race remained the issue in the campaign, and the polls consistently showed an electorate that was polarized along racial lines in its candidate preferences.

If as Jones and Clemmons asserted, the essential task in a deracialized campaign is one of solidifying the natural (black) base of support while not alienating the white constituency, then the Young campaign would have been a success, albeit a likely moderate one. Young was able to hold on to a majority of black votes, though his support among this group was not particularly enthusiastic given his failure to court their support actively, and he did nothing to alienate the white vote. In fact, Young spent a great deal of time courting even the most unlikely white voters below the "gnat line" in conservative south Georgia. Alienation of white voters was simply not the issue. White voters simply could not be sold on voting for a black candidate. As southern farm country lore would have it: "You can take a horse to water, but you can't make him drink."

The North Carolina case reaffirms the limitation of the deracialization strategy. Gantt also launched a deracialized campaign based on race-trandscendent issues, and he aggressively pursued the support of white voters. Despite a strong showing in coalition-building efforts and his apparent tapping of a relatively sizeable tide of discontent against Helms, Gantt was unable to overcome the constraints of a traditionalist political culture, which bound together racism and opposition to other progressive elements represented by the Gantt campaign, the Gantt campaign revealed a significant level of change in a Deep South state and significant vulnerability for an elder son of Old South politics. However, the Gantt campaign showed that the injection of race into a campaign by a popular opponent can have the effect of transforming the tone of the entire campaign in a manner which a black candidate cannot effectively combat.

What then might we conclude are the benefits and implications of deracialization as an electoral strategy? In terms of its manifestation of the changing relationship between black political leaders and mass-level blacks, deracialization as an electoral strategy advances and serves the maintenance needs of black politicians. It offers greater assurances of entry into and longevity in the political game. To their primary support base of black voters, black politicians deliver what they can, largely symbolic benefits and rewards. Deracialization also appears to resolve another strategic dilemma for black politicians. Implicit in the retreat from insurgency and the adoption of a deracialized strategy is the resolution that if a social reform agenda is unobtainable, then it should be set aside. Further, deracialization promises to resolve the complaint advanced by both black political leaders and the masses, that blacks hold too few elective offices, largely because whites generally refuse to vote for black candidates. With deracialization, this impediment at least promises to be overcome.

The majority of cases of deracialized politics, including cases not analyzed here, such as the election of black mayors in Seattle, New Haven, and Denver, have entailed what has been characterized (in Chapter 10) as the liberal Democratic variant. However, in the case of Gary Franks (and others identified in Chapter 10) we see a cadre of practitioners of deracialization who combine this strategic shift with a philosophical/partisan shift as well. The new black Republicans seek to obtain entry into the ranks of the black leadership in a manner which allows them to assert an independency of strategic thinking and partisan ties which they suggest hold the key to alternative and viable paths to economic and political liberation of the black community. Whether wittingly or not, their conservative stances render them servants of the strategic efforts of the Republican party in its goal of altering the terms of discourse regarding social policy issues, thereby legitimizing a different set of policy responses. We are reminded in Chapter 11 that neither variant represents an ideological shift in black politics. Indeed deracialization maintains and even expands the commitment to the ideology of liberal integration. In effect, deracialization as a strategic shift might well be a natural outcome of this ideological perspective given that its political progeny, electoral politics, has evolved as the major strategic fulcrum for realizing social change. Deracialization also achieves greater prominence when viewed within the context of other developments which have recently helped to shape the form and substance of black politics.

A CHANGED ETHOS IN THE BROADER CONTEXT OF AMERICAN POLITICS

This volume began, in the introductory chapter, with an allusion to the impact of the Reagan victory in 1980 and the resulting shifts in domestic politics and policy as prime forces in driving new directions in black political efforts, specifically the Jesse Jackson campaign of 1984. This causal linkage is not to be denied or diminished. However, when one simply juxtaposes the major political developments of the 1980s—the three Republican wins of the White House, the further nationalization and emergent deracialization of black politics, one gets an interesting perspective on a broader path of American political development. American politics generally, and black politics specifically, were both redefined during the 1980s.

The Reagan regime abandoned the New Deal ethos of social reform which had been defined and implemented through a strong role of government in improving the lives of needy individuals. Deep cuts were made in social programs, with some, federally subsidized housing for those of low income, for example, essentially eliminated. These cuts hurt blacks more because blacks are disproportionately represented among the nation's poor. Attacks on affirmative action policies were a further diminution of the federally protective role. Perhaps more important than these policy shifts in the long run were the underlying delegitimating of certain claims on the roles and functions of the federal government in the public sphere.

The diminution of the governmental role in the domestic policy sphere represented a major political defeat for main components of the old New Deal coalition. Major social policies formulated from the early 1930s to the late 1970s represented the cumulative policy responses of government to the varied problems of poverty and discrimination. These policies as well represented a payoff to black voters and others for their allegiance to the Democratic party. Perhaps more importantly, the social policy network effectively represented a political settlement agreed to by all parties involved in policy-making activities as an alternative to profound social change. Thus black politicians and their supporters understandably saw the social program infrastructure as the small "piece of the pie" owed to a major segment of their constituent group over the alternative of nothing at all. Moreover, domestic policies and spending acknowledged the legitimacy of claims by the needy on governmental functions and the public purse. Thus to make the political victory and its concomitant policy shift more decisive, the Reagan regime shut off the traditional black leadership from access to the White House, and the regime's top policy appointees thus shunned these articulators of certain claims on governmental functions in regard to the plight of the poor and disadvantaged. The Reagan regime instead attempted to "raise up" an alternative black leadership which would obey and agree along more favorable philosophical lines. While these efforts emanating from the Reagan regime helped to redefine black politics, perhaps equally consequential were efforts pursued by black politicians themselves which redefined black politics, or which at least reconstituted the mix of its primary ingredients.

THE JACKSON CANDIDACIES AND THE RESTRUCTURING OF BLACK POLITICS

In regard to black politics, the 1980s began with a great disappointment over the Carter presidency and its refusal to pursue aggressively realization of the black agenda. This disappointment was braced by a generalized bitterness over a perceived refusal of the Carter regime to acknowledge fully the pivotal role of the black electorate in the 1976 Carter election victory. For many reasons, the Carter election had been met with great expectations by many African-Americans as an opportunity for the final realization of dreams deferred. The very promising policy responses of the Lyndon Johnson presidency had been influenced by the apotheosis of black political mobilization based on protest activities. However, the tremendous momentum in support of the domestic policy agenda which characterized the early years of the Johnson presidency had been lost to the escalation of the Vietnam War, and the black agenda had been set aside. The Carter election was greatly influenced by a second black political mobilization, this one based on a greatly enhanced voting power. For many black politicians the black agenda had been set aside again under the Carter presidency.

This then was the central grievance of the first Jackson candidacy for the Democratic presidential nomination—the continual setting aside of the black agenda—and it was compellingly captured in the highly resonant Jackson theme of "our time has come." Jackson's first candidacy was thus an insurgent-style candidacy, with a stated objective of redefining the status of the black presence in the Democratic party by provoking a more policy-responsive posture by the party. However, more so than anything else the two Jackson candidacies helped to redefine black politics and set the parameters for its future manifestations, including the recently triumphant strategy of deracialization.

Up to the point of the first Jackson candidacy, contemporary black politics had been run along an interestingly dual track. At the local and state levels where most advances have been made, black politics had been predominantly characterized by an insurgent-style politics, held by many observers to be a largely "independent" black politics. The stars of this show were big-city black mayors but the full chorus line consisted of hundreds of small-town black mayors. At the next level of high visibility were members of the Congressional Black Caucus (CBC), also elected locally. Somewhere below were a host of black elected officials in diverse and sometimes obscure offices at local levels. Except in rare instances, the factor which defined and sustained this level of black politics, which gave these elected officials an air of, and claim to, independence, and which facilitated and in some instances dictated an insurgent style, was a demographic factor of a decisive majority or near-majority black voter base. Even most members of the Congressional Black Caucus were elected from predominantly black, safe districts. Big-city black mayors and caucus members laid different though similar claims to being part of the national black leadership and frequently played pivotal roles in national-level black politics.

National level black politics were played by leaders of major black organizations such as the National Urban League, the Southern Christian Leadership Conference (SCLC), the NAACP, members of the CBC, and some big-city black mayors. National-level black politics was primarily directed toward affecting the platforms of presidential candidates and the outcome of presidential elections. The defining dynamic of this level of black politics, which had been honed to the level of a fine strategy, was one of pressure group politics, a behind-the-scenes negotiations and leveraging process which Walters has aptly labeled the "dependent-leverage strategy" (Walters 1988). In this process a cadre of recognized black leaders would generally agree on and announce a set of goals which blacks wished to pursue in a given election season. They would then negotiate, primarily with the Democratic party, for support of that agenda, promising to deliver or withhold the black vote accordingly.

While Jackson's first candidacy combined elements of both an independent insurgency and dependent leveraging strategies, the cumulative impact of his two candidacies was a significant redefinition of black politics. The Jackson candidacies entailed a shift from delivery of mass-level black votes as the primary currency in bargaining, to capture and retention of delegate votes with planned delivery of that delegate support in return for support of certain policy positions in the party's platform and in the winning candidate's campaign themes. This was a different kind of dependent leveraging tactic, one which directly pitted Jackson against much of the party leadership and one which produced very visible strains within the black leadership corps. Much of the black leadership—big-city black mayors, a majority of the CBC, and the heads of the major civil rights organizations—opposed the first Jackson candidacy. Many of them had committed to other candidates, but most also saw the Jackson candidacy as a high-risk venture which threatened to disrupt the predictability of the traditional relationship between the black leadership and the Democratic party and the benefits which flowed therefrom. Most importantly for the future of black politics, the traditional strategy was redefined and pressed to its limits, and the objectives of the Jackson candidacy, predicated on a Democratic win of the White House, were not realized. Moreover, while analysts agree that Jackson succeeded in injecting into the campaign debate a progressive perspective on domestic and foreign policy issues, they also agree that Jackson failed in not being able to get these perspectives into the 1984 party platform (Smith 1990). Thus a great deal of unfinished business remained.

The second Jackson candidacy of 1988 presaged the definitive shift towards deracialization in black politics. While the first candidacy had advanced a multiethnic theme as incorporated in the concept of the Rainbow Coalition, the second Jackson candidacy embodied a definitive shift towards deracialization tactics. The second candidacy was less insurgent in its tone and appeal, and more mainstream in its issues and rhetoric. The Jackson campaign staff in 1988 was largely comprised of white advisers as opposed to an almost exclusive reliance on blacks in 1984. A moderate white southerner from the Carter regime, Bert Lance, was a key Jackson adviser (Smith 1990). Moreover, in addition to pressing a litany of general social reform issues resonant of the 1984 campaign, Jackson in 1988 abandoned dependent leveraging as a strategy, and ran an autonomous campaign with the objective of winning both the Democratic nomination and the presidency. The model of the independent black candidate as solo broker (and not a member of a larger brokerage group), had thus been established, though the full realization of the implications of this development was again set aside by Jackson's loss and by the Democratic loss of the presidency.

However, having transformed much of national-level black politics into a process defined by an independent, solo political broker, Jackson was interestingly unable to reap fully the rewards of his labors. Perhaps inevitably, certainly in 1988, Jackson had emerged as *the* black political leader; the man to be dealt with, and the man who became the political surrogate for all African-Americans. Treatment of Jackson was seen as reflective of attitudes towards African-Americans. Acquiescence to many of Jackson's specific issue positions was seen as detrimental to the hopes of white Democrats as Jackson as an individual was seen as unduly engendering the anxiety of white voters who remained critical to a Democratic win of the presidency. This created a dilemma for the Democratic party. Again, the dilemma became unfinished business due to the Democratic loss of the presidency in 1988. However, Jackson remained in the minds of many, an unpredictable threat to the party's hold on the black vote.

The election of Douglas Wilder as governor of Virginia promised to resolve at least part of the dilemma of the Democratic leadership regarding the issue of race and the status of blacks in the party. Wilder's election further legitimated the model of the independent, mainstream black politician, but with some significant differences. Wilder garnered strong black support and he had a style proven to be widely acceptable to a broad segment of white voters. Wilder is the consummate political insider and has won a series of state-level elective offices. He downplays the significance of his race as an individual politician and avoids casting issues in racially divisive terms. Wilder was very active in the early days of his governorship in establishing his presence in national-level Democratic politics. In short, Wilder has emerged as an alternative to Jackson in terms of rhetoric, message, style, and claim to black leadership. While one cannot conclude that Wilder will supplant Jackson in national-level political influence or in influence among African-Americans, it is clear that with the election of Wilder as the nation's first black governor and his catapulting into the national leadership corps, the general terrain of black political leadership has changed significantly. This is even more so the case when one takes into account the overall expansion of black elected officials in varied settings. We thus see a significant change in the very character of black politics, away from a systems challenging posture to an emphasis on a more mainstream appeal to a broader voter base, and a concomitant diminution of a black social reform agenda.

Given the recent evolution of black politics as sketched above, part of the dilemma of black politics becomes apparent. While the election of the likes of Douglas Wilder might represent a major accomplishment along with the cumulative presence of some 7200 black elected officials, the significance of these developments pales when juxtaposed against the persistent and worsening plight of the black underclass. The dilemma, the profound question then, is what should be done with the growing strategic fulcrum created by black political power? Barring a major redirection, we have effectively witnessed the apotheosis and decline of black electoral politics as a mechanism for social change. Thus in a significant sense, the somewhat rapid escalation of the black electoral politics strategy has reached a somewhat unexpected conclusion and has brought black America again to the point of agenda setting—a time for redefining goals and plotting new strategies. While the old agenda has not been substantially realized, it has unquestionably lost much of its momentum, and current federal policy initiatives do not provide a context for its advancement. So what might the future hold? The discussion now shifts to examination of positions expressed by the leadership of two major civil rights organizations as indications of a rethinking of the future course of black political efforts.

THE FUTURE: A TURNING INWARD?

The keynote addresses of Benjamin Hooks and the Reverend Joseph Lowery, respective heads of the NAACP and the SCLC, at the 1990 annual meetings of their organizations offer some interesting insights into the likely future directions of at least one level of black politics. Both addresses incorporated a call for a turning inward within the black community. However, the address by Reverend Lowery incorporated a relatively well defined reconceptualization of black politics.

The Hooks address contained the following major points:[1]

A reflection on the "almost magical changes" (in ending segregation) which have taken place all over the South, and the impressive achievements in electing blacks to political office

A lamenting of the continued plight of the black underclass who remain "unaffected and unimpressed by the progress" of black elected officials

An assertion that blaming the system and white folk does little to solve the tremendous problems of black America

A call to emulate the struggles and sacrifices of our black ancestors

A call for a moratorium on excuses as to why black America, spurred by the black middle class, cannot do more to help itself

An assertion that blacks must take responsibility for their own lives, for their own destiny

A call for black Americans to "rebuild the altars of strong family support, renovate community pride and unity, turn to each other and not against each other"

A call to advocate passage of the Civil Rights Act of 1990

A lamenting of the assault by hostile government forces against black elected officials as reflected in "convenient and selective prosecution of black leaders"

A call to build bridges of hope, faith, tolerance, understanding, coalition, and cooperation, and bridges of a drug-free and crime-free society

Perhaps the signal declaration of the Hooks speech was the explicit acknowledgment that the plight of the black underclass has not been altered by the relatively tremendous achievements of the past two decades in electing blacks to political office. This "contradiction" is of course at the heart of the dilemma of black politics. It is, however, a rather telling observation that Mr. Hooks sees the solution to the dilemma, the path to complete black liberation, to lie in a turning inward; what he apparently sees as a return to black self-help efforts, led by the black middle class. As the Hooks speech was lacking in any call for government initiatives to assist the poor, one must conclude that he has abandoned such hopes, either out of frustration and a sense of the futility of such pleas, or out of a change of conviction about the ultimate desirability and outcomes of such efforts. In terms of strategies for future efforts directed toward uplift of the black community, one must conclude that Mr. Hooks sees black self-help initiatives as the appropriate course of action.

The address by the Reverend Joseph Lowery contained the following major points[2]:

A characterization of the American mainstream as a polluted stream and a call for black America not to spend the next 25 years in the American mainstream

A declaration that integration "as defined by the American body politic" is not to be praised but to be buried because it is a confused notion which has been a one-way street, dislodging black role models and destroying the cultural identity of black children

An assertion that the Voting Rights Act was passed not just to change the color of government but also its character; thus all officials, black and white, must be held accountable

A lamenting of the assault on black elected officials as an attempt to destroy the results of the black vote

A strong call for a "spiritual renaissance" to purify the black community and the nation

A call for a commitment to "economic empowerment as an immediate outgrowth of a spiritual renaissance" by all institutions within the black community

A lamenting of excessive targeting of the black community by alcohol and tobacco firms, while acknowledging that these firms provide crucial financial support to black organizations

A challenge to chewing gum, potato chip companies, and others to engage in "equitable reinvestment" in the black community

An assertion that "blackness is a culture, and experience, an attitude toward life, self-respect and identity born of a common experience and not a color. The conceptualization of blackness must never be integrated out of existence."

Lowery, too, calls for a turning inward within the black community, not just as a strategy for self-help, but as an explicit rejection of mainstream, liberal integrationist philosophies and practices. This was a rather interesting message, made more important symbolically by the fact that Lowery's speech was given in Richmond, Virginia, in the presence of the newly elected black governor. Lowery's call for a turning inward was joined to an explicit cause, a spiritual renaissance, to rid the black community (and the nation) of many ills, and to serve as a catalyst for a total commitment to black economic empowerment. It is clear that Lowery, too, harbors some profound misgivings about the achievements of black elected officials, alluding to the necessity to keep them accountable to the black community. However, the most telling statement of the Lowery speech was his apparent need to reaffirm the significance and trandscendence of blackness as an identity and cultural phenomenon. His assertion that blackness is not just a color strongly suggests that he perceives a non-negligible threat to the core and defining element of African-American culture and identity in the United States. However, his speech offered no explicit explanation of his apparent grave sense of alarm.

AN END TO INSURGENCY?

In terms of the economic, social, and political liberation of African-Americans, the continuing question is what strategy, what style, is likely to be effective? While this question is obviously a compelling one, responses to this question inevitably emerge in significant part out of the general sociopolitical context and the tempo of the times. Unquestionably the general sociopolitical context within which black political activities are shaped has been profoundly transformed by developments of the past several decades, including the recent developments such as the Jackson candidacies and the deracialization movement. What do recent developments portend for insurgent-style black politics so vividly associated with social reform efforts?

Insurgency can perhaps be best understood as sustained protest. It involves and requires a railing against something. Broad-based insurgency therefore appears to be temporally determined, manifested at epochal intervals. The present period can best be seen as an interregnum in that regard. There appears to be little evidence that mass-level driven insurgent action of the type which propelled the early stage (post–Voting Rights Act period) of black electoral politics will emerge again in the near future. However there are some issues which may give rise to localized insurgency as a means of creating opportunities and resources for aspiring politicians. The politicization of health-related issues and related corporate advertising targeting the black community is one such issue with potential for inspiring localized insurgency, which may in turn, result in conflicted positions for some black political leaders.

Interestingly, even as Reverend Lowery of the SCLC called for a turning inward and urged the beginning of a spiritual renaissance, he found himself and the SCLC at the center of an issue which poignantly illuminates an overall transition away from the possibilities of mounting collective action to transform the black community.

In his speech, Lowery alluded to a controversy which has slowly but steadily pierced the collective conscience of the African-American community: the undue reliance of many black organizations on financial support from alcohol and tobacco companies on the one hand, and on the other hand, the disproportionate number of deaths and physical impairments in the black community attributable to alcohol and tobacco consumption. The fact that an undeniable, specialized targeting of the black community is pursued by some companies is made more heartfelt by the fact that major civil rights organizations frequently serve as channels for promotions of alcohol and tobacco consumption by African-Americans. Alcohol and tobacco companies are prime sponsors of many functions and activities of many black organizations, providing support for a variety of luncheons, dinners, receptions, and prayer breakfasts, as well as substantive initiatives such as literacy programs. These companies naturally obtain very high-profile promotional advertisements in organizational brochures and printed materials in exchange for their financial support. Indeed the ties between these companies and black organizations are well-established. As Lowery said: "You can get on the phone in almost any emergency and call one of these beer companies and get a contribution. I know them (special company representatives) all by their first names."

The potential political quotient of the issue of excessive promotion and use of alcohol and tobacco products within the black community is one which is laden with varied forms of exploitation. It entails elements of financial exploitation in terms of the "high pressuring" of consumers, most of whom have low incomes; the exploitation of low levels of educational awareness of the health risks attendant to alcohol and tobacco consumption; exploitation of particularly low levels of self-esteem prevalent in low-income black communities in suggesting that alcohol and tobacco consumption contribute to "ultra cool" lifestyles; and exploitation of the tenuous financial status of black organizations in their willingness to, in effect, be cosponsors of the promotion of alcohol and tobacco consumption. It is thus an issue at the core of any comprehensive conception of black liberation. In terms of its moral quotient, the issue is not appreciably unlike the issue of major institutions holding stock in companies that conduct business in South Africa. Indeed the response of some institutions to the alcohol and tobacco issue has been similar to the morally driven response of the South African divestment issue. In early 1991, Johns Hopkins University's Board of Trustees voted unanimously to sell all of its stock in tobacco companies because such investments were seen as undermining the university's efforts to fight cancer. The university's stated position was that, "The holding of tobacco stock is incompatible with the university's mission to disseminate information on the treatment and prevention of disease and illness" (*Atlanta Constitution* 2/23/91, p. A14).

This issue is also one which has the potential to split, or at least realign, the black leadership. Several black activists in several major cities have launched a veritable crusade against the high profile and intensive advertisement of alcohol and tobacco products within the black community. While the issue provides leverage for emerging activists with moral commitment and the need for a forum in which to establish their credentials as leaders, it is not an issue which has been embraced by established black leaders for the simple reason that they are in some ways financially tethered to alcohol and tobacco companies. Interestingly, those activists who have embraced the issue were initially joined by Bush appointee, Secretary of Health and Human Services Dr. Louis Sullivan, who vowed to use his office as a "bully pulpit" to speak out against the "sinister efforts of the tobacco industry to peddle disease, disability, and death to black Americans." It was to this specific declaration by Sullivan and the resulting discomfort it provoked among the established black leadership, that Lowery directed the thrust of his comments, asserting only partially in jest that "we need to talk with old Louis." As a medical doctor, Sullivan acutely recognizes the futility and hypocrisy of advocating improved health care for black Americans without simultaneously advocating mass-level education against alcohol and tobacco consumption.

Thus, the issue of corporate exploitation of alcohol and tobacco consumption within the black community and the disproportionate levels of adverse health consequences attendant to such consumption is the kind of issue which underscores perhaps the major dilemma of black politics: the increasing inability to pursue effective collective action in the face of problems which, due to the continuing legacy of racism, dictate a need for collective action. It is also the kind of issue which might significantly structure the future of black politics. If black activists are successful in galvanizing the black community behind a campaign to throw off the ruinous exploitation by alcohol and tobacco companies, it will by definition be a largely low-income mobilization, thus emphasizing the class-based cleavages which are well-entrenched within the black community but which have been traditionally papered over by racial solidarity. It is therefore the kind of issue which might support a rebirth of insurgent-style black politics. While one cannot predict that this specific issue will rise to a level of critical salience, though for many reasons it should, the dilemma inherent in this issue and the nature of its moral and political quotient are illustrative of the possibilities for a reconstituted black politics which might emerge out of a period of reflection and agenda rebuilding.

TOWARDS A RECONSTITUTED BLACK POLITICS?

What then might reasonably be expected as a likely scenario for a reconstituted black politics? Again the juxtaposition of major developments of the eighties is telling in regard to the future of black politics. Unquestionably the Reagan years embodied a turning away from a social reform ethos in regard to the broader context of American politics. Interestingly, black electoral politics took a similar turn. This was foremost manifest in the move to deracialization in the elections of 1989 and 1990, which as a political strategy was effective in extending the reach of black politicians beyond their predominant tether to a concentrated black population base, but accomplished by shifting to an emphasis on mainstream issues designed to attract greater white voter support. Deracialization thus embodied a redefinition of black politics: the demise and delegitimation of insurgent-style black politics and a transition in which blackness no longer signalled or defined a politics of liberation, but one in which blackness was transformed into a tool for marketing a candidate's appeal to a broader range of voters.

While one cannot yet identify a total transformation in black politics, there is ample evidence to suggest a *greater crystallization* of black politics along two major tracks: electoral politics, and what we might call black advocacy politics. Deracialization will undoubtedly be the preponderant strategy in black electoral politics in the future as it has acquired great legitimacy, and because it promises to be a winning strategy in an expanded political arena. However, much of the momentum of this strategy will depend on increases in victories in statewide races where this strategy faces both its greatest challenge and prospects. Given the nature of the issue agenda which fuels the deracialization strategy, black electoral politics based on this strategy will increasingly become a politics of symbolism, providing a necessary kind of gratification for African-Americans and many whites, and offering as well affirmation of the principles and myths of the egalitarian nature of American politics. Also, given the issue positions of conservative black Republicans, one might expect their ascendancy to accelerate, not in locales with significant black populations, as most blacks do not share philosophical affinity with this group, but in predominantly white settings where their issue positions will more readily override the negative valence of their racial identity. Overall, any expansions on the electoral politics front will likely be offset by losses of several big-city black mayoralties, most likely in Los Angeles, New York City, Philadelphia, and Detroit.

Black advocacy politics will likely be the primary domain of the traditional civil rights organizations, with agitation from less well established black activists. Although this is a significantly familiar role for the established black organizations, in the future it will likely be an altered and diminished role. The diminished role of the traditional black leadership in national-level (black) politics will ensue from the demise of the dependent leveraging strategy and the collective deliberation and advocacy which attended this strategy. Individual African-American candidates involved in electoral politics will significantly and independently define "the black agenda" as it gets factored into the calculus of national-level partisan politics. The "black agenda" will thus be defined by the campaign rhetoric and issue positions of select black candidates pursuing elective office. Utilizing a deracialization strategy will by definition dictate a retreat from a systems challenging social reform agenda.

However, black advocacy groups will be able to pursue strategies directed toward addressing the ills of the low-income black community. They might well be able to operationalize the "turning inward" strategy which they envision as a viable path to black liberation. Interestingly, this bifurcation of black political efforts between electoral politics and advocacy politics will necessarily dictate that advocacy groups target both black and white elected officials in the advancement of black interests. It will also result in a transition away from an undue emphasis on electoral politics to a more diversified strategy for African-American liberation.

NOTES

1. A typewritten copy of the Hooks speech as it was prepared for delivery was provided to the author by the national office of the NAACP. Delivered on July 8, 1990, at the 81st Annual Convention of the NAACP, Los Angeles, California.
2. A video of the Reverend Lowery's "Statement of the Movement" address was provided to the author. Delivered at the 33rd Annual Convention of the SCLC on August 6, 1990, in Richmond, Virginia.

REFERENCES

Cruse, Harold. 1967. *The Crisis of the Negro Intellectual.* New York: Morrow.

———. 1987. *Plural But Equal: A Critical Study of Blacks, Minorities, and America's Plural Society.* New York: Morrow.

Gosnell, Harold. 1935. *Negro Politicians.* Chicago: University of Chicago Press.

———— 1937. *Machine Politics, Chicago Model.* Chicago: University of Chicago Press.

Moon, Henry. 1948. *Balance of Power: The Negro Vote.* Garden City, NY: Doubleday.

Reed, Adolph, Jr. 1986. *The Jesse Jackson Phenomenon: The Crisis of Purpose in Afro-American Politics.* New Haven: Yale University Press.

Smith, Robert C. 1990. "From Insurgency Toward Inclusion: The Jackson Campaigns of 1984 and 1988." In *The Social and Political Implications of The Jesse Jackson Campaign of 1984.* Ed. Lorenzo Morris. New York: Praeger, pp. 216–230.

Walters, Ronald W. 1988. *Black Presidential Politics in America: A Strategic Approach.* New York: State University of New York Press.

Wilson, James Q. 1960. *Negro Politics: The Search for Leadership.* Glencoe, IL: The Free Press